Praise for *Your Home Sweet Home*

"So many factors and emotions are involved in determining the best living situation for any individual or couple. Penelope Tzougros offers a clear, easy to follow guide to help individuals, couples and families make this decision. You will find the interviews, lists and charts invaluable. **This is *What Color is Your Parachute* for our generation as we reach retirement!"**

—**JUDY JOSE-RODDY,** Executive Director,
Sophia Snow Place Senior Living Community

"Our home is the biggest symbol of our personal freedom and independence. Penelope Tzougros has written a monumental book that will safely guide you through the labyrinth of practical and emotional questions you struggle with when deciding whether to stay or move in retirement. *Your Home Sweet Home* is filled with all the helpful tools, wisdom and resources you will ever need to make a decision in your best interests. Penelope's book is like a trusted friend leading you by the hand through the dark corridor of fear into the comforting light of a brand new adventure."

—**BILL HEIGES,** author of *Aging With Attitude* and
Founder of the Aging With Attitude Movement

"If you should be fortunate enough to live into and past retirement age, will your post-work future be rosy? With the guidance financial advisor Penelope Tzougros offers in her new book, planning for how and where to live out your later years can leave you feeling comfortable and secure about your future. **A must read for every retiring individual and couple."**

—**SUSAN HEITLER, PhD,** author of *Prescriptions Without Pills: For Relief from Depression, Anger, Anxiety and More*

"What a great resource for those near or into retirement age! Many of my long-term clients are now contemplating the decision to invest further into their homes to 'age in place' or to sell their home to find something more suitable for their needs. I will recommend this book to help them make that important decision."

—**TRICIA SINN,** Owner of Sinn Design Build, Inc.

Your Home Sweet Home **is a must read** for those pondering the questions of retiring from work and planning their next living arrangements. Through the telling of personal stories, Tzougros gently poses the questions you should be asking yourself in order to make the best personal and financial decisions for you. You may be surprised at your options."

—**DOROTHY DRAGO,** Consumer Product Safety Consultant and author of *Living Safely, Aging Well*

"Retirement should be viewed as a new beginning instead of an ending, and the real question is whether your home is going to enhance or encumber your retirement. When people retire, they need to have a plan as to how they will spend their time. **This book really makes you think about what you want your life to look like after your retire,** and where you want to spend it. A five star plus book!"

—**SHARKIE ZARTMAN,** professor, former All American Athletes, radio show host and author of the Amazon bestseller *Empowered Aging*

"I found *Your Home Sweet Home* to be **chock full of sound, useful information**. If readers ponder the questions asked throughout the book and take the time to answer them honestly, they are bound to arrive at an answer that will serve them in good stead for years to come."

—**PATRICIA DAVIS,** Financial Coach and Manager and author of *Going Broke is No Joke!*

"Penelope Tzougros' book asks the tough questions, questions that retirees and so many others need to ask themselves. The honest responses to these introspective questions could mean the difference between merely making ends meet and enjoying an income stream that enables older Americans to breathe more easily. **Recommended reading**."

—**WILLIAM M. FRANCAVILLA, CFP**, author of *The Madoffs Among Us: Combat the Scammers, Con Artists and Thieves Who Are Plotting to Steal Your Money*

"Moving from your home, especially for those approaching or in retirement, isn't easy. You'll find this book to be **a great source of information** about the financial aspects, current housing options and whether a move now is right for you."

—**CARMEN M. FRANCESCHINO ABR, CDPE, CRS, SRES, SFR, MBA,** REALTOR®/Associate Broker, RE/MAX Preferred

YOUR HOME SWEET HOME

YOUR HOME SWEET HOME

How to Decide Whether You Should Stay or Move in Retirement

PENELOPE S. TZOUGROS
PhD, ChFC, CLU

WEALTHY CHOICES®

Dr. Penelope S. Tzougros, ChFC, CLU
Financial Planner, Author, National Speaker

Your Home Sweet Home:
How to Decide Whether You Should Stay or Move in Retirement

Wealthy Choices®
130 Turner Street, Building 3, Suite 230
Waltham, MA 02454

Email penelope@wealthychoices.com
Phone 781-893-0909 ext. 238
Fax 781-893-3565

Financial Planning offered through Wealthy Choices® and Bay Financial Advisors, Inc.. Dr. Tzougros is also affiliated with Bay Financial Associates LLC (BFA).

Securities and advisory services offered through LPL Financial, Member FINRA/SIPC.

Investment and advisory services offered through Wealthy Choices® and Bay Financial Advisors, Inc., Registered Investment Advisors. Wealthy Choices' and Bay Financial Advisors, Inc. are separate entities from LPL Financial.

Publisher's Cataloging-in-Publication data

Names: Tzougros, Penelope S., 1944-, author.

Title: Your home sweet home : how to decide whether you should stay or move in retirement / Penelope S. Tzougros, PhD, ChFC, CLU.

Description: Includes bibliographical references and index. | Waltham, MA: Wealthy Choices, 2018.

Identifiers: ISBN 978-0-9709870-3-7

Subjects: LCSH Retirement--Planning. | Retirement communities--United States. | Home ownership. | Older people--Housing--United States--Decision making. | Moving, Household--United States. | Life change events in old age--United States. | BISAC BUSINESS & ECONOMICS / Personal Finance / Retirement Planning | BUSINESS & ECONOMICS / Real Estate / Buying & Selling Homes | SELF-HELP / Aging

Classification: LCC HQ1063.2.U6 .T96 2018 | DDC 646.7/9--dc23

Τὰ Σὰ ἐκ τῶν Σῶν Σοὶ προσφέρομεν,
κατὰ πάντα καὶ διὰ πάντα.

Contents

INTRODUCTION

What do you think when you see a framed needle-point or embroidered pillow with the words, *Home Sweet Home*? Depending on your feelings about your current home, you may smile fondly or, on the other hand, if you view your residence merely as an address, you may think this phrase isn't important. Still, for many of you, the notion of *Your Home Sweet Home* opens up a world of memories. *Sweet* sums up what is desirable, comforting, compatible, nurturing, and simply a lot of good stuff.

When you think of your sweet home, what do you remember?

Maybe what comes to mind are all the celebrations—birthdays, graduations, promotions, good report cards, Thanksgiving, and every other memorable family event. Do you hear the laughter of the people you love? Do you see the notches on the door frame measuring a child's growth spurts? Do you sense the relief of finally getting home and being able to sink into a familiar chair and shut out the aggravations of the day?

There's something peaceful and reassuring about the routines of taking out the recycling, changing the clothes in the closets as the seasons change, watering the lawn, filling vases with flowers cut from your own plants, or preparing meals with the tomatoes or herbs you've grown.

But maybe some of your memories are not so sweet. You were sitting at the kitchen table with all the bills spread out, and you knew that the balance in your checking account couldn't handle the kids' braces and the roof repair as well as all the regular bills. Maybe the needs of the house created a big strain. You were going to use money from your home equity line for a tuition payment, but that money was already spent to pay for a new furnace when your old one unexpectedly gave out. The house you love is a haven, but it is also potentially a money pit. There probably have been unanticipated costs that strained your budget. These sorts of stressful surprises can show up again tomorrow, or a few years from now.

As much as you may feel that your house is satisfactory for all your needs, and as much as you may love all that your home means to you emotionally, you shouldn't proceed further into retirement without taking a clear-eyed look at five key questions about your home in relation to your retirement. In this book I will be discussing:

1. Is your house a retirement asset? (Chapters 2, 4)
2. What tests should your house pass for you to stay there? (Chapters 3, 5)
3. Are there better places to live during retirement? (Chapters 8, 9, 12)
4. What does it take to make a change—physically, emotionally, and financially? (Chapters 6, 7, 10, 11)
5. Whether you stay where you are or move, what will you do every day? What are your goals and most desirable

outcomes? What does your decision say about you? (Chapters 1, 12)

By taking the time to consider these questions and answer them honestly, you'll be better able to determine whether you should remain in your home during your retirement, or revitalize your retirement by moving to another part of the country, or to another type of residence.

The desirable outcomes are for you to live well financially, physically, and emotionally. Mulling over these questions will help reassure you that you're on track for your goals. If you determine that somehow you are not headed in the right direction, you'll find advice so you can make a course correction.

It is perfectly reasonable that you, like many others, have always thought of your house as a retirement asset. Calling this assumption into question at the very start of this conversation may be unsettling, irritating, or unacceptable. But this is a critical question that may affect the quality of your retirement.

When you compare your house to your other assets, you may think of your house as holding its value while other assets fluctuate daily. In fact, the market value of your home has most likely gone through one or more cycles of decline and recovery, but because those cycles can take years, not hours or days, you view your house value as stable.

While that perspective seems logical, your house is a real, physical building which changes in value and also needs ongoing upkeep. Look at it this way: you wouldn't be happy if most of your retirement savings went to fixing your roof or re-doing your plumbing instead of paying for entertainment and vacations.

Is your house becoming a physical challenge either because your bones are creaking, or *its bones*—its structures—are breaking down? Are you assuming that you will stay in the same house for many years into the future?

This tension between your house and other retirement assets

may surprise you if you have not yet retired, or if you are in the first few years of retirement.

While you are still working, somehow you figure out how to pay for something like a roof repair. In your early retirement years, when the pool of money for retirement seems ample, you may not worry about big expenses.

But what happens as you and the house age, and your retirement assets are weathering the storms of the markets? What *can* you do? What *should* you do? How do you create a favorable outcome for you, your retirement money, and your house?

How do you evaluate the many additional questions about your comfort, lifestyle, health, emotions, family dynamics, expenses, safety, and options? While it may be tempting to ignore these questions and just let what happens actually happen, that's not the wisest choice.

Is there an easy, non-threatening way to analyze where you are now and what could support your wishes for the next ten, twenty, or thirty years? Yes there is, and that's what this book offers you. As a financial planner, I have helped many clients by laying out the strategies that I will show you in the following pages. My clients and I were a lot younger when we started working together. We faced disruptive market conditions, changes in their lives, and revision of their targets for retirement. Through all those years, planning for a "good" retirement was our consistent goal, even when college funding, estate planning, long-term care planning and urgent discussions about investments took center stage.

In time, retirement consumed our conversations. It was expected, planned for, but suddenly here. The **usual** questions from couples and singles were asked and answered:

- When should I start receiving Social Security?
- How do I apply for Medicare?
- If we retire before we are eligible for Medicare, what health insurance should we apply for?

- How do I move the money out of my work retirement plan?
- How do I invest it?
- How do we protect our assets from taxes, creditors, etc.?
- The life insurance plans we have at work end when we retire; do we still need coverage?
- Do we need an irrevocable trust?
- Should we revise our wills?
- Should we buy a retirement home some place that has a lower cost of living, and then rent it, until we are ready to sell our family home? Can we afford to have two homes and manage them efficiently?
- Does keeping the "family" home make economic sense? We wanted to will it to the kids. Are there better choices?
- Can I lose the house to Medicaid?
- Should we take a home equity loan to build an in-law apartment for Mom, who is now widowed?
- How much of my retirement money can I invest if I want to start my own business?
- My daughter is going through a bad divorce: how much can I afford to give her monthly?

However, there were also **new** questions. Healthy, active about-to-be retirees wanted to know all their options. Those who had been retired for many years were struggling to maintain their homes. Perhaps, retirement communities became attractive because they promoted having all the comforts of home with less work and more fun. With about 10,000 Baby Boomers retiring every day (that's seventy-six million born between 1946 and 1964), the media has a big audience to speak to about where to retire, when to retire, why retire, how to afford retirement, and what to do during retirement. Clients started asking.

- What can you tell us about places for those over the age of 55+?

- Can I afford to buy into a community? What if I don't like it?
- Aren't those senior places much more expensive than my house?
- Will I be able to continue to pay for it? Are rates fixed?
- If I have a medical problem, will they force me to move out?
- Even if I wanted to move, what would I do with all my stuff?
- How do I get my husband to agree? He won't even let me talk about moving. (Yes, in my research, it's mostly the men who did not want to move.)
- What are the "experimental" communities like?
- I don't like the sound of it, but what is "aging in place"?
- What does it cost to adapt my house so that I can stay in it?
- My spouse/partner will be home all day when I'm home. How will I manage that?
- What should I do? I just don't want to worry about money, or the house.

Since I had guided them this far, I needed to help them with this transition. My scholarly habits went into full research mode to make sure that I provided strategies that would fit their particular situations. *Your Home Sweet Home* grew out of those intense conversations and years of research. What I have learned has helped my clients, and it is my hope that my advice here will serve you well also.

Retirement planning is not just a financial equation about how long your money will last if you draw out 4.5%, and the money earns a hypothetical 8%, and you factor in other variables like taxes, longevity, and inflation. Retirement planning rests on exhausting questions like the ones just listed. They become intertwined, confusing, and stressful. They need to be prioritized and structured with the answers tailored to your situation.

This book addresses a range of life experiences and gives you practical steps so that both your transition to retirement and the stages of retirement will be easier. Retirement, like starting a career, has stages, and one critical stage is deciding where to live during retirement. You may face that choice early or later on in retirement.

Your Home Sweet Home is a step-by-step guide for you to assess how your house, your assets, and your abilities may change and what you can do to create a more comfortable and stable retirement. Your unique *Move-Stay* answer will be informed by considering the questions in these chapters, which highlight one area of concern at a time. By taking on the issues slowly and methodically, you will find your *Move-Stay* answer becomes clear or clearer. The Chapter 12 Summary: *Your Home Sweet Home* Decision Guide reduces the many questions raised throughout the book to the key issues, and guides you through an orderly review so you can gather your thoughts in one place.

WHEN

When should you start thinking about this tension between the house and your retirement money? Now! Do you find yourself asking these questions?

- Can I retire?
- Will my money last during retirement?
- What are the risks I face?
- What risks can I remove or minimize?
- Where do I start to figure this out?

If these are some of your questions, what you do with your house is an integral part of the answer.

Perhaps you'll move three or more years from now, or you'll find that your current home can be properly adapted to your changing needs so that you'll never have to move. There is comfort and relief in having a game plan, and having thought about what might happen. As you face the unknowns in life, you can at least work with your current circumstances and make reasonable projections. After all, isn't that how you have done most of your long-term planning? Think about some of your major decisions, like buying your first house, your career moves, or choices about your health; did you have all the facts? Were you 100% sure about the outcomes? Probably not. We plan with the information we have at hand and continue to be creative, optimistic, and flexible.

WHO AND HOW

Who are the people you will get to know? How did they figure it all out?

I interviewed many individuals so that you could benefit from their discoveries, fears, frustrations, family interactions, and strategies. You are not alone if these questions make you feel like a piece of knitting that is unraveling. You pull one strand, and the whole garment comes undone. The stories of how others have managed may make you laugh, cry, or guide you to your own decision.

Here are previews of some real-life examples that will be detailed in later chapters.

- Gretchen and Bert, who are in their mid-seventies, recently retired and have started working on **The House** question. They have about $50,000 left to pay on their mortgage. Their four children have graduated from college. Both the house and the real estate taxes are too much for them. What's next? What do Gretchen and Bert want for themselves, now that they finally have time, and have no major financial obligations? They want to live more simply, and since they are in good health, they want to travel. "More simply" suggests that they may cut expenses, but "more travel" probably requires more money. How will that get worked out? In Chapter 2 we'll follow an unexpected turn in their story.

- Having retired while his wife is still working, Mike has had time to think about what is a worthwhile use of his time. He realizes, with some amusement, that he and his wife will have to figure out how to be in each other's company all the time. While both of them were working, that intense time together was rare. What will change for them? (Chapter 6)

- Angela's parents are in their eighties, and no matter how much she expresses her concerns about why it is not safe for them to stay in their home, they will not listen. Her father is furious with her because she has been trying to get them to move out of the house he designed and had built. **No way!** However, they can't manage the house either financially or physically. Now what? Was there a better time for Angela to talk to them about moving? What do you do when someone is in harm's way and won't listen? Is the anxiety of adult children sometimes on target, sometimes misplaced, self-serving, or not in the best interest of the parents? How do we sort out the children's motivations and also retain the dignity of the parents? Chapter 7 draws together stories from the adult child's point of view as well as from the Mom or Dad's.

- For Charlotte and Ed, the problem was *the stuff*. What to do with forty years of treasures, barnacles, and memories? Answering that question was psychologically draining, disturbing, and intimidating. Initially, they felt that it would be better to stay put. "Let someone else deal with it when we are dead." Then they realized that doing nothing to sort and organize their stuff would leave their sons with a costly and time consuming mess. They did not want to burden them. Once they learned that there was help for going through the process of sorting, selling, and giving away, they took on the project of the move. It was a slow process because, though Charlotte was eager to move, Ed was resisting as much as he could. After five months, they got it done. You'll see in Chapter 11 how much support there is for the practical matters of the move, the sale of the house, and the choice of a new home. Once you are ready for the move, you will not have to do it alone.

- Rebecca has been widowed for about two years and finds the house maintenance worrisome and wearing. Though she loves her home, she is looking for a way to stop the excessive demands of the house. (Chapter 3)

- Geralyn was diagnosed with Multiple Sclerosis *(MS),* and at age sixty-one, she realized that she could no longer live in her own home. How did she manage the actual move, since she had become less physically able? How did she learn to accept being helped? (Chapter 6)

WHERE AND WHAT

Where to live?

Many of those interviewed are working and nearing retirement, yet thinking very creatively about where to live when they retire. Do they want to live in the same part of the country? Do they prefer rural, suburban, or urban settings? What about communal living? What sorts of housing options are there? Chapters 8 and 9 provide an overview of the range of housing ideas, from independent to communal; from self-sufficient to assisted; from informal *"families"* to multigenerational families in one house; from *"fix, adapt, and stay in place"* to *"live everywhere in a motorhome."*

Architects, developers, designers, retirees, real estate companies, cities and towns keep coming up with ingenious variations for residences. You are fortunate to be thinking about housing at such an innovative time when there are so many options to choose from.

What?

What can you take away from *Your Home Sweet Home?*

Your Home Sweet Home is a practical guide filled with advice so that you can make an intelligent, informed, and appropriate decision for your particular situation. For those who like charts, numbers, and checklists, there is a lot to dig into. For those who feel more grounded by hearing the voices of others, there is a treasury of insights. Along with clear and tested financial planning strategies, this book is packed with anecdotes from people who are grappling with questions like the ones you have, and with stories from those who have already made a decision. They may convince you that how well you live in retirement depends, in part, on where you live during retirement.

However, retirement is not a *thing* like the house.

Retirement is clearly not one uniform product that everyone buys. You may have already noticed there are actually three or four stages of change during retirement. You may or may not experience all of those changes. In retirement, people are as different as snow-flakes. The differences among us are more obvious in retirement because of our physical well-being, accumulation of life experiences, settled temperament, investable assets, and habits of mind that lead us to interpret our experiences through a framework of beliefs. You have grown into who you are now, and you are still growing.

As you will see in greater detail, retirement planning is not just about The House, assets, and having enough money to pay for things. It is essentially about who you are and how you want to structure the hours that are freed from the constraints of work and formal obligations. And so, Chapter 1 begins with the question: *Retirement—what do you want it to be?*

CHAPTER 1

Retirement—What Do You Want It To Be?

Retirement is withdrawing from schedules and demands imposed on you by a job and reimagining what to do with your time and energy. Of course, what you can do and what you want to do depend on whether you're single, single with lots of family responsibilities, part of a couple stressed by different retirement dates and different hobbies, or you are both in sync and cheerfully planning where to travel and what to do. Whichever group you're in, when you remove the structure of the work day, you gain the richness of time to spend in a new way.

That switch to redesigning how you use your time and energy also presupposes that you have some money to pay for daily expenses. If you have time, energy and money, then you are fortunate both in where you live and when you can retire.

1

Here are a few thoughts to frame the discussion of what your being *"fortunate"* might mean:

1. According to the World Bank's, *New Ideas About Old Age Security,* "only 15 percent or less have access to a formal system of retirement income support" worldwide."[1]
2. The National Institute on Retirement Security finds that $14,500 is the median retirement account balance for American households nearing retirement.[2]

Historically speaking, retirement is a recent concept. For centuries, people just worked until they couldn't. What happened after that? Those who had families found room in someone's home and contributed to the life of the family by doing various tasks. For those without money or family, there were over 2000 Poor Houses in the United States in the early 1930s, housing about 135,000 people. Some poor houses, by the name of county homes, continued into the 1960s.[3]

The poor house is where you ended up if you had no way to support yourself and were aged, severely handicapped, mentally ill, widowed, or orphaned. If you were well known in the town and considered *"worthy,"* you might be given some aid to enable you to stay in your own home, instead of living out your days in the poor house.

"As late as 1932, only about 5 percent of elderly people in America had any kind of retirement pension."[4]

In 1903, the Massachusetts legislature discussed a bill that would probably have been the first to provide state assistance for the aged. It did not pass. The mindset of those voting was that "the thrifty and worthy did not become destitute and that if you take from children the obligation of supporting their parents you would destroy the family."[5]

With the passing of the Social Security act in 1935, the reliance on poor houses significantly declined. Social Security was enacted in the middle of the most severe depression in the United States. From 1932 to 1934 the unemployment rate was over 20 percent.[6]

With urbanization, people lost the security of being clustered as extended families on farms where they had some level of self-sufficiency and the benefit of each other's help. Charities could not handle the crowds.

President Franklin Delano Roosevelt explained the rationale for Social Security: "We can never ensure 100% of the population against 100% of the hazards and vicissitudes of life, but we have tried to frame a law which will give some measure of protection to the average citizen and to his family against the loss of a job and against poverty-ridden old age."[7]

Social Security was to provide a measure of protection not *all* of the income needed in retirement. However, today, it provides **all, or nearly all,** of the retirement income for about 33 percent of those over sixty-five, and it is the major source of income for 61 percent of retirees.[8]

The board game, *Monopoly*, became available in 1935: the same year Social Security was enacted. There was a card that said, "Go to the poorhouse! Lose a turn."[9] Since you have not drawn that card, you have the happiness of envisioning the special retirement you want. If you are already retired, you have had some time to enjoy and revise your daily choices. From the perspective of history and the worldwide population of working people, your circumstances are very special, maybe even enviable.

Unlike so many other people, you can consider how to shape your retirement.

Whether you are living with a spouse and other relatives or managing things on your own, you have inexhaustible choices. Which of these scenarios captures more closely what you like to do? Which one would be an example of a favorite way to spend the day?

SCENARIO 1

Staring at the sunrise with your cat on your lap.

Not thinking or planning; wondering what the bird chirps mean.

Leaving some of the milk in your cereal bowl for the cat.

Reading. Listening to the radio.

Getting ready to get ready to think about what you might like to do.

Calling a friend or two to make plans for shopping, tennis, lunch, a bike ride, or something else.

Sharing that experience with friends until late afternoon.

Returning home to enjoy a quiet evening.

Paying a few bills, doing laundry, and watching some favorite shows or a movie.

SCENARIO 2

You're the family's "*activities director*," and you're excited about what you've lined up because all of you share these interests. You're really good at finding things that each of you likes and can manage physically.

Brunch at a favorite local diner.

See the new plantings at the nearby experimental "*farm-to-table*" garden.

Compare notes with others who are trying to cultivate heirloom seeds.

Lunch at the museum.

Take in one of the classic movies in the museum series.

Head off to a casual BBQ at a cousin's house.

SCENARIO 3

7:00 a.m.—up, and out by 8:00 to volunteer for a cause you care about.

Noon—get the errands done: grocery store, dry cleaners, photocopies for flyer for a charity event. Lunch on the run while you are driving between things.

3:00 p.m.—pick up grandchild from daycare and change, feed, and play with the little one until the parents come home from late meetings.

8:00 p.m.—return home and catch up on emails and phone calls. Finalize the plans for a trip you are taking to South America.

Practice a new piece of music or spend time on one of your many hobbies.

Burn a little midnight oil. Realize you should get some sleep.

SCENARIO 4

Off to the gym for a combination of exercising, lifting weights, and swimming.

Read the newspaper over breakfast in the café.

Back to the house to continue working on the scooter for Max.

Leave so you can get to work by 1:00 p.m.

Work for 4 hours. You've officially retired from a position you held for many years and now you're working part-time for one, or several, of these reasons:

- You like to be around people.
- You are feeling slightly isolated.
- You miss the daily "*have to*," or purpose.
- You don't have as much spending money as you'd like.
- You're getting on your spouse's nerves being home all day.
- You're bored.
- You've found something that's fun to do.

Here are a few examples of new work for some recent retirees:

- A teacher who left the classroom is restoring old boats. Another teacher became a nanny.

- A hospital administrator, whose real love is travel, funds her trips by working as a nanny.
- A fireman has become an emergency medical technician (EMT).
- An administrator who worked in Washington, D.C., started her own dog walking service. A similar service to exercise dogs was started by a man who used to be a postal service mail carrier.
- A physical therapist for babies and a dancer, now in her eighties, leads tours at an art museum.
- A man who headed a drug addiction program bought a franchise that provides play and education space for kids in the form of a bus that rolls into neighborhoods. The familiar yellow school buses have a retired chiropractor as one of their new drivers.
- An engineer whose company built missiles for the government leads nature walks.
- A sales rep for famous photographers enjoys a less stressful position as driver for Uber.

There are thousands of similar colorful and mundane stories that show that retirees can be clever and unpredictable—just like teenagers.

Entering retirement is like adolescence, but without the acne. Consider a few of the similarities. High school seniors face very big open-ended questions: *What job will I land? Will I marry? Will I fit in? What college should I go to? Can I start a business? How will I manage on my own?* The retiree, likewise, faces big unknowns: *Now that I don't have a job, what do I do with all the time? Will my retirement money last longer than I will? Will I stay as healthy as I am now? Will I be able to do the things I dreamed of doing?* For both groups, there is a sense of excitement, worry, vulnerability, and a realization that their identity is shifting.

These major life transitions generate lots of questions and emotions.

Where will you live? This may be the one question that you thought was settled and not up for discussion. If you want to maximize your retirement, you will want to dig into this question. How well you live in retirement depends, in part, on where you live during retirement.

In the four scenarios just sketched, notice that there was hardly any housework—but is that realistic? Is your house taking up the time that you would rather spend doing other things? Let's see how much time you and/or another family member are giving to the house, and how much to leisure.

Estimate the amount of time you spend on average each week on the following activities. If you'd like to spend more time doing that activity, add a "yes" in the **increase** column. If you want to spend less time, put a "yes" under **decrease**. If you want **no change**, put a yes there. If you want to pay **someone else** to do that task, or arrange for it to be done, add a "yes" in that column.

Whether you are just retiring or have been retired, how do you want to spend your time?

Activity	Hours I/we spend a week on this (week= 168 hours)	I/we want to **increase** time spent	I/we want to **decrease** time spent	No change	I/we want **someone else** to arrange this or do this task
1. House repair projects					
2. Regular house maintenance					
3. Routine house cleaning					
4. Meals—shopping for, preparing, cleaning up					
5. Laundry, dry cleaning, altering, sewing buttons on, etc.					

Activity	Hours I/we spend a week on this (week= 168 hours)	I/we want to increase time spent	I/we want to decrease time spent	No change	I/we want someone else to arrange this or do this task
6. Attending sporting events/ concerts/theatre					
7. Watching television					
8. Participating in sports/exercise—dancing, running, skiing, golfing, tennis, etc.					
9. Listening to, playing, or creating music					
10. Meditating/praying/ quiet time/daydreaming					
11. Volunteering					
12. Shopping—or window shopping—at a mall or online					
13. Traveling—weekend trips and/or major trips					
14. Gardening					
15. Building things, sewing, crafting, repairing things, etc.					
16. Interacting on social media/ playing games					
17. Spending time with friends and family					
18. Phone calls/Skype/facetime with friends and family					
19. Sleeping					
20. Hosting out-of-town guests					

Of those twenty activities, how many do you want to increase? Particularly, how did you respond to the first three items, which focus on taking care of the house? Figuring out the hours devoted to repair projects and maintenance may be difficult because weeks of intense, nonstop work have to be averaged in with weeks of little or no work. Nonetheless, you probably have a sense that the house either doesn't need much work, or it always needs more attention than you want to give it.

If you indicated that you want to decrease the first three items, or you want someone else to be responsible for them, then, right now, the house is taking up more of your time than you would like. That time drain is likely to get worse.

Which activities do you want to increase? Those increases express what sort of retirement you want. We each have the exact same finite bank of 168 hours a week. If, on average, you sleep seven hours a night, then everything else is squeezed into the remaining 119 hours. Since time is precise and limited, the analysis of the role of your house in retirement starts with how you want to spend your hours—your most precious, non-reproducible asset.

NEXT, WE LOOK AT HOW YOU SPEND YOUR MONEY.

Will the activities you like best cost more than you are now spending on leisure activity? You need to spend very little money if you choose reading, listening to music, daydreaming, meditating, or praying. If your favorites are skiing, traveling extensively, and attending sporting events, you'll be drawing much more from your retirement income. Can your budget handle all of that?

Clarify what you want to do. Then, analyze your retirement income. Can it support one big trip every year? Can it support just one *"trip of a lifetime?"* Can you spend a month away from home watching your favorite baseball team in spring training? What are all the costs: tickets, hotel, travel, food, boarding a pet, etc.? Add another 30 to 50 percent to the estimated costs, for the unexpected. If you want to live out of the United States for three months, remember to add in traveler's health insurance. Chapters 3 and 4 will help you analyze your income and answer these sorts of questions.

If something in you clamors, "I've got to do this!", what are the tradeoffs that you are willing to make to seize that particular **Must Have** experience and still be financially okay?

The best outcome is to fulfill your wishes, continue to be able to pay your bills, and count on your income carrying you through retirement. As you know, careful and thorough number-crunching is a critical tool that can help you avoid unpleasant financial realities. Getting what you want is fun; verifying that you can pay for it is a drag. That **Must Have** experience needs to be backed up with the **Have Money** resources.

Picturing what kind of retirement you want helps you deal with your emotions, your identity, and your time. As you start to plan what you'll do, you feel more in control, more excited about what will happen in the future, and less attached to whatever job identity you had at work. The loss of a work identity can be a major adjustment, but creating new plans can speed up the transition because you are looking forward—not living in the past.

If you are already retired, your routines may have become dull and tedious. The house *"got to take care of..."* list gives you something to do, but it's no longer fun. Have you given in to being stodgy because it's easier than making a change? Moving would be too much work, even if a new residence would be better for you. Is being bored an acceptable outcome?

IS YOUR HOME ENHANCING OR ENCUMBERING YOUR RETIREMENT?

Mary was very clear in her reaction to the first three house items on the chart. She's retired, but still works ten hours a week just for pin money. She wants no part of any the constant fixing or doing for the house. She said, "I just want to write a monthly check and have someone else take care of the place. I don't want to own a house anymore." Does Mary's outlook echo yours? She hasn't moved, but she is actively looking for a good rental and will move when she finds it.

Your fun may be the opposite of Mary's. You may find it satisfying to fuss over your house: painting, polishing, and repairing it. If that's enjoyable, then the house enriches your retirement.

The Physical Energy the house requires of you is just one of three ways to evaluate whether your house is a keeper.

Another way to evaluate the house is to understand how much **Mind Share** it takes. What's **Mind Share**? The following examples will clarify.

What happens to your stress level if you discover that squirrels have made a nest in the attic; or you've returned home to see that the huge white oak tree came down in the storm and smashed the porch and part of the kitchen; or those bugs at the base of the house are not ants, but termites; or the sump pump failed and you have two feet of water in the basement?

What's your reaction? You worry. *How much will the repair cost? Do you know a reliable contractor who can fix the problem at a reasonable price? What will the insurance cover? Will the repair be done right the first time? How much follow-up will it take?* Question after question grabs your attention, grabs **Mind Share**. While you are going about having breakfast, doing routine things, the current problem has taken a share of your mind and will not let it go.

Even on less dramatic days, the house claims some **Mind Share** because there is an undercurrent of things you need to keep in mind: you have to change the batteries in the smoke detectors, change the filter on the furnace, have the heating and cooling system checked, fix the garage door opener, wash the windows, repair the fence, remember to schedule the cleaning of the gutters and chimney, and plan when to paint interior rooms, when to paint and caulk the windows, when to clean the rugs and drapes, etc.

The cost of the house is not just what you pay for real estate taxes, utilities, and a mortgage. It is what it costs you in Mind Share and Physical Energy. The house costs Dollars, Mind Share, and Physical Energy. In good weather and bad, you may feel that your house is worth every bit of "*cost*" in all three dimensions. That is true now, but as you and the house age, will you change your mind?

What if you've always been lukewarm about the house? You're basically comfortable with it, but some things are very dissatisfying. You've overlooked them ever since you bought the place, but if you could make the changes without a lot of disruption, construction dust, and cost, you would tackle those projects.

What are two changes that you would make in or around your house?

1. What is the change?

- Why would you make that change?

- What do you think it might cost?

2. What is the second change?

- Why would you make that change?

- What do you think it might cost?

If these changes can't be made, would that motivate you to move? When? Is the house interfering with you enjoying your leisure? Is it costing too much in Dollars, Mind Share and Physical Energy? If it is costing too much, what will you do about it?

SUMMARY

The questions in this chapter help you to evaluate the role of your house by looking at your leisure time. How do you want to spend your days, and to what extent does the house support your vision of retirement? One of the key goals of this book is to guide you to identify and clear away impediments to your enjoying life. That process may also increase your financial and physical safety.

Whether you are just retiring or have been retired for a long time, does your house nurture your vision of retirement? Completely? Somewhat? Less than you would like? Before you make that call, read the next chapter and consider *how suitable your house is, and how expensive it is.* The answers may surprise you.

CHAPTER 2

Is Your House Still the Right House for You?

A house is a building that is reshaped and revitalized by its family. A visitor may see only wall colors, the placement of furniture, and the décor, but when **you** walk through the rooms, you see items that were gifts, such as a child's framed birthday card, or an antique that you bought for a steal. Things are not things; they are embodiments of stories and relationships. Rooms are not their dimensions or function; they are spaces packed with memories of parties, conversations, music, and maybe even arguments. Though you may seldom stop to think about all the life lived there, those experiences subtly tie you to the place. They make it home. They make it a place that you want to stay.

Businesses want to know if you will stay or move, so it is not surprising that surveys are being taken continually to anticipate what you will do with your house. A recent study conducted by Merrill

15

Lynch and Age Wave challenges old ideas about what retirees want. "Home in Retirement: More Freedom, New Choices" finds that about 64 percent want to move.[1]

A vastly different estimate comes from a survey by Bankrate. com, which finds that 80 percent of those over sixty-five **don't** want to move. Even with the different methodologies of the surveys, the range of results likely reflects the evolving and mercurial mood of those over sixty-five.

You may be attached to your house because of the garden that has taken years of care to give you fragrant roses, a good yield of tomatoes, a mostly green lawn—all very pleasing. Then there are the neighbors: some, like you, have stayed. Over the years, you've shared meals, drinks, or coffee with them. However, there are also new neighbors that you hardly know because they are always so busy. They're friendly, but something familiar and warm that you took for granted is missing.

You chose the house for virtues other than the basic house, such as how close it was to whatever you needed—good schools, a supermarket, the main road, a house of worship, a shopping center, a doctor's office, a favorite take-out place, and a well-stocked hardware store.

If the contentment just described fits your circumstances, even if the particulars differ, then it is understandable that you want to stay where you are.

What has changed?

What if the children have all gone off to college and/or their own apartments? There was a time when their constant motion, projects and friends made the house seem too small. Now there is too much space.

Ed reflected on their active house. With his three children and their friends, there were lots of young people running in and out.

"We had a lot of fun there, but now I was looking at an empty house. And it was a big one. I'd go upstairs and see three empty bedrooms and no one ever in them, so you say to yourself something is wrong with this picture. I'm older and I can't keep up with some things as I used to do like fixing things around the house. So, I hired people to maintain the house. One day I was sitting around by the pool by myself and thinking that here's this beautiful house and garden and nobody even looking at it and enjoying it.

My wife and I both talked about it. It was a sad time for her because she raised the kids there. We lived there 28 years. But it was time to go, time to move on.

By the time we sold the house, most of the people living around us were much younger than we were. They were at a different stage of their lives. We moved into an apartment and she was devastated. She wasn't used to someone living on top of her, or around her. I was. She was not comfortable with it. We knew we were going to move again. We just didn't have it all lined up and didn't know what we wanted to do with our lives.

We moved from about 5000 square feet to 1200 square feet. There was a lot of stuff to get rid of. The kids took what they wanted. That wasn't much. We gave other things to charity and threw everything else away.

The kids were emotional about our selling part of their past; we're ending part of their lives too. They don't think that now that we are growing up and leaving, Mom and Dad are going to sell the house. They don't think like that.

We left the apartment and now we're in a freestanding home. It's not an over-sixty-five development. It's what's called a planned unit development. All the grounds are maintained. It's a lot easier. It's all new and there are not a lot of repairs that need to be done. I had the basement finished for the grandkids. So, they had place to go to play games, watch TV, play ping-pong and get away from the boring old people."

Ed and his wife made their decision to sell the family home with the empty bedrooms, but Matt and Ginny wanted to keep the big house, which had "guest" bedrooms with only occasional guests. Matt and Ginny dream of holidays when all four married children will *come home*. That phrase is powerful because it has emotional words that try to capture the past and make it a present reality. However, it can be psychologically limiting—and maybe even *damaging*—to try to keep things as they once were instead of encouraging the changes and new adventures appropriate to each of you.

Matt and Ginny haven't changed the kids' rooms and are maintaining a very big house for events that fall into the category of "just in case."

Other parents are not dealing with "just in case" but rather with "boomerang" adult children returning home to live with them. From 2005 to 2014, "the fraction of young adults age 18 to 31 who lived with their parents rose 15% according to a study by Federal Reserve Board economists. Not only is this rate of change unprecedented, but the percentage of young adults residing with parents has reached a historic high of 36%."[2]

Reasons for their returning home are difficulty finding work, paychecks than don't cover debt and rent, divorce, medical conditions, being laid off, or just liking the nest they grew up in.

As much as parents in both situations may care about their children, they might be spending more of their retirement money than they should to support their adult children who have returned home.

For Matt and Ginny, maintaining the big house might cost more in utilities and real estate taxes than a house that fit their own current needs. If they moved to a residence tailored to their needs, the money saved might be sufficient to pay for hotel rooms if and when the children come to town. Parents supporting these *boomerang children* may be adding to their expenses for such things as food and utilities.

For parents who want the freedom to focus on their own priorities, who want to say, as Gretchen did, "Now it's my turn; time for what I want," the return of children may inhibit the parents' fulfilling their own desires. Gretchen and Bert are in their mid-seventies and just recently decided to retire. They want to travel. They want to live simply. Their house which was the right size when there were three children growing up is now too big. They are toying with the idea of selling the house, banking the money from the sale, and traveling as much as they can while they are still healthy. One dream is to live overseas for five months or more. Do they store their furniture and rent a place when they return? They are confident that they can analyze that sort of question and come up with a good answer, but a more complex question has begun to worry them. Should they postpone their dream trip because their eldest daughter's marriage seems to be headed for a bitter divorce? If that happens, they would want their daughter and grandson to live with them for a while until they are both more emotionally and financially stable. Do they put their dream on hold—*again*? Can she live in the house while they travel? Does their daughter need them present to cushion the emotional trauma on herself and her son? Can they afford the travel that they wanted without investing the proceeds from the sale of the house? More financial and emotional calculations confront them.

Even though it is lovely to have a welcoming home, a big house can cause financial and emotional strains.

OTHER WAYS A HOME GOES FROM BEING THE RIGHT PLACE TO THE WRONG PLACE TO STAY

As wonderful as your house has been for all these years, it may put you in debt—not in Dollars, but *social obligation*. Marguerite's story explains how several factors can come together, creating a forceful reason to move. In her case, the record snowfall of 108.5" during the winter of 2014-2015 was a powerful motivator.

Marguerite's decision process

"Oh, the big snowstorm. I was alone in my house. Across the street from me was another lady from Nova Scotia—Rose, and she was a little older than me: I was in the low 90s and she was in the high 90s. I said to her, 'I don't know what you're going to do next winter, but I'm not going to be in this house. I am going to sell this house and find a place to go because it's not fair.' Our neighbors were two nurses—a man and his wife, and they had two little boys. I was right next door to them— and Rose lived across the street—and they took it upon themselves to take care of us. I said, 'That's too much. I'm not doing it. I am getting out.' Well, anyway, Rose was sitting and she dropped dead just sitting and eating a piece of pizza. So, she was gone, and it was just me. When John and Carroll [her son and his wife] came home – they spend every winter in Florida –I said, 'John, I don't know where I'm going, but I'm not going to be in this house this winter.' And he said 'Have you thought about it? Are you sure?' I said, 'I gave it a lot of thought. I just got to find a place to go, so I won't be dependent on the neighbors because that snowstorm just scared me to death. I thought, 'Gee! How can you get old and depend on neighbors to take care of you?'"

Was being dependent on your neighbors the only reason you wanted to move?

"Well, I sort of had it in my head that I would move. I always had a garden. I had a big rose garden and I did a lot of work in the yard. I loved working in the yard, but I just knew, in time, that I wouldn't be able to do it, but it came after that snowstorm. I said, 'No way. I'm getting out.' So, just one day, John and Carroll came up and he said, 'Okay, we're going looking.' Well, we went north of here, went to different places, but I had already known about this place [Sophia Snow Place] because people from our church—I go to Stratford Street Church—, some of them are here. I had been here to visit and heard how nice it was. Anyway, we did a lot of really looking... I just want something small. I said, 'I only need a comfortable bed and three good meals a day. That's all I require.' So, that is what I have here. I had to sell my house, of course, to get in here, to have the money to come in here. That's fine."

Even though Marguerite, now ninety-three has been in her new home for only seven months, she is on pace to knit the hundred hats that she donates to her church every year. She knew when she was tending to her roses that she would lose some of her physical abilities. That, coupled with the snow storm, her dependence on neighbors, and her friend's death, led her to find a setting where she did not impose on the kindness of others, but still had appropriate support. She is now content and active in her new home.

Marguerite's indebtedness to her kind neighbors is like Evon's view of her friends caring for her. Both of them truly appreciated the help at the time, but they feel that certain kinds of care should come either from their families or a professional.

Evon's process:

For many happy years, Evon, a teacher, lived in a large house in Georgia with her young sons and her parents. Life changed: Her parents passed away, and her sons grew up and found work in the northeast.

She was startled into action by her own observation: *"I found in that three-bedroom house with three stories that I was living in a corner."*

What did she do about that? She started looking at rentals, independent living places, and smaller houses.

"I do have severe osteoporosis and I break very easily. I had purchased this small, two-bedroom house in a new community and it was actually fit for a person with a handicap. It was handicapped-accessible. I found a lady builder who had built a house for one of her relatives who had a difficulty. She started building all of her houses that way, and it was amazing that many of the other builders, seeing what she did, started doing that also – bigger doorways, bathrooms that were accessible, etc. I lived there ten years alone. I could have continued to live there. People in the community were my age, so I had no problems, but I kept falling and breaking and needing assistance, and I started thinking, 'How do I handle this? I have no relatives, only friends here? I need to be near one of the kids. I don't have anything that's actually holding me here.' So, I started looking. It wasn't that difficult for me to give up my home. The only emotional thing that I had was I had very close friends and I still have ten of them. I go visit them all the time in Atlanta, fifty-some-odd years I still have friends there, but no family connection, and friends said,

'Well, we'll take care of you.' I broke one hip and I was in rehab, the kids were trying to come back and forth, and I had a friend who was doing my laundry and taking care of me. She's my age, and I thought, 'What do you do when you don't have family and your friends are all your age, and you're getting older?'"

How she made her decision:

"Now, I was ten years in the little house, and for about three or four of them, I was thinking about, 'Well, what do I want to do? What should I do? I didn't have to do anything. I was settled, but I had a dog, Daisy (a border collie) and she and I were growing old together and when she sat down one day during our walk because her hip couldn't go any further, I said, 'Okay, I'm not doing this to you anymore,' and I had to put her down. Then, I started getting the house ready. I had a wonderful minister, his name was Haught Purcell, he gave me some advice (and I really did follow his advice). He said, 'Don't wait until you get too old to move.' And that made sense."

Evon, now 86, moved to Sophia Snow House ten years ago in 2006. She looked at more than ten places and took her time to make the move. She discussed it with her sons, who agreed with her decision. She's an avid Red Sox fan, and she is doing very well—better than her team, on most days!

In these stories, we hear how some individuals answered the question, "Is my house still the right place for me?" You may not want to ask that question. If you do ask it, you may shy away from a critical answer. However, for the sake of your safety, your independence, and your health, please consider the warning signals that your house is giving off. These warning signals can help you evaluate your house with clear eyes and less bias.

Ultimately, you want the decision to be your decision. You certainly don't want to be forced to move out against your will.

WARNING SIGNALS FROM YOUR HOUSE – USE, SAFETY, LOCATION

It wouldn't be surprising to realize that your house might not serve you well in ten or fifteen years. After all, houses are generally designed for the able-bodied and young. If both of those descriptors don't fit you, then it's wise to look at how you're using your house now, and what might change.

Although there are many more warning signals, you should be conscious of at least a short list of them coming up next. As you visit the homes of friends who are also your age, you may notice these warning signals more quickly. That's good, because it may prime you to recognize the same obstacles in your house. You can fix some problems easily and inexpensively.

Use

Is your house useful? Does it need to be adapted so that you can use it more easily?

Right now, you may be able to carry the laundry up and down the stairs. If your knee starts being a problem, or your energy level is always low, this normal activity could become a strain. Then, what would you do?

Look at the entrance to your home. If someone you love wants to visit, and that person uses a walker or a wheelchair, how does that person manage the stairs or a high threshold? Does the very structure of your house prevent visits from people you love?

If you needed to use a walker or wheelchair, would the door sills be hard to roll over? Would the doorways be wide enough? Would you be able to turn a wheelchair around in the hallways? Could you get into the shower? If you used a wheelchair, could you chop vegetables on the countertop, or would it be too high for you to use safely and efficiently?

Can you access all the shelves in your closets? Can you kneel or bend to pull out pots and pans from bottom shelves? Are kitchen bowls, colanders, big pans and appliances within easy reach? Do you regularly use a step-stool to reach for things you need?

Architects, kitchen designers, stair lift companies, carpenters, and other professionals could change the structures and make the house more useful. Those changes cost money. Could you withdraw enough money from your retirement account to pay for such adaptations? If you withdrew that money, would you still have enough money to cover your usual expenses?

Safety

Electric cords. Do you run extension cords because there are not enough electrical outlets where you want them? Older homes were not designed for the load of appliances and gizmos that we now regard as necessary. Are the cords the right gauge to carry the electrical load? Are you likely to step on the cords and damage them, or trip on the cords and fall?

Scatter rugs and falls. Small rugs, called *throw rugs* or *scatter rugs*, can add the right spot of color to a room—an artful touch. But for 50,000 people over sixty-five in 2013, rugs were the reason for a fall. Annually, falls from all sorts of causes result in over 2.5 million seniors being treated in an emergency department, according to the Centers for Disease Control and Prevention.[3] "Falls are the number one cause of injury, hospital visits due to trauma, and death from an injury among people age 65 and older."[4]

What factors contribute to falls? There are many, such as clutter, scatter rugs, uneven depth or rises of stairs, wobbly stair railings, and poor lighting that makes it harder to see the transitions in floor surfaces from a carpet to a wooden floor, or from a wooden floor to ceramic tiles.

Those external factors tell only part of the story, however. Our changing bodies tell the rest. Not surprisingly, falls can result from loss of balance, poor eyesight, dizziness caused by medications, body weakness, foot pain or inappropriate footwear.

Some low-cost and quick changes for the external problems are: removing scatter rugs, clearing away clutter, and getting rid of the electric cords that could trip you or cause a fire. Even if scatter rugs have non-stick pads underneath them, the difference in texture and height can catch a slipper and cause a fall. You can increase lighting and add electric outlets to reduce the need for extension cords. Add railings to both sides of the stairs and add grab bars in the shower and tub.

As for your body—exercise at any age helps. Balance and strengthening exercises help to prevent falls.[5]

Burns. While taking a shower, has the water ever suddenly gotten very hot? Both the very young and old have in common the fact that their skin is thinner, and so, very hot water can burn them. Some medications, medical conditions, and poor circulation can distort your ability to gauge the water's temperature until it has scalded your skin.

Has the thermostat for the hot water been set below 120^0 F? Has an anti-scald device been installed? These measures can protect the person in the shower, so that the water will not suddenly turn too hot or cold if a toilet is flushed, the dishwasher is started, or the washing machine is turned on.

Location

Do you get out of the house most days—say, five out of seven? Can you get out of your house easily and navigate the streets near you? If you say, "not so easily," are you dealing with mobility, vision, and/or hearing problems that make negotiating the outdoors much more challenging than staying in your own living room?

Are there sidewalks, and are they in good repair? Is there good lighting if you want to walk at night? Are you fit enough to walk for exercise? Are you afraid to walk around the block at night? If you feel safe, what is within walking distance? If you were no longer able to drive, would you be able to walk to shops for food and other routine needs? If not, how convenient is public transportation?

When few of your old neighbors remain, you may feel that there is no one to call on when you need a favor, or just want to chat. You may miss the casual conversations, beers, cups of tea, and group events that made you feel part of a community.

A Gallup poll in November 2015 reported that 45 percent of American women over fifty are afraid to walk within a mile of their homes at night.[6] That fear, coupled with not being able to drive, poor public transportation, and losing familiar neighbors could add to the isolation that many seniors feel, but do not express.

You may still love your house, but not where it is located.

Answering the questions in this chapter can help you recognize how your relationship with your house has changed, or could change in the coming years. The warning signals may be loud and clear at the moment. Think about how you can respond to them if you want to stay in your home. Then consider those solutions in relation to the next chapter, which discusses what it costs to run your house.

SUMMARY

Is your house still the right house for your retirement? It's tough to deal with this question because it stirs up uncertainty, anxiety, and fear. Being aware of warning signals can help you identify potential dangers before they harm you.

The stories of Ed, Marguerite and Evon show people who have made successful and happy transitions. However, if you want to stay in your home and be just as happy and content as they are, consider carefully the short list of warning signals and evaluate your home so that you can stay in your beloved home safely and independently. The next chapter removes the emotional component, and focuses on neutral numbers which verify what your house really costs.

You want to make a smart decision about where to live, and determining the cost of running your house is one critical part of preparing for that decision.

CHAPTER 3

Would You Be Just as Happy If Your House Cost You Less?

Two very popular views about owning your own home are:

- It is a great asset because it holds its value
- It is the least expensive place for you to live in retirement.

These views reinforce the feeling that there is no reason for you to move, but have you examined both ideas? What if they're wrong? What if, by relying on their being true, you undermine your finances, and make your retirement stressful?

Let's start with the view that your home holds its value. Which *value*? The value from the real estate tax assessment, the mortgage lender, the property insurer, the Realtor®, the appraiser, or your unrealized appreciation?

Let's look at the value meaning your unrealized appreciation.

Your house has appreciated in value if you bought it at one price and now its value is much higher. If you have not yet sold the house that appreciation is not yet realized. Inflation is one factor for your current higher house value.

If you bought your house in 1968 for $24,700,[1] which was the median price for a new single-family house in the United States—and you are selling it 50 years later in 2018 at $179,540[2] that sale price would match the rate of inflation. In 1978, a median one-family house might have cost $55,700, and in 2018 its inflation-adjusted value might be $198,382. You may feel like you have a gain of $154,840, and $142,682 respectively. From this perspective, if the house has kept up with inflation, it has kept its value.[3]

Certainly, houses are unique, and you may have been very fortunate in buying a house at well below the market price. And now, you are equally happy because your area has appreciated rapidly, and you have done better than inflation.

The difference between gain and profit: The gain is the difference between your purchase price and your selling price, but how much of that is a profit?

What is your profit when you take into account the costs of the house? Subtract from the gain, the real estate taxes, repairs, regular maintenance, mortgage interest, insurance, cost of home equity loans, and refinancing cost. What is the profit?

What is your gain, and then, what is your profit? Even if, at this moment, you are not feeling up to the task of filling out this chart, just look it over and take away the concept that what you have *made* on your house is whatever you clear after all that you spent on it. For those of you who love numbers, dig into calculating your gain and profit. Perhaps you will confirm for yourself that, even after accounting for all of the expenses, your house is showing a significant profit. If you are lucky, a good sales price can help to repay you for all those outlays.

DETERMINING THE PROFIT ON SELLING YOUR HOME

	Estimated Current Market Value $_____	Year _____
Minus	Purchase price of your home $_____	_____
=	$_____ Gain in price if you were to sell now	
	Minus cumulative real estate taxes $_____	Real estate taxes this year $_____ Cumulative taxes over _____ years Subtract that cumulative tax amount from the gain
	Minus cumulative annual maintenance $_____	Maintenance Cumulative cost
	Minus cumulative repairs $_____	Repairs Cumulative cost
	Minus cumulative mortgage interest $_____	Cumulative cost
	Minus cumulative cost of refinancing $_____	Refinancing
	Minus cost of home equity loan or line $_____	Home equity loan or home equity line
	Minus interest on home equity loan or line	Interest on loan or line Cumulative cost
	Minus property insurance $_____	Cost of property insurance this year_____ Cumulative cost of insurance
	Minus estimated selling costs $_____	Is there a mortgage or loan to be paid off at the closing?
	Minus Other... $_____	
=	Profit $_____	

If the Dollars you committed to your down payment had been prudently invested, could you have paid rent all those years and had a better financial outcome? Perhaps, yes. Many new home buyers are facing that question because current house prices are beyond their reach. Their problem may also be yours. If your house is not at the right price for a starter home, will you be able to sell it? Will your asking price be lowered significantly to attract the new home buyers? The demand now is for starter homes.[4] The current market offers big homes with high prices and high maintenance, but fewer homes for those starting out.

After you rough out the numbers above, do you conclude that you have made a profit? Bravo if the answer is, "Yes." For some of you, there may be neither a gain nor a profit. You may have bought at the top of a market cycle, or overpaid for your house, or your house value has not recovered from the Great Recession of 2007-2009. If that is your reality, your house may not have appreciated as much as inflation, and even worse, it may have lost value.

Even if your house has lost value, perhaps you should sell. Understandably, selling your house and taking a loss may feel too frightening or too financially damaging. That may be how you <u>feel</u>, but get out a calculator or your computer and follow this next section on costs. The ongoing carrying costs for your house may be putting you further behind than you think, and may damage your overall finances more than selling your house at a loss. It may be hard to accept this view, even if it is true.

Let's move on to carrying costs, and explore a popular assumption: "I can't live anywhere else for as little as I spend now." That sounds so comforting and attractive, but is it accurate?

Is your home efficient and economical to maintain? Can you afford to stay there? Will your retirement money be sufficient for everything you want to do during retirement and all the repairs and maintenance that the house will require? Before you settle into an answer, consider the questions in this chapter on maintenance and cost.

HOW WELL ARE YOU MAINTAINING YOUR HOUSE? IS IT EASY TO TAKE CARE OF?

Rebecca, a widow of two years, showed me the list of small and larger projects for the house. It tires her just to plan for and schedule the work to be done. Some years ago, her husband would have taken care of all those details without her so much as noticing. Mr. Fixit has died, so <u>she</u> has to figure it all out. She called the electrician they had always relied on but he has retired and did not have a referral for another electrician. She asked her neighbors for recommendations and gradually worked through the tasks. She is capable, but she does not want to be worrying about fixing the house. She wants to spend her time differently.

Mike used to look forward to weekends in his workshop with time to build, repair things, and be creative. He has regained a lot of skill since his stroke, but he is limited in the tasks he can take on. He is optimistic that, with more rehab exercises, he will be able to do more. In the meantime, the house is beginning to show signs of Mike's neglect.

Whatever its size and architectural charms, your house responds to the weather and the activities of daily living, and as a result, it needs more attention than dusting and vacuuming. The house is the house. It's sturdy. The longer you've lived there, the more you're likely to take it for granted. Maybe you don't see what's wrong. For your purposes, things are working fine.

WHICH MAINTENANCE TASKS ARE ROUTINE FOR YOU?

Which easy and accessible maintenance tasks are you taking care of? Are you observing small things, so you can catch them before they become costly projects?

ROUTINE HOUSE MAINTENANCE

Task	I notice and do something about it	I have some-one else take care of it	I haven't paid attention to this
Leaky faucets			
Water filters Is the drinking water safe? If there is a water filter system for the whole house, is it properly maintained? Is a sink water purifier changed on schedule? How often is the filter changed in a pitcher that has a water purifier?			
Toilet that does not fill properly or runs too long			
Changing the batteries in smoke detectors and carbon monoxide detectors			
Sink and tub drain sluggishly			
Frayed electrical cords? Outlets working?			
Clothes dryer doesn't dry as quickly. Do vents and hoses need cleaning?			
Windows—is caulking good or deteriorating?			
Chimney—cleaned how often?			
Gutters—cleaned when?			
Exterior painting and repair to siding or shingles			

There are many more tasks and each house will have its own special issues. [See Appendix A for more maintenance tasks.] The tasks range in cost as well as the skill needed to do them, but what they have in common is that they shouldn't be ignored.

A study of very specific houses in a particular time and place was conducted by the University of Connecticut and Syracuse University. It found "that for the typical homeowner, maintenance adds roughly 1 percent per year to the value of the home..."[5] Though the one percent increase in value may not be exactly applicable to your house, or every house, the finding of the study is important for highlighting the function of maintenance in determining the house price. Maintenance is not just fixing the worst problems, and it's not about trendy aesthetics. It's a steady course of action for the sake of the house itself. Are you willing to do that? Are maintenance tasks both more irksome to think about and more difficult for you to address, either financially or physically?

Suppose you are the homeowner who is getting older and less able to maintain the house: you are only fixing the worst problems. What do you think will happen to the house value?

Here's one outcome: years have passed, and you've done little upkeep. Finally, you decide to sell. The kitchen and bathroom are perfectly functional, but have not been updated; the gutters need repair, the windows are drafty, and there's a list of other items showing that the house maintenance has been neglected. At the very time you need the maximum profit from the sale of your house, it has declined in value, and the prospective buyer is looking at making a low offer for what looks to the buyer like a fixer-upper.

That, of course, is not a welcome outcome for you, the homeowner. What can be done? You can stop that imagined storyline from playing out by changing one thought. Change your thought from "I am never leaving this house because I can't live anywhere else for less," to "Where can I live that will give me the best circumstances for my retirement?"

Even if you really don't want to move, what if, for the next sixty-six days, you gave yourself permission to think about other choices? What if there was a surprise? What if there was a place that would please you even more than your home does, and cost less to maintain?

Have there been other times in your life when something turned out better than you thought it could? A parking spot opened up just when you needed it. The dentist's bill was less than you expected, and the root canal didn't hurt. The new restaurant served tastier food than you expected. Granted these are minor issues, but pleasant surprises. What else has worked out better for you?

This exploration of a *possible* change in thought is a two-step process. Those steps will give you an opportunity to consider the journey from "I am never leaving this house because I can't live anywhere else for less," to "Where can I live that will give me the best circumstances for my retirement?"

First, let's verify the claim, "I can't live anywhere else for less." Second, allow yourself to hear about and imagine other settings that might suit you and please you even more than where you are now. You may be skeptical about both steps, but for the sake of your happiest retirement, please give both an honest try.

After an unemotional analysis, you may find that your house is not as cost-effective as you thought. That doesn't mean you want to leave, or that you must move, but it does give you a relevant data point.

YOUR HOME SWEET HOME COST ANALYSIS

When I ask my clients what their house costs to run monthly, I get a preliminary list that looks like this:

- $2,000 Mortgage
- $150 Heat—Oil? Gas? Heat and cooking gas?
- $400 RE taxes
- $150 Yard work, snow plowing
- $100 Electric
- $50 Water and sewer cost
- $170 Cable, internet, phone
- $150 House insurance
- $20 Pest control: wasps, ants, rodents, squirrels, etc.

That adds up to $3,190. When the mortgage is paid down, it would seem that the costs might be only $1,190 monthly, but the picture is incomplete. What's missing? The maintenance and repair costs.

A short and incomplete list:

- Seasonal tune-ups for the heating/cooling system
- Chimney, flue cleaning
- Appliances—repair, or replace
- Faucets and other plumbing repairs
- Deck or porch—waterproofing, new floor boards.
- Interior and exterior painting or touch ups
- Windows properly caulked
- Curtains or blinds cleaned
- Carpets and other floors—cleaned or polished

Once all the repairs, desirable improvements, and routine maintenance are averaged into a monthly view of running the house, the **total cost** will increase. Note the focus was just on the house, and not the landscaping or garage, etc., which add more cost.

If you are managing to pay for all of the items listed above without any strain, that's good. If you are paying for repairs or one-time problems with a home equity loan, that strategy might be dangerous. When you were working and you had regular income and some raises, over time you could pay off the loan. Do you have those same buffers of additional income when you are retired? Whether you have a surplus or are counting on a home equity loan to cover increasing costs, you should know the **total cost** of your housing, including prudent, scheduled maintenance.

For those of you who are always aware of all your expenses, you are the *Penny People.* You are happiest recording your income and outgo down to the *penny.* However, many more people are *Gyroscopes* in relation to their expenses. Just as a gyroscope stabilizes an aircraft by responding subtly to its motion to keep the plane moving the right way, the *Gyroscope People* likewise balance their spending by cutting back *here* when they sense they've overspent *there.* They seem to do it unconsciously. They don't balance their check books. They accept the ATM's view of what's available to spend, and they spend roughly the same amount every month without any detailed record keeping. Both *Penny People* and *Gyroscopes* can be successful personal money managers. As you would expect, it is tougher when the two different types are married to each other. That's a story for another day.

No matter what your usual style of managing money is, at major points of transition—like retirement and deciding where to live—you will benefit from creating a detailed analysis of total costs. If it's your heart's desire to stay in your house, you are depriving yourself of one of the tools that can help you check your assumptions about current expenses, and adjust your financial plan for the years to come. That tool is an accurate total cost analysis, which can become your *reliable baseline.*

Look at what can happen without an accurate total cost analysis. Using the example above, you might be saying to yourself, "My house only costs me $3,190 every month. Any income above that amount I can spend on food, clothing, travel, etc." However, when the house costs exceed the $3,190, you may have to reduce your spending on other things, lean on your credit cards, or take out bigger *extra one-time payments* from your retirement money. If you reduce your retirement money, you will probably be reducing the income it can generate for you. How then would you keep up with regular expenses?

On the other hand, when you develop an accurate total cost analysis, you can use that as a tool to verify ongoing costs and evaluate how well your income might cover those rising or unexpected expenses. You can adjust your portfolio and prepare yourself both psychologically and financially for the changes. This is about maintaining your independence and keeping your stress levels low, not about being mean-spirited and fuming over every bill.

Here are the key questions: Over the next ten years or longer, will your income rise faster than the costs of running your house, or will the house costs increase faster than your income? Will your desire and ability to take care of your house increase or decrease? *Your Home Sweet Home* Cost Analysis addresses all those questions. This analysis is very likely more comprehensive than any you've done before, and ultimately, it is a better baseline for projecting future needs.

Those of you who are *Penny People* will relish the next chart, and those of you who are *Gyroscopic People* will think about the concepts, which may intrigue you enough to start writing in some numbers after a while.

Your Home Sweet Home Cost Analysis (Appendix B) is unique because it evaluates the cost of your house in three ways: **Dollars, Mind Share, and Physical Energy**.

DOLLARS

The first measure: **Dollars** is the easiest to assess. This is what you pay for repairs, maintenance, real estate taxes, water, sewer, and much more. Notice that the cash flow analysis pages start with the expenses for the house and the grounds around the house. Anything that is not strictly a cost of repairing or maintaining the house and property is in the next category of Needs and Wants.

The cash flow analysis has two columns for the Dollars spent monthly or annually on the house. Some jobs, like painting the exterior of your house, are not annual expenses. Estimate how much it would cost and divide that by the number of years between paint jobs. For many types of exterior finishes, every five years might be right. The climate, the quality of the paint, and the sun exposure play into how frequently you paint. Good painters will check on critical issues, like the caulking around windows, mildew, rot, etc. So, if you estimate that the full exterior paint job would cost $10,000 and you paint every five years, you would list $2,000 in the annual column, and $167 for the monthly column. By adding it to your monthly expenses, you remind yourself how much you should be saving for that project.

Mind Share

The next column is **Mind Share**. It is a unique concept for a cash flow analysis, since most cash flow sheets state only Dollars in and Dollars out.

Mind Share is measured in time. However, time and money are tied together in financial planning. *How much of your time will the house project take?* An attentive homeowner is likely to be consciously or subconsciously aware of the ongoing needs of the house.

Mind Share is the cost to your sense of calm. How much of your attention is consumed by problems with the house? How much time and mental exertion do you spend on figuring out what is wrong, who to call, arranging for the work to be done, and figuring out how to pay for the work? You might also lose hours from your part time job, if you have to stay home while the work is done.

Here is a simple example. It is not a hazard, but you can see how the questions escalate the claim on Mind Share, keeping your mind busy:

You see that the wood fence at the back of your yard is leaning into your neighbor's yard. Why? What happened? Does it need to be braced? Did the wood rot? Could it be carpenter ants or some other insect? Who knows enough about insects? If it's infested, does that mean the whole fence needs to be replaced? If it has to be pulled down, should you replace it with chain link? Will the new neighbors object to the change? Will they want to see a formal survey to be sure you are not infringing on their land? Who does surveys? How much do they cost? Do they have a legal right to ask for a survey? What are the city or town regulations about fence height?

You find yourself in the midst of responding to emails, drifting off course and searching for local surveyors, fence costs, pictures of carpenter ants, and on and on.

Rebecca, the widow mentioned earlier in this chapter, has a long list of house projects, including fence repair. Most of the items on her list generate spirals of questions like these. They worry her and make her feel weary.

PHYSICAL ENERGY

The next column on the cash flow sheet accounts for the time you spend actually doing a task for the house. It is your Physical Energy—your *sweat equity*. The reason why you do the work yourself could be that you really enjoy it, you would rather not pay someone else, or you can't afford to pay someone else. You are substituting your time and energy for paying out those Dollars.

What does it cost to run your house?

What does it cost to run your house? It is not only the regular predicable expenses, it is the mental and physical work that changes how you spend your time, and how relaxed you feel. So, if you assert, "I can't live anyplace as inexpensively as I live here," it is worth your being thorough about the *Your Home Sweet Home* Cost Analysis and then comparing those real costs with other places you might live.

It's critical that you know what your house costs. Why? Two reasons:

1. You don't want to run out of money as a result of your own faulty projections about how little your house costs to run. You mistakenly thought you had a lot of *surplus*, so

you remodeled a bathroom, finished a basement, bought a boat, or took the whole family on an expensive vacation. You wouldn't be able to blame the investment markets for your running out of money, if the reason you were *broke* was your choosing to spend more than you could afford. You don't want to look back and admit that you could have avoided the problem, but you didn't, because you didn't know the facts.

2. You don't want to miss out on something better for you. What if there was a place that was nicer and less expensive than your present house? Perhaps no one has brought that option to your attention because you always say that you don't want to move. Would you be happy about missing out on a great new option?

What if you look again at the hypothetical example of basic expenses and compare them to those in another residence?

Basic Home Expenses

If current home costs	If new residence costs
$2,000 Mortgage	$2,000
$150 Heat Oil? Gas heat and cooking gas?	
$400 RE taxes	
$150 Yard work, snow plowing	
$100 Electric	
$50 Water and sewer cost	
$170 Cable, internet, phone	
$150 House insurance	$170 House insurance
$20 Pest control wasps, ants, rodents, squirrels, etc.	
Total $3,190. monthly	Total $2,170 monthly

Annual additional expenses	Annual additional expenses
Seasonal tune-ups for the heating/cooling system $400	
Chimney, flue cleaning $400	
Appliances — repair, or replaced	
Zero to $2,000	
Faucets—leaks $100	
Deck or porch—waterproofing, new floor boards. $300	
Interior and exterior painting or touch ups $2000	
Windows caulked and/or replaced	
Zero to $15,000	
Carpets and other floors—clean, polish $100 to $500	$100 to $500
Total annual estimate: potentially from $1,300 to $19,500?	Total annual estimate: potentially from $100 to $500?

Which housing would you prefer?

- The current house, with basic costs of about $3,190 and the potential, in any year, to add costs of between $1,300 and $18,700?

OR

- A different residence, with basic costs of $2,170 and the potential added cost, in any year, of between $100 and $500?

In these examples, the new residence would allow you to spend more money on keeping yourself in good shape psychologically and physically, and less on keeping your house in good shape. What's the best use of your money: Keeping you thriving and happy, or maintaining your house?

Of course, your own expenses are different from those just listed. However, once you complete the *Your Home Sweet Home* Cost

Analysis, you will have real numbers in the left column to compare with real numbers on the right. The right-side column will list the real costs of another housing option. Would you like to free up Dollars, Mind Share, and Physical Energy? Moving to another home might help you do that.

SUMMARY

The *Your Home Sweet Home* Cost Analysis of Dollars, Mind Share, and Physical Energy reflects you as an integrated person who makes financial decisions, has preferences and worries, accomplishes necessary tasks, and copes creatively with the unexpected.

The clarity and valuable information that comes from completing *Your Home Sweet Home* Cost Analysis can help you make smarter decisions.

In **Appendix B,** you'll find the worksheet to complete the *Your Home Sweet Home* Cost Analysis of your current home. You can then summarize that information on the *Comparison Worksheet* in **Appendix C** which will help you compare your current home to the costs for another residence.

Even if you choose not to move, completing the *Your Home Sweet Home* Cost Analysis can help you manage your current expenses and income better. This is a tool to help you work towards maintaining your independence and financial stability. Your future is worth devoting time to completing the analysis as well as you can. If you are a *Gyroscope Person*, find a *Penny Person* who can help you gather the information.

The numbers do not need to be exact as if you were preparing for an audit, but they should be close enough to guide your decisions and protect your future.

CHAPTER 4

Can You Hold onto
Your Retirement Money
and Your House?

In contrast to your big, solid, and sturdy house, your retirement money is represented by small pieces of paper or digital statements online. The stock and bond investments represent a world of change, uncertainty, and fragility. The contrast between these assets can make you feel sure of your house and worried about your retirement money. It is understandable to feel a security bias towards doors and windows you can open and close, but the house can interfere with your well-being during retirement just as the much as your retirement investments can.

No matter where you invest your money, your money is always at risk. Even if you hide money under your mattress, you can lose it. A friend's grandmother found that out when her house burned down, destroying all her savings which were actually hidden in the mattress.

Not all money risks are that dramatic. Because the risks that may affect your portfolio and your house don't catch your attention the way a house fire would, this chapter draws your focus to five of the key risks that are particularly relevant to retirees who want to continue to live in their homes. The ideal plan is to have you, your house, and your money well-coordinated for a serene retirement.

Picture this: you have settled into your comfortable couch and you're wrapped up in a movie. There's a vigorous wind, and the rain is pelting your house relentlessly. In the few seconds that the movie has no music or dialogue, you hear an odd sound in the house. You try to ignore it. In another quiet moment in the movie, you hear that sound again. You reluctantly pull yourself out of your cozy, warm, and relaxed mood to search for and identify the sound.

Oh no, the storm that you heard outside is now dripping inside. What do you do next? You find a pail, a pot, a basin—anything to catch the drips. And next? You worry. Did the wind rip off some roof shingles? Did a branch hit the roof? Is there a lot of damage? Is the insulation getting wet? Who do you call to fix it? What will it cost? How will you pay for whatever has gone wrong?

Since there is nothing you can do about the damage until the storm stops, you go back to the movie feeling less peaceful, and more worried.

If you have plenty of money, the repair will be manageable, and you will not be financially stressed. In your case, your retirement income can cover this repair easily. However, for many households, an unexpected bill of $1,000 would be a blow. It might require adding to a credit card balance or trying to economize by delaying the refill of an expensive prescription, canceling a dental appointment, postponing a car repair, or eating out less.

If you look at a continuum that has, at one end, people who have plenty of money, and at the other end, those who struggle with every unexpected expense, where would you place yourself?

Plenty of money	Some reserves	Not much extra	Struggling
Not a problem	Just for the house	Borrow from a friend or add to a credit card	Stress

If you did not place yourself on the extreme left of the continuum, then how will you handle multiple house *events* like the roof damage? That answer fits into the bigger question: "How much retirement can you buy?" It sounds odd to say, *buy retirement*, as if it were a piece of clothing or a car. When you think of *buying* a two-week vacation package, you have a reasonable idea of what it could cost. You've talked to a travel agent, or you've checked airline and hotel prices and you know roughly what you will spend. Retirement is a very long vacation. How prepared are you to pay for it?

What lifestyle can your retirement assets support?

When will your retirement income run out?

Do you have answers to those questions? If you do, how did you develop them? Hopefully, you are not relying completely on a calculator that you found online. Unless the assumptions embedded in the online calculator are explained so that you understand what your answers mean, you may have a very optimistic, very incomplete, and possibly very misleading view of your retirement.

Let's assume for the moment that you have Social Security income. You know that there is an annual $10,000 gap between what Social Security covers and what you need for retirement. How much do you need in retirement savings to cover that gap? *Penelope's Rule of 20* is a quick way to give you an order of magnitude. If you are sixty-five, multiply the gap number (in this case $10,000) by 20. The answer indicates that you need about $200,000 in investable or income-producing assets to make up the difference between what Social Security provides and what you need to cover your expenses.

Your net worth (all of what you own minus what you owe) may be much greater than $200,000, but if that value is tied up in property or investments that do not produce income, don't count them. Count only the assets that will help you buy groceries and pay for regular expenses.

Penelope's Rule of 20 is a step toward answering the question, "How much retirement do my assets support?" No matter how much you have saved for retirement, you want to be aware of the risks dogging that retirement money.

I'll show you five of the risks that can batter your retirement assets, and therefore, your ability to keep your house. You want to maintain your house and your retirement assets.

Why do I want to focus your attention on what is threatening, or potentially harmful? By understanding those risks, you can better assess how your money might hold up during retirement. This assessment may give you more confidence in the reasonableness of your financial plan, or it may show you that you should make some course corrections. If you feel you need more than a *slight* course correction because the struggle to maintain your house and a comfortable lifestyle is getting more difficult, then this section may show you solutions that you were not aware of. It could be that no one has brought to your attention the ways to eliminate the tug-of-war between the demands of the house and the needs of the portfolio. Maybe you haven't known what or whom to ask. If that's the case, then the next section offers you guidance.

WHAT'S RISK?

What is your first reaction to **Risk**? Is it both good and bad? Is it frightening? Do you think of yourself as a risk taker, or are you a risk taker only in some activities? You may take physical risks like rock climbing or skiing down a mountain, but you want your investments to be guaranteed. Your acceptance of risks in physical activities may be higher than your tolerance for financial risks. Whatever your comfort level with risk, consider the impact of these five financial risks. What happens if these risks reduce the money you have available to take care of your house and yourself? Would you cut everything that was not an absolute necessity? Would you move? Would you find part-time work?

RISKS TO YOUR RETIREMENT MONEY

1. Risk to Principal.

You bought an investment at $30 a share, and today, the price hit $15. You lost money **if** you sold it. If you did not sell it, then you have not locked in that $15 value. The loss is just on paper; it has not affected you in your pocket. Today, it is at $15, and tomorrow, it may be at some other price. It may not make you feel good even though it is only a paper loss, and not an actual, realized loss.

However, if you absolutely had to sell the investment because you needed money to pay for tuition or a large medical bill, you would have lost principal because you locked in and sold at the $15 price.

The changes in prices for stocks and bonds, ETF's, and many other investments are reported daily—in some cases, even minute by minute. It is understandable, then, if you think of these assets as volatile and risky, but your house value as stable. It probably isn't, but you may only be aware of the change in the value of your house when you refinance it, or when another house in the neighborhood sells. Otherwise, you don't focus on the price of your house. Instead you go about your business mowing the lawn, shopping, and having dinner.

However, house values change. Significant decreases for many homes started in 1990, 2001, and 2007. You may not have been concerned about the broader trends[1] because you were not ready to sell, so you did not think you had lost principal, or that you were experiencing a risk to principal.

Suppose, however, that in 2008, you were very keen on knowing your house value because you were preparing to move. Your house was worth $300,000. The following spring, when you put your house on the market, it was worth $38,000 less. Did it develop a major defect in that year? Not likely, but it was caught in the trajectory of the Great Recession (2007-2009). The S&P/Case-Shiller U.S. National Home Price Index showed that the market value of houses declined by 12.75 percent in that timeframe.[1]

You would have been lucky to find a buyer at $261,750. Would that have covered the mortgage and allowed you to sell with a gain? If, for whatever reason, you could not postpone the move, and you had to sell at the lower price, you lost money. A house, just like a stock, can lose its value. So, is your house your best investment? Is it your safest investment? Very conservative investors may say, "Yes." They rule out any participation in the stock market because they fear the risk to principal which they associate only with the stock market, and not with their homes.

Investment values change frequently, but unless you must sell, the changes are like background noise that you are aware of, and ignore.

What to do about the risk to principal? When you buy any investment, think about your need for cash. Can you let the investment sit for two years, ten years, six months? Match the type of investment to the time frame. Risk is about time. If you are holding a good investment, and can wait out a downturn, you will not feel you have taken on risk. If you must sell into a downturn, is the investment bad, or is your timing bad?

2. Risk to Purchasing Power

Your money is always at risk—that's scary but true. I'll say it again for emphasis. *Your money is always at risk.* If you're thinking that your money is safe because it's in the bank, you're right that it is protected up to certain limits by the Federal Deposit Insurance Corporation (FDIC).[2]

The principal is protected, but not its value in relation to inflation.

If you were to leave $100 in your bank account and inflation averaged 5 percent on an annual basis for twenty years, your $100 would be able to purchase only about $37 of eggs, milk, yogurt, bread, etc. At that future date, you would have less purchasing power.

What about loss of purchasing power now, and not twenty years from now? Suppose your $100 earns 1 percent a year annually, then it would earn one dollar of interest. However, if inflation is 2 percent, that would mean your $100 should earn two dollars to keep up with inflation. If you could keep up with inflation, you would probably manage with ease the increases in real estate taxes, fuel costs for your house, etc.

If you must spend $102, though you only earned $101, you will have to pull more out of your savings to cover your bills. You spend down your money faster.

What to do about the risk to purchasing power? If you want to keep all your money in the bank, then be aware that other parts of your portfolio must help you adjust for inflation. You will want to own something that grows more than inflation. Perhaps you are knowledgeable and have made smart buys in stocks, real estate, art, antiques, or some collectibles. You bought those items with the expectation that they would appreciate, and you could sell them at a significant profit, then you would add those proceeds to your cash on hand to pay bills. If this has been your tactic, then you have created your own way to keep up with inflation. Fine, you've found a way to maintain your purchasing power.

3. Risk of low interest rates

From 1984 to 2001, bank certificates of deposit of one-year and five-year durations averaged between 3 percent and 12 percent.[3] Renewing a certificate of deposit in that timeframe was attractive for a saver who wanted to avoid risk to principal. In the past, maybe your $1,000 one-year certificate of deposit earned 12 percent compounded daily. At the end of the year you would have $127.47 in interest. If today, a one-year certificate of deposit earns 2.30 percent, you would accumulate $23.27 instead of $127.47, for each $1,000. How do you make up for having $104.20 less?[4]

What to do? If you absolutely need more income to cover your expenses, then learn about other investments even if they require that you take on a little more risk. Being too risk averse or conservative can reduce your spending money.

Here are just a few of the many options available to you.

- While dividend payments are not guaranteed, there are stocks that pay dividends and have increased dividends yearly for twenty-five years. One way to identify those companies is to review the S&P 500 Dividend Aristocrats https://us.spindices.com/indices/strategy/sp-500-dividend-aristocrats. Click on the tab "constituents" to see the specific companies. Continue your research from there. It's also important to know that companies may reduce or eliminate the payment of dividends at any time.

- Another set of choices to provide more cash to live on could be short-term bond funds, which you can research in financial magazines and newspapers and websites like www.Morningstar.com. Be aware that an increase in interest rates may cause the price of bonds and bond mutual funds to decline.

- For those of you who can set aside cash that you will not need for three years or more, there are fixed annuities, which are long-term contracts that you purchase from insurance companies. Though they are not FDIC insured, the principal used to fund the annuity and the interest rate credited are guaranteed by the insurance company.

Fixed annuities are long-term investment vehicles designed for retirement purposes. Gains from tax-deferred investments are taxable as ordinary income upon withdrawal. Guarantees are based on the claims paying ability of the issuing company. Withdrawals made prior to age 59½ are subject to a 10% IRS penalty tax, and surrender charges may apply.

- For those who have a lump sum of $5,000 or more to invest, there are many different types of annuities, from equity indexed annuities, deferred annuities, variable annuities, to Single Premium Deferred Annuities(SPIA's). Each of these has guarantees backed by the insurance company.[5]

If these suggestions feel overwhelming, consult someone you trust who is familiar with these investments, and who can explain them clearly. They may or may not be a fit for you. If you have been investing for years, but just did not consider these options, give yourself time to learn about them. For many of the clients I've worked with, we were able to increase their income by using strategies that combined various types of investments. That might work for you too. Don't resign yourself to the *hardship* of low interest rates.

4. Risk of ill health.

If you are well now and able to enjoy all your normal activities, you're likely to assume that your good health will continue. Optimism is fine. Exercising and eating properly are even better. With average good health, a couple who is sixty-five years-old can expect to spend $280,000 out of pocket on health care costs during retirement. This is according to a 2018 Fidelity Benefits Consulting study.[6]

Have you accounted for health care expenses in your financial plan? If you've completed the *Your Home Sweet Home* Cost Analysis, you can answer, "Yes." You have begun to break down and pay for that $280,000. *Your Home Sweet Home* Cost Analysis has lines for the insurances related to Medicare (Parts A, B, C, D, and Medicare

Supplement). In addition, you will want to account for out of pocket costs for doctor visits, co-insurance, co-pays, deductibles, and for procedures and medications that are not covered by your plan.

The estimate of $280,000 does not include three significant expenses:

1. Long-term care.
2. The inflation rate for health care costs which, since 1960, has been rising annually at 6.9 percent.
3. The costs related to such items as dental services, hearing aids, acupuncture, and treatments for chronic illnesses like diabetes, arthritis, and heart disease.

LONG-TERM CARE

As for long-term care, in 2017 if you had been on vacation, would you have been comfortable spending $267 a night on a hotel room? That's what the daily cost was for a private room in a nursing home. The annual national median was $97,455.[7]

Can your portfolio cover all your normal living expenses, and then also pay out another $97,455, to take care of your spouse in a nursing home?

Will you ever need to be in a nursing home? We have no crystal ball, only a statistical answer. You may be among the 70 percent who will need some long-term care after the age of sixty-five.[8]

Medicare pays for acute care for a condition that will improve, like a broken hip. Medicare does not pay for custodial care, which is what stroke and Alzheimer's patients need. Alzheimer's is the sixth leading cause of death in the United States. One in nine people ages sixty-five and older has Alzheimer's, and "Every 65 seconds someone in the United States develops the disease."[9]

What to do? If your loved one must be moved to a nursing home, it's as if you're suddenly maintaining two homes. If your portfolio is substantial enough to pay for the care of a spouse who is in a nursing facility and for the healthy spouse who is at home, you can self-insure. If there is not enough money to do both, then consider one of the three ways to add a safety net. Shift your potential risk to the insurance company. Ask a financial planner or insurance agent about: 1) a long-term care policy; 2) an annuity with a long-term care rider; 3) a life insurance policy with a long-term care rider.[10] A combination of these choices may construct a safety-net as well as address part of your estate planning.

If your retirement money cannot produce enough cash to pay for these two homes, what happens?[11] Would you take in a border—an Airbnb guest? Would you move? Would you spend down your savings and apply to Medicaid? Because "medical problems contributed to half of all home foreclosure filings in 2016,"[12] it is worth creating or reinforcing your health care safety net.

5. Risk of longevity

Should your money run out before you do? No! That's not the outcome anyone wants.

How long is your vacation, aka, your retirement going to be? You don't know. So how do you go about answering questions, such as, How long will your money last? What lifestyle will your assets support?

A comprehensive financial plan answers questions like these by relying on long-term patterns of inflation, taxes, rates of return on investments, and future views of the capital markets. The analysis looks for irregularities and exceptions. Most importantly, it focuses on what you want to do, what you value, what worries you, and who you are. The answers are in the shape of, "If this happens, then that is the likely outcome.

The answers are like a compass that keeps the ship pointed in the right direction, though it can't control the winds.

What to do? Have someone who is knowledgeable,

trustworthy, and attentive to your concerns prepare a financial plan for your retirement.

This financial plan can give you a reasoned and conditional answer to how long your money will last given the lifestyle you want.

If your money is not expected to last as long as you would like it to, you may have to change where or how you live. It is very possible that no one has helped you identify viable alternatives for improving your portfolio or finding other places to live. Your home may not be the most cost-effective place to live. Make changes that can help you maintain your lifestyle. Is taking care of **you** more important than taking care of a house?

If you are worried about outliving your money, you may want to consider shifting some of the risk to an institution that is built to deal with fifty and one hundred year time frames. There are many new types of annuities that insurance companies have created. Many guarantee to pay income to you for as long as you live so that you will not outlive that portion of your money stream. Learn what the guarantees are based on and what the guidelines are for investing in these long-term instruments.[13]

Why is it worth understanding how annuities work?

If you have money in a bank account (or a mutual fund) and you spend all of it, it is gone. If you invest in an appropriate annuity, it continues to pay you as long as you live, even after all the money you invested has been spent or paid out. Certain types of annuities can perform this unique job for your portfolio.

That all sorts of investments and insurance have proponents and opponents is normal.

It's critical that you look with an open mind at any investments and strategies that can help you. Reject those that don't. Ask questions. Investments are tools—a means to an end. A hammer is not a bad tool because it can't do the work of a saw.

Often, people do not realize that their situation can be improved. They become resigned. Don't give up on creating better outcomes for your particular situation. You don't have to do all the research yourself. Ask for help.

How else might you deal with your money not lasting as long as you need it to?

When you were working, you might not have thought too much about the sort of risks we just discussed because regular paychecks were coming in and you had other, more demanding things to worry about.

You could add up your main expenses, subtract them from your take home pay and know that you were managing to stay afloat. That straightforward arithmetic was sufficient. You figured out how to cover a needed repair for the house, even if it used up some of your *rainy day fund*. But what happens when you're retired and more than one thing goes wrong?

For those with very substantial retirement accounts, the repairs don't present a problem. But if those repairs are coupled with health hazards, market corrections, and illiquid assets (i.e., a house or asset that no one wants to buy), even those who think that they have plenty of money may find that a *perfect storm* could have a staggering effect on them.

Stress testing both your portfolio and your assumptions is a prudent process, no matter what your net worth is.

If and when money gets tight, it is worth asking what you will do. Would you borrow money? If not, where would the money needed for the repair or medical care come from? There are no overtime hours, bonuses, or raises if you're completely retired.

Depending on how much money you might need, some usual choices are:

- Withdraw more than usual from your retirement assets.
- Use your credit card or cards
- Find part-time or full-time work.
- Apply for a home equity loan (lump sum), or home equity

line (HELOC a maximum amount from which you draw down money as needed).

- Refinance the mortgage.
- Borrow from a friend or family member.
- Borrow against a life insurance policy that has cash value.
- Sell collectibles or real estate holdings.
- Apply for a reverse mortgage.

In 2014, only 29.75 percent of Americans of all ages owned their homes free and clear.[14] Of those over sixty-five, 30 percent have mortgages. These mortgages were 82 percent larger in 2011 than they were a decade earlier. The loan has increased in relation to the value of the house, so the home owner has less equity. In the same time frame, the mortgage debt for those over seventy-five has grown from 8.4 percent to 21.2 percent.[15] Many senior citizens have larger mortgages and they're struggling to pay them. In addition, many are burdened by credit card debt: "...the one age cohort with more credit card debt in 2015 than in 2003 are those over the age of 67."[16]

You may need to borrow because your current debt payments for the mortgage and credit cards are using up your extra income— but if you borrow, you may create a downward spiral. If there isn't enough money now to pay for things, and you are living on a regular monthly income, where will the extra money come from to pay the newly borrowed money?

Will you cut back on all the luxuries and frills, and save up the extra money needed? That could work if you have been indulging in lots of luxuries and frills. However, many people would say that they are already frugal. If that's the case, adding debt may help in the short term, but lead to financial insecurity later on. Instead of adding debt, figure out why you need more cash. What is the root of the problem?

Would a reverse mortgage be a better solution than taking on the other sorts of debt on the list above?

Reverse Mortgage is the popular name for the Home Equity

Conversion Mortgage (HECM) program from the Department of Housing and Urban Development, which is administered by Federal Housing Administration (FHA). New rules for HECM were enacted October 2, 2017, so only pay attention to information or articles written after that date which are based on the new regulations. You can download the official booklet on Reverse Mortgages from the National Council on Aging website (https://www.ncoa.org/economic-security/home-equity/housing-options/use-your-home-to-stay-at-home), or call (571) 527-3900 and ask for a copy of "Use Your Home to Stay at Home." It is clear and comprehensive.

A very brief overview of HECM: The eligibility requirements include:

- You are age sixty-two or older.
- You own the home.
- The mortgage balance is low.
- Your finances are deemed by the lender to be sufficient to carry the house.
- You must enroll in counseling about HECM.
- You must maintain the house within FHA guidelines so that you keep up the value of the house; *maintenance matters.*
- You pay the real estate taxes, homeowner's insurance, usual bills- electric, water, etc.

With an HECM, your home's equity is being distributed to you. As you deplete your home equity, your loan balance grows. Be aware that the interest due on the loan is compounded and the loan amount grows. When the house is sold, the loan is repaid. The result could be that there is no equity left—nothing to leave to the children or other heirs.

An even more significant worry is foreclosure. If you cannot keep up with the real estate taxes, etc., then you could lose the house.[17]

A reverse mortgage is a complex product and, though it could be useful in some situations, it should be approached with great caution and a lot of scrutiny.

Most HECM loans are administered by FHA, and they are insured against the lender defaulting. That is good, but it is also something you are paying for. The total cost of the HECM is typically higher than the cost of a home equity loan. Be aware that there are lenders who offer reverse mortgages, but do not work through FHA. Those loans are not Federally insured, nor are their fees regulated.

Borrowing extra money from any of the sources we reviewed has consequences that you may not like. First, the loans may be band aids, not long-term solutions, because the root of the problem was not addressed. Second, more debt could harm your credit rating. A lower credit rating can lead to paying higher interest on car loans and credit cards.[18]

SUMMARY

You set aside money for retirement with the hope of ensuring comfortable years ahead. Turn that hope into confidence by analyzing your assumptions and understanding what your portfolio can and cannot do for you.

Consider the five risks in this chapter: *risk to principal, purchasing power, low interest rates, health and longevity.* For each of these risks, there are defensive actions. Know the risks, and realize that you can do something positive that can help you strengthen your portfolio so that you can maintain your house and your lifestyle. In addition, by completing the *Your Home Sweet Home* Cost Analysis, you can see whether the house is giving off early warning signs of dangers ahead.

Your retirement portfolio should pay for your needs, wants, and luxuries. A well-designed portfolio also has something set aside for emergencies. If the repairs and maintenance of the house deplete that emergency fund, the tension between the house and your retirement money grows. When the tension is at a breaking point, do you want to be pushed to choose between eating and heating, or between recreation and real estate taxes? No. Ideally, you want your portfolio to address all the risks and be resilient. You don't want your portfolio or you to be trapped by circumstances.

CHAPTER 5

Do You and Your House Pass the Test so that You Can Stay There?

Have you ever said to yourself, "I never want to leave my house?" As popular as this feeling is, it can trip you up and make for a small and unpleasant life. That is not what you want. You want a safe, comfortable, and independent life in a home that you love. You can have that. There are steps you can take to make staying home a good, enriching experience. In addition, you can quiet the voices of any friends or family members who are urging you to move out of your house.

These voices come from well-intentioned people who are uneasy about you as a couple being able to manage, or you living alone being able to take care of the house and yourself. From their point of view, you are not aware of your situation. What does *aware* mean? It could mean that you are not doing what they think they would do in your situation. Are they looking at your circumstances from your point of view of age, experience, preferences and resources? Are they evaluating your situation in terms of what would be more convenient for them, or what seems more *logical* to them?

During a leisurely afternoon's conversation with residents in a Continuing Care Retirement Community(CCRC), I asked whether most of their friends were happy in their homes. Most people said that they were. The exception was Ada—a woman who was moved there by her family. She grumbled about the coffee not being hot enough and the food not being salty enough. Her room was too small. She didn't like the view. There were lots of ways she expressed her dissatisfaction.

The residents did not yet know the details of Ada's move, but we can look at two common paths that may have led to her unhappiness, and loss of independence. The first sequence could have started with the family talking about the house being too much for Ada to maintain both physically and financially. She could see the truth in that, but she wasn't ready to make the move. The family members kept the pressure on her to move, and finally she was worn down, so she agreed. Because they had pushed hard to get her to move and sign the papers for the facility, Ada did not feel that it was really her decision. If she had been allowed to work gradually on making the transition, maybe she would have embraced the solution, and made the change with a better attitude.

Another path that could have led Ada to moving against her will is that the family determined that she was not competent. One or more family members may have decided that she could not make responsible decisions concerning legal matters, her health care, or her finances.

Someone in the family, or an attorney they hired could have gone to the Probate court with evidence for Ada's being incompetent. If the case were solid enough, the court might decide to appoint someone as a guardian for Ada. If the guardian had made the case that Ada was not safe in her home, she could have been moved.

None of us wants to be forced to do something so life-changing. One way to show that you are aware and in control is to review as objectively as you can what is happening with your house, your health and your money. Address these five areas of concern: **Safety, Use, Maintenance, Health and Money**. You will feel self-assured, and you may be able to silence the voices of those who doubt you are making good decisions. You may convince them that you really are in control and okay. That is what you and those who care about you want.

Malka Young, who oversees the Healthy Aging programs offered by Jewish Family Services, explains that safety is a balancing act. "There are different ways to increase safety which is in general a concern of the adult children...the interest of the older adults themselves generally falls on the side of autonomy." In addition, Young reminds us to focus on more than physical safety. Be aware that a safety review should cover emotional and financial safety.[1]

SAFETY, USE, MAINTENANCE, HEALTH, AND MONEY

Safety, use, and location are concerns introduced in Chapter 2, and the maintenance discussion started with the cost analysis in Chapter 3.

I presented these topics earlier with the intention of revisiting them and layering on more complexity and dimension now. Where to live during your retirement may feel like a daunting question, so you need time to think and see it from many sides. The chapters are gradually exploring the personal, physical, and financial aspects of the question so that you can develop your unique answer.

Here, the topics are made more vivid with a few stories, and then with the observations of professionals. Seeing your house through their eyes may help you prioritize what you should do to stay in your house, and help you identify which projects and upgrades are worth your money. Will a sale of the house recoup those costs?

After you go through the following review of **Safety, Use, Maintenance, Health, and Money**, if your house doesn't get a passing grade initially, you can fix the problems and then feel comfortable about staying. If the needed changes are too expensive, or they are too intrusive on your daily life—like months of hammering, sawdust and inconvenience—then those may be reasons to move.

Safety

Mildred lives in a beautiful home with a bright and modern kitchen. The colors are coordinated down to the very scatter rug, which picks up colors in the wall paper. She was getting breakfast ready one morning, and as she turned to get the eggs from the refrigerator, her slipper caught on the rug. The next thing she knew, she was in an ambulance going to hospital. She had to have hip surgery and then she spent weeks in rehab to recover her mobility.

Could something similar happen to you? Because everything about your house is familiar to you, you don't notice that scatter rug any more than Mildred does. Other safety issues could be easily ignored too.

Look at your stairs and railings. Do you have sets of stairs with either no hand rail, or one that is not secure and wobbles?

Do you have a combination tub and shower? Is it hard to step into it? Are there sturdy grab bars? Is there a shower mat to create a surface for firm footing?

What to do?

You can walk through your house with the safety checklist in Appendix D. Make a note of any potential hazards and then talk with someone who can recommend how to fix them. Another approach is to ask someone who is not familiar with your house to make a safety assessment. This can be done by a geriatric care giver, home inspector, visiting nurse, social worker, professional home organizer, someone from the fire department, or an architect. These individuals would bring a perspective from their expertise and help you identify safety hazards.

Use

We ignore the fact that we change, but the house doesn't. Our bones change, but the *bones* of the house stay the same. Your capacity to do things can change gradually and you don't notice it. The house becomes less useful and more of a storage place.

Terry invited friends over for dinner. She wants to make her favorite stew but realizes that she hasn't made that stew for a long time, and her good stew pot is on a high shelf. It is heavy and hard to get down. She talks to herself about this, "How come I haven't used that pot? It's one of my favorites. Oh, I remember now. The last time I got on the step stool, as I started to pull the pot off the shelf, the weight of the pot shifted my balance and I felt a little shaky. I had trouble steadying myself and getting down the steps. It frightened me. I've got to figure something else out."

Terry recalls the incident. She put it in the back of her mind because it made her so uneasy. Now that she is remembering what happened and is about to get on the step stool again she is very clear that she needs a different solution for where that pot is stored.

Another common utility issue is expressed by Margaret. She came downstairs one morning and was starting to make her coffee when she realized that she had forgotten to bring down a package she wanted to mail. She says to herself, "I'll get it later. It will probably get there on time for Michael's birthday if I mail it tomorrow."

Why is Margaret reluctant to climb the stairs again? Is it the pain in her knee talking? Is it her back acting up? If you've found yourself unwilling to make another trip upstairs or downstairs, what is that telling you? What should you do about it?

Are aspects of the house, like the stairs, becoming obstacles? Would a chair lift solve the problem? Would an exercise class or physical therapy be a better solution?

What to do?

Terry and Margaret both need help to make the house more user-friendly. Perhaps a professional organizer, home remodeler, or architect could suggest modifications to make all the rooms and the shelving more accessible.

Maintenance and repairs

Here's what happened to Myra and Dan one morning.

"Myra, did you start running the laundry while I was in the shower? It went cold."

"No, but even if I did, there should be plenty of hot water anyway."

Dan goes down to the basement and finds a puddle of water under the hot water heater. He comes back up. "Where's the phone number for the plumber?"

"Hi Randy, this is Dan. How ya doing? Can you come by? The hot water heater just... You what? Oh, how nice for you? Great to be retired. Who can you recommend... no one. Oh."

If checking the water heater had been on a maintenance schedule, this couple might have caught the problem before the water heater failed. They were operating on the mindset of repairs—not steady maintenance. Because of this, Myra and Dan started the day with no hot water and no plumber.

What to do?

Maintenance and repair problems are manageable when you have reliable, good tradespeople who show up on time and do the job right. Unfortunately, that's not always the case. Nonetheless, if you want to stay in your home, keeping it in good condition is imperative, both for its eventual resale value and for your health, safety, and comfort. If you are aware of what to monitor and have a list of workers with a variety of skills, you have a great foundation for intelligent maintenance. You're not going to wait for serious damage before you act.

Depending on the style and location of your house, there are more than forty regular maintenance items. Will you do those tasks yourself? Can you afford to pay for that routine maintenance, or would those expenses reduce the income you need to live on? The tug-of-war between the house and the retirement assets persists. (See Appendix A for a maintenance list)

Forty maintenance items may seem like an endless list, but some maintenance tasks are more important than others, as Claude McGavic, Executive Director of the National Association of Home Inspectors, explains. He prioritizes your tasks:

> "The primary cause of damage in any house is moisture damage. It can be everything from water damage to even high humidity in the house that creates conditions for the development of mold... If the roof is leaking and you don't get it fixed, then the ceilings are going to start leaking. If ceilings start leaking, then you're going to have dry wall or plaster damage and then you're going to have mold. One of the things you need to do inside and out is to be aware of moisture and related problems. The next major issue is going to be related to the heating and cooling equipment. That's because the cooling equipment produces moisture, it produces condensation and an air-conditioner can dump as much as twenty gallons of water a day on the outside of the house. Twenty gallons is a lot of water. If it's dumped next to the foundation and it starts leaking into the basement, you're going to have a problem. And if your air conditioning unit is in your attic and it starts leaking, it's going to leak through your ceiling."[2]

Ultimately, all the maintenance issues are about keeping your house in good shape so that it can command top value when you sell it, or your beneficiary or estate does. You may not like this idea, but remaining in your house if you can't care for it may be degrading its value. You'll see why as you hear from the experienced professionals in this section. David Doering makes two key points about maintenance: One is about using all of our senses and the other is about elders making upgrades.

As David Doering reminds us, we react to houses with all of our senses. He has worked as an appraiser for over thirty years, and has served as the President of the National Association of Independent Fee Appraisers (NAIFA).[3] Maintain your home not just for what the eyes see, but also for what the nose smells. He provided an example of his own house built in Jefferson, Missouri in 1860:

"My wife is a veterinarian. And we have a lot of dogs because we end up adopting dogs that get dropped off on us. And yet people always remark that our house always smells so fresh. Well, it's because we stay on top of it. We have our guy that we pay to deep clean our carpets, which we do about every two or three years. He has an ozone generator, and it basically attacks the odor in the air and neutralizes it. So, there may be some benefits to having things professionally cleaned. The more you can remove the negative influences within a house the better. They may be visual or perceivable through other senses, like a banister that's sticky. These are things that just grab someone and make it difficult for that person to have a positive experience going through the home and maybe wanting to make a good offer. I've been in homes where I could eat off the bathroom floor it's so clean. I just feel completely different about those. I know I'm not going to have to worry about health and sanitation issues."

If, after evaluating your house on the basis of *Safety, Use, and Maintenance*, you come away with a long list of things that need correction, don't be alarmed or assume that costly upgrades are the best solution. Consider David Doering's advice: *maintenance, not upgrades*. Clean, and not fancy wins, in his opinion. Doering says,

"Many older persons may not be able to afford $15,000 to $20,000 to remodel their kitchens and bathrooms and things like. While those changes may make the house more marketable, I don't know that the return on investment would be there for that seller. Suppose a buyer is comparing a renovated house and your lovely sweet grandma's house. She's lived there for the last fifty years and you could eat off the floor it's so clean, but nothing's been updated and it still has the pink tub and sink in the bathroom and it has the Formica countertops, but a very clean porcelain sink. Instead of worrying about upgrades, she could be realistic about those features of her house that are not up to date and be prepared to discuss them intelligently. She could acknowledge that the kitchen and bathroom haven't been changed, and provide written estimates showing the remodeling cost. The buyer might add up those estimates and compare that to a house across the street that has been updated. The buyer might still find that your grandmother's house is a better buy even adding in the remodeling costs. The buyer can remodel to their specific level and taste, at their own speed. But if you leave everything to the imagination, every buyer has a tendency to think that every repair or change is going to be monumental, when every seller thinks they're inconsequential."

Doering emphasizes that maintenance for seniors is more important than upgrades for the value of your house. Right now, you may be disinterested in the value of your house because you are saying to yourself, "The house is fine in whatever condition it's in. I am not going to move. Not now. I'm not ready." But what if, in the back of your mind, you also hear yourself saying, "Well, maybe sometime down the road I'll have to move because I'll need help." With that internal dialogue, you have constructed a *health time-line* that acknowledges possible changes to how you manage your daily activities.

Just as you have a *health timeline*, so does your house. John S. Marrazzo teaches appraisers, owns his own appraisal firm, and has appraised properties for thirty-five years. Coming from that background, he explains your home's timeline. The terms *total economic life*, and *effective age* may be unfamiliar to you, but they are important in the appraisal of your house, and therefore its value to a buyer.[4] Each property—your house included—has a *total economic life*, which means, "how long that property will have economic ability from the day it was built." That concept of *total economic life* would be important to a lender, because a lender doesn't want to provide a thirty-year mortgage on a house that seems like it will collapse in fifteen years.

It would be normal for a home inspector to comment on the condition of the roof by saying that twenty-year roofing material has a remaining ten years of life left, or the dishwasher has five years of life left. In either case, the new buyer is put on notice to budget for a new dishwasher and/or new roof.

Marrazzo adds another concept that can help you have a more objective view of the right asking price for your house—if, and when you are ready to sell it. *Effective age* is closely related to *total economic life*.

> "Effective age is not the chronological age of the property but it's the way it appears to be. Let's say it's two years old but it looks like ten years old because in the first two years it wasn't taken care of. In fact, it was abused. So, if a property has a fifty-year total economic life and has a ten-year effective age, what's remaining is forty years.
> The concept is very important because if you are dealing with elderly people who are on fixed income, they have a tendency not to repair their property as often. The effective age [the look] becomes greater and the remaining economic life becomes smaller, which affects the value."

If, for whatever reasons, the maintenance on the house has been deferred so long that serious problems are endangering your health and the health of the house, then as much as you don't want to move, it may be wiser to move. Here are two ways that some people were able to structure good outcomes.

Marrazzo spoke of one client who asked him for help; "I can't maintain this house. I should probably sell and move into an apartment. Can you help me?" So, he looked at the property, worked up some estimates for what it would cost to stop the rotting; especially the window sills, which were in very bad condition. The window sills were so bad that the rot could go from the outside to the frame of the house. Marrazzo emphasized that the owner can't cover that up with vinyl or paint.

"If your frame goes, the house collapses." He estimated that, for the homeowner he was working with,

> "by spending that $6,000 today, he could just prevent this house

from falling apart in the next five to ten years. This person unfortunately did not have the $6,000 dollars available because they were on fixed income, but he did have the ability to borrow the $6,000 through a home equity loan... Now the property was secure. Now, here's the remarkable part of that...[if] the person were to sell the house today [a year later] he would probably pick up $10,000 to $15,000 more."

The client's being able to access a home equity loan lead to a good outcome. Another approach to a better solution has been offered by some Realtors® who have encountered similar problems. They have helped the distressed homeowner make the repairs, and then the Realtors® recouped their investment through their commission when the house was sold.

Both the appraiser and the Realtors® are suggesting strategies that help the homeowner address critical repairs, and reap a greater benefit on the sale of the house. The homeowner with a team of thoughtful advisors can move from dilemma to attractive outcome.

If you want to stay in your home, and your house passes the review for safety, use and maintenance, then the next areas of concern are your finances and your health.

Finances

Chapter 3 asked for a more detailed view of what it costs to run your house. By completing *Your Home Sweet Home* Cost Analysis, you may discover surprising information that is critical for your future. Up to now, you have not taken the time, had the interest, or needed to add up all the expenses. Once you look at **all** those costs, you may say that your house is worth every penny. Great. You have the money and you are spending it on what you love.

Health

What could spoil your love affair with your house? Your health slips from, "I still feel like I'm forty" (or whatever your best decade is)", to, "I need a ride. I can't drive anymore because of what's happened with my eyes." A lot of activities you managed easily a few years ago are now an effort and require coordination with other people. When you have to fit into someone else's schedule, you may have to wait to run all your errands. You may have to pay for rides or for help with tasks that used to be easy for you to do. You may go out less and less.

Can you properly evaluate your own driving skill? Should you give up your license? If you could not drive, would you become isolated? Are you within walking distance of everything you need? Are you able to walk to those places?

Many people routinely put money aside monthly for a new car, or their next car. They know at some point the car they currently drive will need to be traded in. How about putting money aside for a taxi fund, or its equivalent Uber, Lyft, limo, or other car service? Some people dislike taking a cab because they view that as an indulgence. However, if you set aside the money for a ride as a necessary expense, it may feel as normal as paying your electric bill. Taking this approach makes this cost just part of *Your Home Sweet Home* Cost Analysis. It would be a way of maintaining your independence.

At a recent awards dinner held by the Greek Orthodox Metropolis of Boston, one of the recipients being honored for her years of service and faithfulness, was a ninety-five year woman. Her independence and competence were evidenced by her driving herself to church several times a week. That's laudable and simultaneously worrisome.

Worrisome because older drivers may be unaware that medications are impairing their responses, that their cognitive responses are slower, that their muscle weakness has reduced their ability to push hard on the brake pedal, or that arthritis makes it harder to turn their heads to check the traffic on all sides. When older drivers are in crashes, they are more likely to die because of their fragility.[5]

Though you may feel that being able to drive keeps you independent, you should be willing to stop driving when you know you've had a few too many close calls, or when someone points out, for example, that you're merging into traffic too slowly, or you are not aware of other cars as you change lanes, or that you are doing something else that is dangerous. It is hard to give up a car, but that's easier than filling out a police report for a life-changing accident. If you have given up your car, you can redirect the money you used to spend on maintenance and insurance to pay for a car service. You can still have your independence. Focus on staying as healthy as you can, which entails healthy eating, exercise, nurturing social interactions, volunteering, commitments to purposeful action, a spiritual context, and activities that challenge the mind. Staying healthy takes activity and thought and, of course, the wisdom to recognize that you don't know what *surprises* your body's chemistry is brewing.

Good health makes it reasonable to stay in your home, but what happens if your health slips? It is possible to stay at home safely, and with good home care, but is it affordable? Would you be relying on a spouse or family member to provide the care? Would that person be trained to care for you and knowledgeable about your conditions? Would that person have the time to care for you on a regular and long-term basis? If you needed to rely on home health care services, could you pay for four-hour time blocks, which have become the norm? The Genworth 2017 Cost of Care Survey cites the national median for a home health aide is $22 an hour. "It is 'hands-on' personal care, but not medical care. This is the rate charged by a non-Medicare certified, licensed agency." An annual cost could run between $34,892 in Louisiana to $63,972 in North Dakota for about 44 hours of care a week.[6] Who, among your family and friends, would watch over you for the other 124 hours?

SUMMARY

If the choices facing you now or in the near future are 1) staying at home and hiring people who can help you with your medical and physical needs, or 2) moving to a residence where that care is part of the program, would you vote to stay in your own home with some extra help? If you say, "Yes, I want to stay home," then this chapter says, yes, you can stay home. It encourages you to do that as long as you have prepared to stay by:

- Consulting with people who can help you remove safety hazards.
- Asking carpenters, home organizers, or architects to adapt the house so you can use it more effectively.
- Evaluating your income and assets to determine whether there is enough money to cover all the costs for maintaining your home and, if needed, the additional cost of homemaker health aides.
- Discussing with your health care professionals what exercises, physical therapy, food changes, and activities could support your staying as healthy as possible.

Are you realistic about your health and well-being? Are you making reasonable decisions about your finances and your health? For your own economic good and for that of your beneficiaries, are you able to accept a professional's critique and evaluation of your house, your health, and your finances? If you answered, "yes," then you are likely to remain in control of your situation and not be pushed to move as Ada was.

The review of your house in this chapter has the same purpose as the tune-up for your heating and cooling system, the oil change for your car, your annual dental appointment, etc.—to keep things in good working order. Maintaining the highest value for your house is critical for you if you want to sell your home and buy elsewhere. The proceeds from the sale might allow you to not only cover the purchase of another property, but also increase your cash flow.

Maybe you're holding on to the house for tax reasons. You don't want to pay capital gains taxes now, or you want to ensure a step-up in basis at your death so that your beneficiaries derive as much value from the house as they can.[7]

If you and your house pass the tests for staying, then relax, settle in and luxuriate in the pleasures of your home sweet home. You have done the work of evaluating your situation, implementing the recommendations of advisors, and putting in place the appropriate support structures for your finances, your safety, and your physical, emotional, and spiritual health. Instead of passively letting circumstances dictate a solution, you have made a decision. That's something to be proud of.

CHAPTER 6

Hear What Friends Are Saying about "Do I Stay, or Do I Move?"

As you read this chapter, imagine you're walking through spacious rooms full of people talking about the very topic that interests you right now. It is a relaxed, friendly atmosphere and they're puzzling about whether they should stay in their current homes or move elsewhere. For many people, arriving at an answer to that question means traveling through a tangle of impediments: fears of change and loss, the death of a spouse, worries about making friends, insecurities about being independent, remaining relevant, making new routines, and doing things that are meaningful. One person will be adding on to what someone else says. You'll get the gist of their messages. You may stay engaged with some speakers for a long time, and with others for only a few sentences.

There's just a brief introduction, then you may hear someone expressing pretty much what you're thinking or someone else may offer a perspective that's new to you. In either case, you're in *your group*. They are simpatico. They know what you are struggling with. They get it. They are not going to be glib about the emotional, financial or practical questions that are running around in your head. Enter this evening's party and enjoy the soiree.

Here's Charlotte. She's in her eighties, living alone in a third-floor walk-up and contending with her kids who want her to move.

"My children keep saying, 'Ma, you won't be able to walk' and they're nagging me to find some place so that *they* can feel more comfortable themselves. I realize that they're right, but I love where I live. I love, love, love where I live, and I have friends here in the condo. I have a plot in the community garden. That's a source of the great joy to me.

I think they have a point, but I feel that if I have a hip replacement or something like that, I would just call one of my friends and say, 'Can I come and stay at your place?' I've already mentioned that to one of my friends. She said, 'Sure.' And she has an elevator building. I think I could manage these things. It's not impossible. So, I'm really not ready to make the move right now.

The reason why it's not positive [to move] is that I can't find a place that I say, 'Oh wow! This is so terrific. I am so glad I'm here.' I have a deposit down on a place near my younger daughter but I don't want to live in one of those places. I really don't.

I'm used to having young people around. That's one of the reasons I like to tutor, because then I have some young people around. I love children. I love, love, love children. So, I would be in a place where there are very few children. A friend of mine is in a place where they have classes and stuff like that, but it's not the same.

I love being a part of the community. I am a very important part of the community because I'm active in local politics. I know people. I can walk down the street and meet people I know.

These are people that I do bicycle trips with and they are very amazed that I can do as much as I can and I keep telling them, 'Keep active, keep active, keep active,' and they do that. We usually go about 20-25 miles.

I know from doing a lot of reading on this that you should not be isolated. If I couldn't drive [at the other place], then I would be isolated. Here I can take public transportation from where I live and get to various places, and I do that. I love being on the top floor. I'm on the top floor and I can look out in the trees and everything else. Beautiful. I don't want to give that up."

Eileen is about twenty years younger than Charlotte, but they share some concerns. Hip replacements—Eileen has already had two, and while she was recovering she became painfully aware of the uneven streets near her house and the inconvenience of having to walk twenty minutes to board the nearest public transportation. Though she is not ready to retire completely, she is clear that the issue is not as much leaving a house she enjoys, but rather where to go next. She wants more privacy and quiet, but Helene, her partner, prefers much more activity and people nearby. Ollie, the Icelandic Sheepdog, did not bark to say which environment he preferred. He will continue to be pampered and loved wherever they move. Eileen makes it clear that her concern about retirement is not just where to live, but how to engage life:

"What would make it meaningful? Starting last year, I thought I should begin to do some retirement like activity. So, I started to take some lifelong learning courses and I also started to write a memoir.

I think my concern is to have activities that feel truly meaningful to me, so, I need to zero in on some kind of volunteer activity.

The best part of what I think happens in good communities where people trust each other and care about each other is that they can model good things and they can encourage each other to do more and to take on life in a very positive way. One of my concerns about the house, the retirement, is that people get stuck and too afraid to make a change. They live in circumstances that keep pressing in on [them], instead of getting liberated out of that to something.

My thinking personally is that it's not the difficulty of making change, it's the difficulty in deciding the next steps. You've got to be real clear about it."

Eileen highlights a category of people who are *stuck and too afraid to make a change*. What could stop the walls from closing in on them?

Maybe the fear would be lessened if the person could see the next steps as enticing, and favorable. Kalliope Barlis, who played golf professionally, has redirected what she learned on the golf circuit to help people get rid of their fears, maintain their well-being, and achieve more.[1]

"Dr. Richard Bandler told me about a famous family therapist named Virginia Satir who once said that the greatest instinct in people is not survival, but that the greatest instinct in people is to keep things familiar.

Most of the time when people fear, whatever it is that they're fearing doesn't even have to be in their presence. Basically, the older parent who is sitting in their home is thinking about not being in their home and being somewhere where they've never been. The person sees horrible things happening. That's what scares them. They're building these pictures of the unknown that are usually life size or bigger than life size. Let's say, in the instance of someone who fears dogs: it's usually a great big dog moving in towards them. It gets bigger as it's moving in towards them, while they're thinking about it. They don't even have to be near the dog.

Instead, we help them make pictures of staying home in loneliness, with hunger because they can't feed themselves. They don't know how to use an oven anymore. Once that sort of stuff is made even bigger, then they'll want to move away from those images and move towards the bigger pictures you create by describing the in-home movies, the in-home activities, the in-home social life [of the new residence].

If a woman likes the company of a man, think of how many boyfriends she can have in [an assisted living]...I'm not kidding. You know I've got a woman who was just moved into a home, and she's already got three boyfriends for herself. You know she's gone on more dates than my nieces and nephews. Once you start building these sorts of pictures inside their mind that are positive, they'll want to move towards that place. Think of how much more connected you'll be with the people around you. Because you'll have likeminded people in the same age group, you can talk about the same good times that you used to share, the same movie stars that were popular, the same music that is anchored in their minds. The new place becomes more of a compelling experience to want to move towards, instead of being a change that they're afraid of. Once you start talking about possibilities of what they'll experience and helping them see and hear and feel it, they'll be able to imagine their future in a better way. The transition will be easier. I mean, acceptance of moving will be more forthcoming to the older parent."

Joyce is not afraid to move, but Karl is resistant. She's trying to figure out their next steps and is cautiously drawing her husband into imagining what the next home might be like. She reasons that the value of their house has

"gone up enormously, but that doesn't help. It's paper money. It's not real money, at this point, unless you sell it, and then you have to think about where else you're going to live and what it's going to cost you.

My husband [in his eighties] still thinks he's twenty-five and that he can still do everything. It's a great attitude, but he doesn't recognize all the things that he can't do, and he really can't and he doesn't want to pay to get anyone to do them. So, it's an ongoing battle. I finally persuaded him a couple of years ago, because I could no longer do it, to get someone to help do the shoveling—the snow shoveling and plowing—and they don't do a great job, but they do an adequate job up to a point, better at plowing the driveway than they are at hand shoveling any of the walks, and I really need them cleared free of ice.

Well, I think we can probably stay here, I would say, another five years and I've thought about alternatives and haven't really decided what we would do. I've looked at a couple of options. I really have. [Karl's] not willing to consider them, but it doesn't matter at this point. I think that I just keep talking about it periodically, not too often, and trying to get him out to look at various places and consider various options and I really don't know at this point whether it would be some kind of a senior community or just what. It really depends on how our health continues, it really does, and what we're able to do or not able to do as we get even older.

Not knowing where, ...well, that would be the biggest thing as far as leaving goes. We'll have to cross that bridge eventually, but not at the moment. At the moment, it's cheaper and easier to stay here and deal with the issues around this house."

Mark and his wife, a nurse practitioner specializing in geriatric care, sympathize with Joyce because they had to make two moves to get to the right house. Mark thinks that their current house will be good for them in the long run.

"I think what people most need to think about is location and it's where they're moving near to, the things they want to be near to, whether it be family or amenities, in our case, the synagogue. Since we moved into a house across from the synagogue, we already know a lot of people nearby.

I think we've found the best of all worlds, which is a house that can easily be lived in on one floor without going into the basement. There's a laundry down there now, but if we get to the point where the stairs are an issue, we can bring that upstairs and just live on this floor. I think this is a house that we could continue to live in until we reach a point where we need to go into assisted living or something, but we're only 60, which is, I guess, young these days."

Is it easy to make friends as you're in your 60s?

"I would say it's not difficult, but you have to put yourself out there. Since I retired early, I face a lot of questions from people about why I did that; especially men came to ask how I could stand to do that because a lot of men are so tied to and identified by their work personas that they didn't know how they would function without it. And I would say it was particularly easy for me because I was becoming so much more involved in synagogue activities. They gave me a ready-made thing that I had to get up and do in the morning. I met a lot of people who immediately had similar values and interests to me. So, I've made a lot of friends. I don't think any of them are particularly deep friendships, but I've got a lot of people that I know and interact with and you've got to be careful not to isolate yourself. I was fortunate that I had kind of a ready-made mechanism to make sure that didn't happen.

I think I'm very successfully retired, and I define it as the ability to continue to have meaningful things to use my time on. You can define meaningful in a whole host of ways, but I have several of them and they fill a lot of time. I feel fairly accomplished, even though they're not things that are money earning jobs for the most part. So, having meaningful activities, that's positive. Then remove the negative things by having a financial plan that you're able to put together and then set it aside and not [be] worried about it. If you have a plan— and I think this is true of life in general, in my opinion—if you have an issue, you have to convince yourself to only worry about it for a certain amount of time, decide whether it's anything you can do something about and then don't let yourself think about it. Retirement financial planning is probably the quintessential example of that—where you've got to have a plan, decide you're comfortable with it, and then only review it once every three or six or twelve months and otherwise don't think about it because you can drive yourself nuts worrying about the things you could need money for and what could happen. ...

We are extremely, acutely aware of the fact that in terms of unexpected things that can happen in your financial planning, probably the biggest hit is needing long-term care and it's not really unexpected; it's sort of predictable statistically. So, I would say a combination of just being aware of the potential problem, and being nudged a little bit, got us to make that decision. The earlier you do that, the cheaper the insurance is."

As a business owner and father, what did you say to yourself when circumstances were really difficult?

"Oh, that's such a great question. I have access to a lot of religious teachers, and one of them, Aliza Bulow, a well-known teacher in the Orthodox Jewish community, posted one day on her Facebook page an answer to that question. Actually, that was shortly after one of her children had committed suicide. Which is, I think, one of the worst things a person can have to deal with. Anyway, this is what she said, and I actually carry this in my pocket and refer to it occasionally. She says that for scary times I say the last line of a prayer in the Jewish literature that reads, 'God is with me. I will not fear.' For confusing times, she'd say, 'There's nothing else but God.' And when she wants to elevate her mood she says, 'This is the day God has made for me. Let us rejoice and be happy.' And when she's brimming with thankfulness, she says,

'Give thanks to God. His kindness is everlasting.' So, I thought, 'Wow! That's such a great collection of things to think about when you're feeling like you're going through difficult times.'"

Your wife will be working for another five years. What will happen when she retires?

"I think it will be different in that we've been very successfully married for 41 years, but we've never had to spend a lot of time together in the same house during an average day. One of us has always been working. So, outside of when we're both on vacation or traveling together, we only spend two or three hours a day together, which, over 41 years, is a lot of time; but being in the same house for 16 or whatever waking hours every day, I think, is a very challenging idea for a relationship, and I think we're going to have to negotiate our way through that thoughtfully or we will drive each other insane.

In fact, we got, not intentionally, with this little house a massive backyard—I mean truly massive, I can't believe how big it is—and she's been talking about building what they call—I don't know what female version of a man cave is—a man cave for herself in the backyard so that she has somewhere to go to get away from me.

I do think that's a real issue. Not just for us, but being sort of in an enclosed space with the same person for long numbers of hours, no matter how much you care about them, is a challenge that you need to figure out some solutions for. Beyond that, I don't see it changing much for me.

I do worry that she's not as good a candidate for retirement as I was. I don't think she has as clear an idea of what to do with her time. I think it will be a challenge for her and my challenge will be helping her and coping with her anxiety, but I don't think it will change the way I spend my time and how I view my retirement much beyond that."

Mark has settled into retirement, but for Bruce, a real estate developer, and Susan, a psychologist, retirement doesn't fit the way they see the world, probably because they have always been self-employed. Susan says, "If retirement means I stop doing the things I love professionally, it doesn't make any sense to me."

Since real estate development is a cyclical business, and Bruce has always been busy even during the many downturns in that market, his son quipped, "*How would we know if you were retired?*"

As they age, Susan observed, "It becomes more and more about family." Bruce added, with a smile, acknowledging his bias, "As you get older, you find your family really has more advantages...you like them better, their children are more interesting. They're the most fun people to be with."

Bruce's harmonious snapshot of his family life contrasts with what Diana lived through. Diana's mother did not want anything to change, which may have driven Diana to become the change agent in her family, and a high achiever in school and her career. Her mother left the responsibility to Diana to take care of her brother, who is now 70, "autistic and retarded." She had to put both her mom and dad into a nursing home. As she raised two sons, one with special needs, she grew into a powerful figure with her own international management consulting firm. She had to be at the top of her game.

> "I filled every single block of time with some things to do, because some things to do means that it's a distraction from—from being, from just being. There's this distraction of human doing versus human being.
>
> There was always a façade in front of the curtain and [me] at the back of the curtain. It's currency in our society now that we're busy. One must be busy. Otherwise, what are you doing with your life? If you're not volunteering, what do you do with yourself? I don't want to spend time carelessly, just like I don't want to spend money carelessly, even though I keep spending money carelessly."

She retired to regain her sense of authenticity. There was "a growing disconnect of authenticity – 'Who am I really?'"

As she moves into an over fifty-five community, Diana has, as part of her spiritual quest, the intention "to be quiet and not be hyperactive." Another change is to be able to ask for help. That is hard for her because she demanded so much of herself as the person in charge and responsible for necessary outcomes. She describes the move itself as a continuous internal process:

> "I think it's really important, and I am saying this to myself as much as I am saying it to you—to be iterative and to achieve the feeling— I hope this is going to be okay. I don't want to move again, but I am willing to move again. I don't know for how long this will be my home. I must appreciate the accomplishment of doing this [move] and allow patience and compassion and see how it works. ...I just accepted that we don't have all the answers in front of us. I wish I had, but I don't."

Geralyn advises people on how to accept their new and unfamiliar home. She tells people who move into Sophia Snow Place:

> "Give yourself six months to a year before you know if you like it or not. You need that much time. No one likes it the first month. They've got boxes. You're moving in and you can't find things. If you're used to a gas range and you get an electric range you've got to remember to take the pots off because it doesn't turn off.
>
> I just fell in love with it [Sophia Snow Place]. I was too young, so I had to wait a year, I sold my house and moved in. I had to move. I knew I was moving from a bungalow to this place. I was in a prayer group at St. John Chrysostom's. And you develop relationships there, and I was lamenting about moving and the prayer group said we'll take care of it.
>
> So, one Saturday, I invited them into the house. It was four of them that came in and they did a garage sale and I went to the library and sat there for a couple of hours and just thought this is really weird. And came back and all my stuff that people wanted was gone. And then they put the rest of the stuff out for the collection the next day.
>
> It's a decision you have to make. So, there's always regrets, but you know you can say, the glass is either half full or half empty. So, I chose to look at the half full side of the whole process. When I moved in, it was scary. Because I'd lived in apartments in my college years, I thought that's what this was going to feel like. And you know, there was just a nice group of people. I was the youngest. I had a lot of grandmothers and grandfathers. But that quickly became not as important as just the friendships. So, ages, you know, became less and less of importance.
>
> I was officially diagnosed in 1990. I had some symptoms in 1988,

but the worst part was my sister always had Multiple Sclerosis(MS). She was five years younger. She never accepted it at all. She never took any of the treatments. When I moved here, it was because physically I was too isolated being in my own house. Here I can get all my services that I need, a la carte. I mean, I feel lucky in that physical therapists come in. I had to give up my car when I moved in here, so I gave it to someone. Moving can't be a loss. It has to be a gain, somehow.

Another thing that I find interesting is when people say I can do it, I can do it. Well, yes, you can do it, but you're spending a lot of time and energy, someone else [can do it for you]; give them the joy of doing it for you, with you.

I remember when I was first walking with a cane, and it was aggravating the heck out of me. And I remember being at the Newton Library, and I was feeling sad, because I was walking with my cane. They have a long walkway to get to their front door.

And I remember this little girl, I don't know, ten years old, skipping around to the door in front of me, and her little pony tail bouncing. She turned around and she saw me; and she smiled from ear to ear and held the door open for me. I realized at that point that I was giving her joy by her opening the door. I mean how how easy was that for me to do, to say thank you.

I was bold and I walked up to this woman [who I guessed was her mother] and I said, 'Can I tell you something about your daughter?' I could see the woman going 'Oh, great what is she doing now.' You know, you just see that on her face. I said, 'I just want to thank you for raising her to be so helpful to me.' And the woman smiled…and I could see that look between mother and daughter, just smiling at each other. She goes, 'Well, thank you.' And I turned away and I walked to my car. I remember this all these years. I remember how that's all it took, you know, was for me to say thank you to the girl and then just, it was just wonderful, you know."

Esther, like Geralyn, celebrates what is special in nature and in people. At ninety-three, she continues to be a renowned and effective Jewish educator; she teaches, writes poetry, and comforts people in her community. She took care of her husband as he died of cancer and subsequently she moved to a retirement community. Esther explains that he would not have wanted to make that move.

"No. Because he was an individualist. He wanted things his way, and no other way. No, no, because he would say, 'I don't want to go to dinner when they tell me to go to dinner, even though you have a flexibility. I don't want to eat what they're giving me.' He was just he was a great guy, but you know..."

The move

"I announced to my kids that I wanted to move to Boston. And they were very surprised. They said, 'Are you sure, are you sure?' because I was very active and involved in the community where I lived. I said, 'Yes I think I'm sure because I want to make life easier for you guys.'

I couldn't bring everything, obviously. But I sort of compromised. This place is maybe half of the space that I had, so I took the furniture from what they call the family room, and the buyers bought the living room and the dining room. They loved the two big sculptures that I couldn't take. So, they got a real bargain. Of course, I had to think about how I would put things together here, so with my son, Andy, we made a floor plan, and we measured every piece, and we sort of knew beforehand what I could take and what I couldn't take."

Are you still growing as a person?

"Yes, because I think, because I read a great deal. I prepare for my sessions.

So, I do research and, and I'm very happy when I do the session and people are satisfied, and so, yes."

Goals:

"If you don't set goals, you float and you don't know what's going to be the next day, what's going to be the next. If I didn't have lectures to prepare, or books to read, it would be very sad. I need that to give meaning to my life."

Like Esther, Mike and Tina loved where they lived. On gift giving holidays:

"we didn't buy a gift for each other. We would take that money that we were going to spend on each other, and do something for the house. Come Mother's Day, we'd go out and buy all new plants, flowers and what not. And I used to do all that sort of thing. Whenever we did something around the house, there was never a thought of—oh, we'll get our money back."

They were fastidious about keeping the house in the very best condition, even painting it every two or three years. In their view, if you aren't going to do that, you shouldn't have a house.

But they were getting tired of keeping that high standard. Mike explains:

"We had three bedrooms upstairs, three bedrooms downstairs. So, the house became quite a headache. Just by chance we were home and I got a call from a real estate person that I knew and he came over and he said, 'Mike why don't you sell the house?' I guess he caught us at the right time and I said, 'Yeah why not?'"

Though they had kept their house like a showplace, and doted on it, within six months they were happily established in their new apartment, which they think is perfect for their needs. No regrets at all. They just decided to move and they moved.

Tamara and her husband were like Mike and Tina in agreeing that they needed to move, but in their case, it was more about unused space:

"I loved the space. I loved the house. We raised our children there. But we just realized that there were rooms that we never went in. ...I think we realized...the boys' rooms were never going to be used again. We had a large finished basement that they used, that we weren't going to be using, and I think we pretty much articulated to each other the fact that it was a lot of space that we loved but that we didn't need."

To those who resist moving, her advice is:

" I'd say take a good look at what you're doing and the energy that you're expending on things that you could do other things with."

Sarah explains that her mother's transition, which took longer than Mike and Tina's, was smooth and she avoided a mistake that many others are making.

"She [Glennie] was seventy-four at the time. And she thought she was too young to move into the retirement community. She was actually thinking about going into an apartment complex in the city instead. It was her decision, but we all voiced that we thought it was stupid to make two moves if she could make only one. It was just going to be a lot easier for her to get situated, and that's finally what she decided to do.

What she knew was that she could not maintain the house that she was in. It wasn't really a cost issue; it was more of just the sheer logistics of managing that big property. And she knew she couldn't do that. She didn't want her whole life to be swept up in doing that. That was the primary motivator for her. It was more about 'I just don't want this headache.'

The only reason they stayed in the house as long as they did was Mom wanted Dad to be able to die there. The last year, when he couldn't take care of a whole bunch of stuff, it was really hard on her. Right after he died, a couple of things happened, which really drove the issue home.

There was a huge storm. They had a house on the river, just south of Richmond on the James River. There was a huge storm that took out the dock. It not only took out the dock, but it took out the power. She was having to start the generator herself and she had to make arrangements to get the dock rebuilt and replaced. If there was any doubt in her mind if she wanted to stay (and there wasn't), that storm just clinched things.

But the big decision that we had to make, or that mother had to make, was how much to put down versus starting with the higher monthly payment [for Cedar Fields]. What was the breakeven to which she had to live. My husband did all of the analysis for her on that. When the breakeven date came, he actually called her and said, 'I just want you to know that this is the breakeven date that you didn't think you'd live for.'

She had moved so many times, moving was not an issue. There was no attachment to houses. She had moved all her life. And what she saw as the reason for doing this was a whole lot more freedom. So, she was able to see the benefit and to see what she was going to as opposed *to* what she was going *from*. I think the key is seeing the benefit in what you're going to as opposed to what you're leaving behind. Resistance to change comes from (a) fear of the unknown and (b) not seeing the good stuff and only seeing the good stuff that is going to be lost."

Marcia Grace, like Glennie, had a spouse whose health determined the decisions about the house. Marcia Grace sold a house because her husband could not manage the stairs anymore. They bought another house where they could build a deck so he could

"enjoy being outside. The bedroom is on the main floor. He passed. I live here alone. I suppose if I couldn't go up and down stairs I wouldn't be able to do my laundry because the washer/dryer is in the basement."

How do you define old?

"Old to me means frail. It means infirm, weak... Age is a number, and that is all it is. It's just a number."

Do you have models in your mind of people who aged well?

"Many, many... [their characteristics] are energy. They're curious. They are go-getters, independent thinkers, creative, passionate."

The house interferes with what she is passionate about.

"I loved maintaining the house until I really got passionate about writing my book [*Calm, Creative, Joyful: Lessons in Transforming Your Life*]. Now I just don't have time."

Marcia Grace and her husband bought into a house that was better for them, but Margaret and her sisters didn't have the authority to sell the house and move their mother to something more appropriate. The transition for Margaret's eighty nine year old mother took a long time because she resisted change. The daughters had to work at making the move happen:

"A few years before that my sisters would come down from upstate and they would try to get her to start cleaning out the house. That's how it started. The other thing was that she started to lose her memory, so over the years it was the cleaning out of the house, and my sister saying, 'You know you should move upstate. What do you need this big house for? There's nobody around you. There's no activity.'

I think it took her a while to come to the point where she was accepting the fact. That's all I can say. I just see my mother as very closed. She's not a very open person in terms of her feelings. So, we didn't know where she was coming from. We kind of knew she was digging in her heels a little bit. But, finally, I think she saw the writing on the wall. It was her decision.

We didn't force her into it. We just kept telling her that, you know, this is probably the best thing for you. She's a very active person, and there was really, at that point, nothing around her to do I think she waited too long. I'm seventy-four, I have said to myself, and I hope I can stick to this, that by the time I'm eighty, I want to make a decision as to what I'm going to do because being in a home, in a suburban community, you are isolated.

I'm going to reach a point where I don't want the responsibility anymore. I don't mind the gardening, but I'm getting to the point where I don't even want to go out there and water my flowers. I do like to garden, all right, but you know...when you live alone, you're the one making all those decisions.

So, for example, I have to make a decision about having my driveway sealed. Now I have to go through the process of trying to find someone to seal my driveway. If I had a list of people at my command that I could go to, it would be easier, but there are certain jobs that I have to look for somebody and that to me is draining. I don't even know where to begin. I went to Angie's List. I got two names, I called those two names. One of them didn't follow up at all. To the other one I said, 'Please I would like to meet the person. I have cracks in my driveway. I want to discuss it with you.' The guy comes and he leaves me an estimate in my box. I'm not dealing with that. Now I have to start from day one. It's things like that that I feel are too much.

I understand now why some older people live in homes that are just in a state of disrepair. Either they don't have the money to fix those things, or just don't have the energy to fix them, and don't have family close by that can help them."

Exceptions to Margaret's observation that some older people don't keep up their homes are Claire and Lois. Even though they were in their early eighties when Claire and Lois sold their three-story Second Empire Victorian, they were tireless in keeping their house in top condition. They were *house poor* from a cash flow point of view, but they used a home equity line judiciously for all the repairs and maintenance. The property appreciated tremendously over the fifty-five years that they owned it, but so did the real estate taxes and the demands for repairs. Had Lois not fallen and broken her hip, they would have stayed in the heart of the city, and not moved to Independent Living at Springhouse.

> Claire: No one wants to leave their house. ...No one wants to...
> Lois: No one wants to leave their life.
> Claire: Leave their home.

Why? Aren't you living better now?

> Claire: No one knows that. No one knows that. They don't know that until they get here.
> Lois: Most people think the same way as what you said, though they would not enunciate it. My life is over and I have to leave my wonderful neighborhood and my neighbors or whatever, and move away and do this, and sequester myself somewhere. That's the way people feel.
> Claire: Can't convince them.
> Lois: And people, it's all right to feel that way. My advice to people is you have to realize that you have to be practical, and that's a terrible, terrible thing to say. Most people are not going to move unless there is an extremely compelling reason such as death, serious illness...
> Claire: Alzheimer's.
> Lois: Alzheimer's, or a change in financial circumstances. It would be nice if the human condition was such that people said, 'Well, you know, when I'm seventy, I really know that I'm going to have move.' No. That does not happen. It would be nice. Some people do it and then afterwards they say, 'Why did I do this?' ...Nobody wants to change

their routine. It takes a major life event to do it. And that's not my advice that you should wait, but I understand. I didn't want to change. Nobody wants to change; they want to stay where they are, where everything's familiar.

Claire: Everybody wants to die at home.

Lois: Everybody wants to have God take them from their seat as they are, and they can wave goodbye to everybody and just say that's the way it is. I've lived my life, thank you all for being here, you can take care of what's left. That's what people want.

Claire: We cried for two weeks. ...

Lois: I didn't want to be here and I didn't want to be there. We didn't know where we wanted to be. I don't know about her, but I know...

Claire: That was the same way I felt.

Lois: What were you crying about?

Claire: I don't know. I could have died that day. I could have died then, and I would have been happy. I would have been, I was really... ready to go. I was ready to go. And I mean...

Lois: Because your life you felt was over. Except you wouldn't have left me.

Claire: No, I wouldn't. I couldn't leave her. ...I mean the people here were wonderful to us...I mean going into this foreign territory, going down to eat supper, was horrible. The people were so nice to us and they just gathered us around. ...They were wonderful. They were like mothers to us.

Lois: Yes, they were. They were very nice to us.

Claire: And within two weeks...I was going down to supper and it was the first time in forty-five years we had not been away on Memorial Day weekend, and I started to cry...and I thought, 'Well, by the time I get down [to the dining room] it will all stop.'

Lois: She couldn't stop.

Claire: I couldn't stop. And I go down there [everyone was asking]... 'Is she okay? What can we do? ...What's wrong?'

'Well, you know this is the first time we haven't gone away.' So, one friend came up, ...'Oh, you don't want to go there this weekend. It's too cold.' And I said, 'Yeah, and the black flies will eat me alive.' And I started to laugh and it was okay. It was okay.

Lois: The community has been kind to us.

Claire: It was hard. The people have been so kind to us and you know, I mean it was just, I can't tell you why, how we were feeling. She was feeling worse than I was.

Lois: I was so depressed.

The laughter, friendships, projects and creative community have made their new address a home where they are nurtured, involved in committees, and enjoying their lives.

The sense of being in a caring community was a major attraction for Marilyn and her brother-in-law, Leon. Within eighteen months, each of them made the decision to move into Brookdale Lakeside. Leon appreciates his new home.

"I feel it's a very good community and I like the variety of things that are offered. I had an angiogram in January, and they said some of the blockages in my heart can no longer be reached. So, my intent was to come here, be ready for anything that occurs with the heart at this point. I think it's wonderful that whatever old age might present to you they have, through their efforts, put together a facility that will take care of your home needs, your health needs, your individual care needs, your food, and shopping and the fact that you may not be able to move as well as you did in the past. Somebody else is available to help wash the clothes, to help clean the apartment.

They explained Medicare and I thought it was a tremendous advantage to have ready for the future. Well, the future is now. I feel that they have activated what I didn't even think I would be using. I think that's great."

Marilyn moved in before Leon did. She had visited many retirement communities, read brochures, searched on her computer, and she recalls:

"I just kept thinking, 'I may have ten years left, I may have six, but I don't want to spend the rest of my life dragging groceries and shoveling snow. No, there is an easier way out there.'

My other sister, [Leon's] wife she died first. So, I lost her, then my husband, then my son, then my daughter, and then my other sister.

Every time I lost one more person, I thought, 'I'm going look for an apartment, I don't need this whole big house.' So, I spent like five, six years, looking for senior places. First, just apartments, you know, and then switching over to facilities where you could get assisted living. I was definitely wanting to stay in the city. And I'd seen so many beautiful buildings and facilities. I was very impressed by one place. It's a little more expensive, and has a really elaborate lobby, and you know, just more impressive. The thing that impressed me, which is stupid, I loved their library. It was huge. Of course, ours here is great, but it's smaller. As I'm thinking of that, I think 'but they have the big library.' And I'm like 'how many books can you read at one time. All I need is one book at a time. I'm not going to read all 3,000 books in the library.'

My nephew was with me that day, and I said, 'Could we go back to the first one I looked at?' I said, 'It just seems like it just had good vibes about it,' and now I don't know why—we walked in the lobby and I was like 'this feels like being home.' There were people talking to each other. When I walked in here, the staff, everybody seemed to know all the residents by their first name.

Well that's it. I went through a session where I really was ill and I was in the hospital on and off for like three months. Up until that point I had never been ill, you know. It was a real shock to find out how weak you can get and how suddenly you find yourself in a position where you can't do anything for yourself, especially in the beginning.

I had already planned to move into an apartment. I didn't want to take care of the house, her house or our house. We just sold our house and I wound up with my daughter's home after she, she was single, after she passed away. Then I thought, 'I'm really lucky I've got two homes that I can't take care of.' It was the middle of winter. We got snow. She had a beautiful lot and a half yard. She was so good with the flowers, but in the good weather there was always cutting the grass. All I could think of was, 'Oh, my gosh. I'll never have any time for myself.'

Then I had to spend more time shopping for groceries and not really wanting to eat dinner anyway, so I would get something frozen because it was easier than cooking a whole dinner. I was looking for a smaller senior apartment, until I got so sick, and then I was thinking that maybe I needed something more than just an apartment for myself. Thinking if I get sick like that again then what do I do, move out of my independent apartment, and look for a place when I'm already sick? So, I thought, no, instead of looking for just a senior apartment I was looking for a facility that could take care of me if and when I needed help. I wouldn't have to pack up again and move everything and start from scratch."

Both Leon and Marilyn are in their eighties and are enthusiastic about their new home. Kristen, the Director of Sales and Marketing for Brookdale, remarked that people make assumptions about independent and assisted living communities:

> Kristen: It's interesting because everyone I talk to has this thought that if they move to a community like this that they will somehow lose their independence and lose that sense of freedom and independence.
>
> Marilyn: That's, gosh no...I warned my grandsons, be careful. I'm in a great place. I don't use as much energy. I may live ten years longer. We have more time to do things that we want to do.
>
> Leon: Very much so.

With their wheelchairs and walkers, a couple of dozen residents went to a Cubs game. Had the residents been living alone in their own homes, that trip and many other outings might not have been possible for them. Being home alone was confining, but being in the assisted living setting gave them more freedom and independence.

Gayle, the Director of Business Development for Brookdale, explains that for some people a concern about being independent is secondary to the gripping fear of making a change.

> Gayle: Change, in general, is scary at times, and when someone's been living in the same condo for fifty years, to just even think about moving is just a lot. It almost doesn't even get to —I'm losing my independence, it's...this is home. I've been here for fifty years. This is where I want to be.
>
> Marilyn: If you've lived the same life for fifty years, and haven't experienced a lot of changes, it must be a terrifying feeling to just move out of your little house where you feel secure. But they don't even realize what they're missing.

For Marilyn, deciding on assisted living took years, but Kathryn knew before she retired that she wanted to move to Independent Living. Kathryn had the advantage of having worked in Planned Giving for Presbyterian Homes, retirement communities.

"Actually, my work made it very clear to me that this was a very good move, because people are never alone. And their needs are met. I used to tell people that statistics really show that those who have good nourishment, good medical care, good socialization, and good diet are going to live longer and have happier, more productive lives. So, I decided it was time to put my money where my mouth was.

I worked until I was seventy-five because I liked working. I loved the routine and so forth. And I wondered what I would do. I volunteer at a Second Time Around shop which benefits Shore Community Services, which is for physically and mentally challenged adults. I can't volunteer where my son is because it's too far. But this one is closer.

It was sort of a joke. I worked in a retirement community. And I said, 'When people start to think that I live there rather than I work there, I think maybe it's time to leave.' ...A resident at one of the homes said to me when I was getting ready to retire, 'Well, knowing when to retire is kind of like falling in love. When it's right, you know it.' And I thought what a profound observation. It was true. When it's right you know it. And I guess I just decided it was right."

Kathryn sold her home about a year and a half after her husband died. What she says to others about making a change is:

"Not to be afraid to make the change, but to find out where you're going and to be confident. You don't have to know anybody in the community. I have a friend who moved to one of the Presbyterian Homes communities. When she was in her former neighborhood, she thought she had reached a point where all of her friends were gone or moving away. But now that she's moved into the retirement community, she told me that she had no idea that she would make so many new, good friends. She said, 'Oh, I've made all these wonderful new friends, and we have so much in common.'

And, you know, age breaks down barriers that we have when we're at the point where we're trying to claw to get to the top, or to be the best, or to be socially acceptable, or whatever our internal clock is doing. ...Don't be afraid of who you are. You'll make new friends."

Marilyn has something to add about friendships:

"One of our residents said to me, 'I have a question to ask you.' And I said, 'Sure.' And she said, 'Do you think sex at ninety-one is okay?' And I said, 'If you feel like it, if it's okay for you, who am I to say no.' If you feel old, it eventually restricts you from what you can or want to do, then you're old, you know."

Sally tacks on her definition of *old people*.

"They're not involved. They're not learning. They're negative and just waiting to die. Giving up on life. I don't know if it's a part of self-worth, if you're saying okay, I'm not worthwhile anymore because the kids are grown, and I've got cancer or whatever, and they forget to live life. There's still life there, you know, make it happen.

Certainly, the aging process, you can't stop it. But you can take better care of yourself, so you can still have fun.

Think positively for one thing. Stay involved with other people. Don't become a hermit. Take part in active learning and keep having fun.

Many people don't want to think they'd move to a retirement community because that means they're old. But then once they get here, they see that it enhances their life tremendously."

Sally and her husband moved to The Clare[2] with a sense of adventure, and no regrets about leaving their condo.

"It was almost whimsical. I mentioned to my husband one day that I heard about this place, and I thought maybe we could buy a place, rent it out until we were ready for it. Then I kept hearing about it. So, we decided we'd go to one of the introductory luncheons. We were still young. We went to that model and we both got excited about the possibilities, and what a nice gift it would be to our kids. And how we wouldn't have to worry about being cared for. We'd been taking care of our parents, in one way or another and we wouldn't have to burden the kids with that."

Sally explains that it is a community, not just people doing activities together. It is people really caring about each other. Her husband died very recently:

> "If I hadn't been here when my husband died, I don't know what I would have done. But they just envelop you; they're wonderful."

About nine years ago, when his wife died, Bob didn't have a big community around him.

> "I didn't appreciate when my mother died. She died at about seventy or seventy-one, and my father was left alone. I didn't understand how deeply that must have hurt the man until I lost my wife, which was way too late then to understand as far as my relationship with my father went.
>
> My wife and I were joined at the hip. We did everything together. Constantly, all the time.
>
> But that was the hardest time that I had. She was taking Spanish lessons up to the time she died. An elderly guy in her group—he was also in his 80's, who had lost his wife—after I lost Celia, he said, 'You know, just remember this, that you never get over it, you just get used to it.'
>
> And he was right. He was right. I mean, I think about Celia all the time. I guess I could have hidden in a corner and been depressed. But I wanted to go on. I took a couple of trips. I went skiing alone.
>
> I had my two kids and my grandkids. Figured they needed me, too. I wanted them to need me. And I needed them. That was one factor. I mean it was a big factor. Was I going to give up on life just because my poor wife had to give hers up?
>
> It felt painful, but immediately I started reading some grieving books and a couple of really excellent books. And my daughters—I talked to them a lot. But you know, there's stuff you can't talk to your daughters about, your intimate thoughts. And they said, 'Hey, why don't you get a therapist?' So, I did. I found somebody, and I went to her for about a year. She was tremendous help. That helped me a lot, just talking things out. How to deal with people; how to deal with my situation. Meeting new people, what to do about that. How to deal with another woman that I met. For some reason, I got sympathy from one of my

wife's high school classmates, and I thought I had feelings for her, even though I never did in high school."

At eighty, Bob continues to ski, plan major trips, and live in the house he and his wife shared. He calls it his anchor.

> "So long as I can keep control and financially it doesn't get out of hand, if things are Steady Eddie, right as they are now, I should be fine. But again, how long can I do it, is what goes through my head."

Even if your house has been an anchor because your husband built it and that's where you lived for thirty years, Nancy shows how quickly that anchor can be lifted. When her husband died, some of their friends went their own way, others were a forty-minute drive away and Nancy, who didn't like to drive, also had an eye problem that made it too hard for her to drive at night. Her daughter's assessment was, "Ma, you can't stay here alone."

> "And after my daughter left I was sitting at my computer, with my little Shih Tzu. And I looked, I said, 'If I don't do something, this is going to be the rest of my life. Sitting alone at my computer playing solitaire.'
>
> And I said, 'I'm too young for this. I've got too much to live for. To live and do.' My daughter kept nagging at me. After another week I finally said to her, 'Yes, I'm ready to move.' In nine weeks after my husband died, I moved.
>
> Put the house on the market. It was listed at 8:30 p.m. one night and it was sold by 10:30 a.m. in the morning. I was meant to come here. And my little doggie I gave to a neighbor, because I now live on the 36th floor. And I don't have a big yard anymore, and he was 13, and he was used to the house and a big yard, and it just wouldn't have worked for us. So, my neighbor took him, which I'm very thankful for."

What was hard about making that change?

> "Well, giving my dog away. And getting rid of all my furniture, I think, because I had done that once before when my daughter's father and I got divorced I walked out of the house, with my suitcase and some dishes and that was about it. And just to go through it all again, that was emotional. And that really wasn't that bad because I was on a lot

of antidepressants at the time because my husband had been so ill and we were barely keeping going. I was over medicated. I will admit that, now. I didn't think I was at the time.

I just make decisions, I just do them. I'm that way."

Jim is good at making decisions, too. He said he would never move into a retirement community, but...

"I worked for about thirty years as a fundraiser for various hospitals. A lot of my work took place in visiting people in retirement communities. The retirement communities were always in the suburbs. And they were little cottages or medium rise buildings. And it was just something about that that I didn't like at all. I'm a city person, and for most of my life I lived in Lincoln Park here in Chicago.

I said, 'Well, what I'm going to do is I'm going to buy a really good long-term care policy. And then when my time comes. I'm going to just hire somebody and I'm going to stay in my apartment, and I'm going to be happy ever after.' I'm single. That was my plan.

Then time went along and I had a friend who was an older person, lived two blocks away. And she got old, she got sick. She was alone. And I had to find care for her. And it wasn't a pretty sight. We kept trying to find people. People would come in and rip her off, tell her sad stories, she'd give them money.

She really shouldn't have been living in the apartment because she couldn't get out. She was becoming feeble; I mean she was feeble. So, it wasn't very nice. She didn't have the wherewithal to go anywhere. She'd spent some time, after breaking a hip, in a nursing home. That wasn't very nice and she ended up dying alone. We found her."

Jim was still working as a fundraiser for hospitals when a friend invited him to a breakfast meeting about The Clare. That event changed his mind about where to move when he retired.

"We went and I won the prize of the day which was *Successful Aging*, a book. And I found out that this place was being run by Franciscan Sisters, when it was built. And I had worked for the Franciscan Sisters, so I said, 'God is telling me something.' And it all started clicking in my mind, that you know, maybe this is an answer.

To me it was an adventure. It just seemed like a whole new thing and I didn't feel like I was moving into an old people's home. I felt like I was moving into a high-rise apartment where I'd live my life the same as I was living before. But when the time came, I had a backup security of the nursing care.

A lot of people don't realize that what you're buying into is health-care as well as a place to live. So, they don't realize that a certain portion of the entry fee is considered healthcare. ...There's a tax advantage to that."

Jim's statement that he would never move into a retirement community could make Elizabeth smile because she said the same thing.

Elizabeth: Well, because I don't mind laughing at myself, I'll tell you, if you don't mind, Bill [her husband]? I'll tell you how this evolved.

My friend from Crystal Lake called me in Maryland and said, 'Can I ask you a question?' And I said, 'Sure.' She said, 'I hear you're coming to The Clare.' And I said, 'What's The Clare?' And she said, 'It's a nice retirement, really nice retirement center downtown.' And I said, 'Ann, I am never moving to Chicago, and I'm not moving to The Clare.'

So that evening my daughter called me and we were chatting and I said, 'Ann called me today and asked me if we were moving to The Clare and I just kind of laughed at her.' And she said, 'Oh, Mom, I heard that's a really lovely place.' And I said, 'I'm not going, I'm not interested.'

And she said, 'Oh Mom,' she said...long story short...'You know I always wanted you to live with us, but I know you'd never do that. I'm going to check The Clare out.' And I said, 'Well, go ahead, Christina, but I'm not moving there.'

My son called a little later that night, and I told him the story, and he said, 'Mom, you are not going to a senior residence, you are too young. I won't let you.' I said, 'Well, you know she said she's going to check out The Clare.' He said, 'Wait a minute, The Clare?' And I said, 'Yes.' 'Oh Mom,' that's exactly how he said it, 'I know that place, it's beautiful. I think it would be great for you.' And he said, 'Mom, it's like no other senior center. You'd open the door every day and it's Lumosity.' Lumosity, the brain games I like to play. He said, 'There are people, all kinds of people going by, children and babies and it's everything, and it's right at the Gold Coast.' 'All right, I'll look at it, but I'll tell you this, I am never moving to Chicago and I am never moving to The Clare.' We came out and looked at it, and three months later we were signing a contract.

Bill: I've always lived in the suburbs in a lot of space and two acre lots and all that stuff. And I've never lived downtown. And I said, 'Well, if we're thinking about moving back to Chicago, I'm not going to the suburbs, and I'll go downtown and look.'

And so, we checked it out and found the apartment that we liked, with a view of the lake, and north and, and that was it. And we just did it for the kids, you know, because I didn't want them to worry about us...

Elizabeth: Well, first of all, we had looked for the kids.

Bill: Right.

Elizabeth: But we, we were not in the state of mind to move yet.

Bill: No. No.

Elizabeth: We'll do it, we're going to do it right, but not yet; we're not ready. You know that sort of thing. Oh, we always knew that we would do something like this because we would not want to burden our kids. I know the emotional stuff you go through and the physical stuff. They're all busy; they all have lives.

I didn't have to take care of my parents. But I did see that with my friends and with other people. I'll tell you one thing I knew as a nurse though. I worked in the emergency room and none of my patients had appointments. You don't know when you're going to need it. You don't know the time, you don't know the hour, you don't know if it can be catastrophic, or if it will be a minor thing, but something happens someday."

Summary

Which speakers did you want to spend more time with? Was there a particular comment that you found useful?

Clearly, some people made the decision to move from their homes quickly and had no regrets. For those who are stuck, too frightened to make a change, there is a suggestion about how to face the fear by replacing the threatening unknowns with positive images of what can be beneficial in the new setting.

No matter the state of your health, or where you live, how you fill your days is critical. All the people at this gathering want to be authentic, live fully, and be the best of themselves. Being engaged in activities for the sake of being busy is not satisfying to several speakers. They want to find meaning and relevance for their activity. In most cases, those quests led to being nurtured by a community, and nurturing that community. Isolation is dangerous to your health, and community is beneficial.

Managing a house, in terms of the demands on your Dollars, Mind Share and Physical Energy, is a continuous process, and in many cases it is the reason for someone moving out of the house. Leaving the task of sorting and discarding the stuff in the house to others at your death sparked anxiety in parents, as well as singles.

Everyone was conscious of not wanting family or friends to be their caregivers. Some took practical steps to assure their preferred outcome. Naturally, a discussion about caregiving leads to observations about aging, grief, and knowing how to accept help graciously.

Creating a similar soiree among your own circle of friends and family can help you and others find answers to the intertwined questions that must be separated out when you ask, "Should I move or not?" Though this is a serious decision, the process of your becoming comfortable with your unique answer can be a celebration. Hold your own soiree. It's about engaging life. High school graduation is not referred to as *The End*. It's a *Commencement*. This soiree is a commencement for what you are doing next. There are even recipes in Appendix E for some of the food that was enjoyed at this one.

CHAPTER 7

Whose Move Is It Anyway?

Who's making the decision about where you'll live next year, or the years after that? Just you? You and your spouse? You and other family members? You and dear old friends?

With couples, one person may be retired and ready to make a change, but he or she can't relocate because of the working spouse's job. In other cases, they agree that they should move, but when and where are up in the air. Not surprisingly, among other variations are *the stalemate* (when only one spouse is eager to move), and *the adventure* (when both agree and know what they want). That's nice.

Ideally, it will be your decision, and not one forced on you by illness, accident, finances, or the pressure from others.

If you've made the decision to move, it's essential to tell those you are close to what's on your mind. Three reasons to communicate with them are:

1. They may have practical suggestions about the process of the move.

2. Since they care about you, it's sort of their move too. After all, they'll want to visit you, and you'll be at a different address. Will you still meet at the same coffee shop for breakfast? Will rush hour traffic change what time of day they're likely to stop by? Will you be too far away for them to make frequent visits? They have to adjust to your new situation too.

3. They'll also be concerned that the new place is good for you. As long as you're happy with it and it suits your needs, then, in your opinion, it's good for you. They need to hear that so they can feel confident that you'll be okay.

Conversations about really important matters are frequently fragmented, scattered over time, dropped, picked up, and finally knit together in a course of action. Our major decisions have bits of facts, emotions, observations, and intuitions. They can develop over months (or even years), and though the decision to move may feel like it's yours, it may involve your adult children in different ways.

THE ADULT CHILDREN AND YOUR MOVE

What to do *with* or *for* older parents is a concern for many families. Karen Wasserman, the Director of Your Elder Experts at Jewish Family & Children Services (JF&CS), has heard many an adult child (generally a daughter) say, "Well, my mom will just come and live with us." With years of experience in counseling elders and their families, and having trustworthy knowledge of the housing options in her geographic area, Wasserman asks the daughter straightforward questions like: "Why do you think your mom is going to live with you? What are you basing that on? Did you discuss this with your husband? Does your mom want to live with you? Is Mom happy where she is with her circle of friends and activities?"

Sometimes, without discussing alternatives with their siblings or parents, someone in the family expects that a particular person in the family will take on the responsibility of caring for the elder parents, or the surviving parent. That's the role this daughter took on. Having encountered so many similar stories, Wasserman is aware that the daughter's assumption that her mother would come to live in her home could be built on a combination of guilt, love, family tradition, a sense of duty, pressure from siblings or other family members, or simply ignorance of other ways to create a good outcome. Her work helps families explore additional options so that the course of action will be as good as it can be for each of those concerned. If you feel stuck with decisions that seem beyond your control and experience, consider talking with someone who has the training to ask the right questions and guide you to alternatives.

OTHER INTERACTIONS WITH THE KIDS

The adult children were once the little kids you raised, or, perhaps, the beloved nieces and nephews with whom you have developed very special bonds. You aren't asking them for permission to move—you are talking to them about it for your sake and theirs.

From Charlotte's point of view there is no reason to move. A community organizer, she lives on her own in a three-story walk-up. "Well, I do yoga three times a week. I walk a lot. There's no elevator, and I take several trips up and down the stairs. I do canoeing. I do bicycling. I do some hiking—not a lot." She is happy with all that activity but her children are worried about it being too much for her.

For some adult children, the parents' move is distressing. Esther recalls, "When we sold our house on Long Island to move to Florida, my youngest son said, 'How could you do that, Mom? I was born here.' ... so, he had more bond than I had."

Erika and her husband decided to move to an independent living community. At first, they were trying to figure out how they could leave the house to their son and daughter and their families. The young families always loved visiting the house in the woods and getting away from the noise and concrete of the city. After talking with the adult children, it became clear that though they loved the house, their lives were too busy to spare the long hours of travel to get there. The house would be more of a burden than a boon.

That honest discussion freed the parents and children from the financial as well as emotional constraints of holding on to the house.

Elizabeth's house presented a different set of challenges—it was *too close* to her loving family. Ten years ago, when she was seventy-two, she wanted her independence. She and her husband had been married forty-six and a half years. He died when she was sixty-eight, and her daughter and her family were very attentive.

"There were only three of us—my husband and my daughter, and when he died, my daughter was married and her kids would come and do everything for me, and I wanted to be independent. So, I saw this place, Sophia Snow House, and I came and I've been happy ever since."

You had their devoted attention, why did you want to move?

"Yeah, but I didn't want their attention. I was seventy-two and I wanted to do my own thing. They still call me every day, but I want to be independent as long as I can."

What was hard about making the decision to move?

"Well, everybody's going to miss their fun life. That's the best time of your life—with your family and children, and stuff like that but when he went, I was alone. I could have gone to my daughter's, but I wanted, again, to be independent, and I wanted to do my own things. They were coming over regularly, fixing my car. They were there every day and sleeping overnight. I didn't need that. I wanted to be independent.

We looked at about four or five places before I came here. I even thought of buying a two-family house. It was a nice house. I was going to put it in my name and my son-in-law's. I'm very fond of him and he's fond of me. My daughter said, 'Well, we will sell our house,' and he said, 'Well, we won't sell the house. We'll rent it though.' I got the feeling that he didn't want to give it up. So, when he said that, I said, 'I've changed my mind.' That was the end of that. It was a nice two-family, but I'm glad I came here."

When should someone make the move?

"I said to my sister, 'I'm not saying I recommend it,' but I said, 'When you hit eighty [she is seventy-six now], really think about a retirement place, because it's a turning point, and a retirement home is like being in your house, except you have people around you and you feel safe.' That's a big word when you get old, it's safe.

Safe from somebody breaking in the house, or if you get sick, you have people here and just everything, you feel safe. In your house when you're alone, if something breaks, or something like that, you think when are you going to get it fixed, and who should you call? Here, the man's so nice and talented; he fixes everything for us."

Evon also took the lead in making the change. Hers was from Atlanta to Boston and she brought both her sons into the process. Leaving Atlanta would mean leaving friends with whom she shared fifty years of experiences. She looked at places in both cities. She decided:

"Yes, I'm going to Boston. 'Okay, what do you like?', her sons asked. 'I like what's being built here, Sophia Snow Place.'

I visited there with and without my kids. The residents were home folks. They were talking. They were about. They were doing. So, we made the last visit and we went to the airport and sat in the airport and talked. 'What do you think, what do you think, what do you think?' and they all came up with this place.

They did definitely want me to move. My son in New York has never really totally accepted it because he knows I love my friends in Atlanta and that's why he sent me to Florida for a month, and my friends came down to visit me."

Evon is happy about being closer to her sons, and she keeps in touch with her friends in Atlanta.

Evon is like many other parents who move to be near their children and grandchildren. That's not surprising, but it's a tough call when the children live in the West, East, Midwest, and outside of the United States. Howard and Esther's two children lived on opposite coasts. They deliberately took a trip to California with the intention of moving there. They found a nice place near their son, only to learn that his career was now taking him to a new job in the East. That's where their daughter and her family are, and that family seemed to be staying put.

They woke up in the middle of the night and decided that they would call their daughter the next day and ask her to find them a place near her. She did just that and called them, saying, "I saw this place. You guys will love it. Should I put a deposit down on it?" They said, "Yes!"

> "Our daughter picked out the apartment, and she knows we are old country people. We lived in the country in New Jersey and Virginia, and whenever we vacationed, it was the country. She said, 'I found this wonderful apartment overlooking the woods.' Later we came here, and we took one look at the place and said, 'We think we'd like it here.'"

A special part of this story is the deep understanding between the parents and their daughter. They could count on her to see the new home as if through their eyes. She knew what mattered to them. She was choosing what was right for them—not overlaying the choice with her own preferences. That's a family in harmony. Another example of the adult child being right on target comes from Carrie's clever campaign to find her mom a house.

> "After my stepfather passed, Mom didn't want the work of the house. So, I started to look for a place for her. I knew of a senior community near her that had little townhouses. I actually had looked for an opening in that community online. They went really fast, so I figured I better find out by word-of-mouth how to get a unit.

I decided to advertise for her and I made up some flyers that said this is my mom and you would love to have her live here and added a picture of her. She's a fun person and a great neighbor and if there's an opening please give me a call. I made up 200 brochures and put them on everybody's doorstep. And a friend said to me, 'There was a place on Craigslist at the condo where your mom wants to live.' So, I got right on the internet and my sister and I went to look at it together. And I saw it was the house with the blue door and that was the one out of the 200 units that I had picked out for my mom. That was the one. The only thing they showed on the Craigslist was the blue door. It was wonderful. We beat out the competition. Seven other people were looking at it that morning. Mom didn't see it until about a month later.

She is perfectly happy with this place. She has no regrets, but she does say that it's hard to live among so many old people because some of them are really crotchety."

As you would imagine, not all transitions are as reasonable, smooth, and genial as they those experienced by Evon, Howard and Esther and Carrie's mom.

In Angela's family, there is great love and respect. There is also Roberto, a patriarch who is a successful, stubborn entrepreneur with a communication style that obstructs discussions of feelings and alternative opinions. Starting about eight years ago, Angela could see that something was not quite right. But what was it? Her guess was that the Great Recession of 2007 was affecting his contracting business, and that meant less income. That made it harder to pay the real estate taxes and heating bill. Roberto and Rosa, his wife, lived in the 5,000 sq. ft. dream house that he designed and had built. It was beautiful, and it was also a statement of his talent and success. He had always been a healthy and energetic man but about three years ago, he started to become exhausted easily. That was not normal for him. He finally went to the doctor and found out that, at some point, he had suffered a heart attack. The stress was damaging his health. There he was in his early eighties, still working and trying to pay all the carrying costs of the house, including a $3,000 a month mortgage.

With the lingering effects of the recession, there were no buyers for the house at the price that would give him the profit he needed. So, in what was a very unprecedented move, he asked his daughter to pay the mortgage, which she did for several years while continuing to urge him to move.

Roberto didn't want to move from his trophy house, but one day, he said, "It's just too much for us to be taking care of it, and it's costing too much for the heat and the taxes. What are we doing here?"

Nonetheless, Roberto alienated members of the family who brought in a Realtor®, and then a moving van. He stopped talking to them, refused to be in the same room with them. It was a nightmare. There was so much work to do to get the house ready to sell, and so many emotions making everything more complicated.

The house was full of wonderful objects and furniture. Rosa saved everything. She kept repeating, "What am I going to do with it?" For three months, Angela's family and her sister's family devoted every weekend to boxing up things that they moved to their own basements, and to storage units that they are paying for. Some items like sterling silver and china will be sold gradually. The hope is that those sales will raise some extra money for their parents. They gave away twenty-five percent of the *stuff*, and left a lot at the town dump where anyone could take what they wanted.

In the midst of all this packing and cleaning out, Angela came into the house one day and found her mother crying.

"'Mom, what are you crying for?'" And she couldn't even get the words out. I thought it's because my father is uprooting her from her hometown where she was born and raised and lived her entire life and now she's going across the country. It's sort of like we didn't really discuss this. We're just going now.

It turns out that she was upset because Dad kept saying, 'You can't take anything with you.' He said, 'I'm going with two suitcases' and she said to me, 'I want to take my pottery wheel.' 'Mom, you're taking your pottery wheel.'

It was like I had to make peace. I turned to my father, 'Dad, Mom's taking her potter wheel.' I said, 'Mom, of course, you're taking your pottery wheel. Of course, you are. You love your pottery. Dad, she's taking whatever she wants, okay? That's what she's doing, Dad.' And so, what happened for me was I crossed the threshold into, now I'm the adult taking care of the parents, which we all get to at some point. My dad is just bigger and louder. We're talking about my father, whom I love as much as life itself, but he would never take advice from anybody, would never listen to anybody, and he just barreled ahead. He is so unlike my uncle. I am very, very close to my aunt and uncle. Years ago, their children were trying to convince them to sell their house in Florida and move into an assisted living, and my uncle would have no part of it. I think what helped to tip the scale was when I said to him one day, 'You know, Tio, I know your kids want you to go see this assisted living place. It might not be a bad idea because that way you could make a decision before someone makes it for you.' And the next thing I know, he's running down to look at this place. My dad doesn't work that way, no. So, I feel like at this point I could be ready for whatever happens next because I'm just going to have to be objective about it. Now, I've got to think about my husband and me, and he's been tremendous in supporting me through this whole thing, but we have got to take care of us now and live our lives and make the decisions we want for our life together, and this has been a big distraction. I mean, I don't say this to you just to tell you more of my woes but I think in terms of when you're creating these scenarios or case studies or however you're going to portray them in the book, it's like there are just so many elements to these things."

What do you take away from Angela's story about her mom and dad? What did you think of her uncle's reaction? Have you experienced similar personalities? What would you have said to any one of them? Do people in your family talk about their emotions? Do they communicate well?

All the members of Angela's family have moved to situations which they initially resisted, but have later found to be very desirable.

Just as the elder adults have moved on, so, too, it is time for the adult children to move on with their lives. As Angela says, "...there are just so many elements to these things." She is a devoted daughter, who, for months, spent whole weekends with her sister clearing out her parents' home and preparing it for a potential buyer. Now she wants to turn her attention to what is right for her husband and herself.

Stubborn parents may provide a lesson for their adult children. Though they did not set out to be a model of what not to do, that's what Ken learned from his parents' transition to a retirement home. His parents, who were in their mid-80's, lived in their beloved homestead and refused to leave it.

> "They finally got to the point where they just couldn't be left living there.
>
> So, a couple of my brothers made the decision to find a place for them. I'm sure they meant well. But the selection criteria, I thought, in hindsight, were off. Because they put them in a beautiful, beautiful building overlooking Tampa Bay. Very plush. They had one dining room. And it was expected that every gentleman would wear a suit and tie. A coat and tie to dinner every night. That was not my father. My father was a meat and potatoes, hardworking man who had worked with his hands all his life. This was just not him. And it took probably three or four months before he passed away. And then, of course once he was gone, Mom started to go downhill, and within a couple of years she was gone.
>
> And so, as my wife and I grew older and we got to the point a year or two ago when we started saying, 'Should we wait and let the children make those decisions for us, or are we going to make them ourselves?' And I think therein lies the whole issue. It's not whether people should leave their big house, or a small house. That's not the issue. The issue is: What are they prepared to do for themselves, and how much are they prepared to allow their children to do for them. And then the third element is, do you really want to impose upon your children the responsibility of making those types of decisions?
>
> But the fact remains that we decided to make the change to move to Orchard Cove because, first, we did not want to impose on our children—put that burden on them—and second, we wanted to make the

change while we had the mental faculty and the ability to make those decisions for ourselves."

The mistake made in taking care of his parents gave Ed and his wife the motivation to act, be independent, and not burden their children.

Ed's parents didn't want to move out of their home. Their sons forced the move and made what turned out to be an inappropriate residential choice. They did not evaluate the place in terms of what was consonant with their parents' lifestyle. They may have been ignorant of all the types of housing available, and may not have known how to bring in services that would have helped their parents stay at home comfortably and safely.

How else could the move be managed? Could a different approach have drawn out the cooperation of Ed's parents? Maybe the following strategies could have worked for that family. Maybe they can work for yours.

DIFFICULT PEOPLE—HOPEFUL STRATEGIES

You think that your husband, wife, mom, dad, great-aunt, or dear friend should move out of the current house and find a safer and more affordable living arrangement. Well, that's your idea, and it is not shared by that other person. In fact, that person is 100 percent opposed to moving. What do you say now? This is not a match of wits, or a competition to see who can scream louder or who can stir up the most guilt. The issue is that one group of people sees the living situation as no longer appropriate and the other set of people does not want change. There may be just one person in each group, or there could be four adult children on one side and one parent on the other. The number on each team doesn't matter. It is not a tug-of war where more muscle will move the rope across the line.

SEVEN COMPREHENSIVE QUESTIONS:

Let's consider some questions that may lead to a successful resolution of *Move-Stay*.

In the mind of the person advocating a move, the first item on the list is a successful move to a new place, but that outcome does not show up on the list of the person who does not want to move. That person already has resolved to stay.

Here are some of the questions that are worth considering. Though answering all the questions may be useful, the order will depend on which team you are on, *Team Move* or *Team Stay*.

1. WHO

The critical and first question is: **WHO** wants to stay in place? Team Move skips over that question, assuming it knows the answer. Team Move is often made up of the out-of-town, less-involved adult children. They are busy and just want the issue resolved. Team Move instead of thinking about **WHO**, asks what seems to them very reasonable: "Why does the person want to stay there?" Unfortunately, if that question is posed to Team Stay, it may sound like, "Give me your reasons and I'll show you why you're wrong."

Does Team Move understand **WHO** the person is, and why moving out could be damaging or disheartening?

A more productive approach might be to explore that person's values, pleasures, abilities, emotional range, and safety-net. What is the person's view of the coming years? Take a new look at **WHO** the person is.

Here are questions that lead to conversations, which need good listeners and time to listen.

Some openers from Team Move:

- *What do you enjoy doing every day?*
- *What would make up a very special day for you?*
- *Tell me about the neighbors you like the best.*

- *Which of your neighbors do you visit, or ask to come in for a visit?* (Another good reason for asking about the neighbors is that you may need to call a neighbor to run over and check on your loved one.)
- *What are some of the pleasures of being in this house?*
- *If there were enough money, what three things would you dream of changing? Why would you make those changes?*

As you can see, the last three questions are searching out the pros and cons of staying in the house. Maybe what is missing or undesirable becomes part of the discussion.

If the neighbors are now strangers, and the house has problems, you have something to explore. Don't pounce, but instead, just ask more questions. And most of all, *listen.*

2. What can you imagine?

Engage the imagination. Try this:
If you could have your home just the way you wanted,
Where would it be?
What would it look like?
What would you see as you opened the front door and stepped in?
What would you see outside your bedroom window?
What would you hear as you sat on the porch?

3. Are you the right person?

Are you the right person to be having these conversations with the person who does not want to move? Are you the patient one? Are you able to engage the discussion from the other person's point of view? Can you say, meaningfully, "I understand how you feel?"

Are you the right messenger to be advocating for a move out of the house? Does the person suspect that you are motivated by what will benefit you the most? For example, the move would mean less worry for you, more assets being saved, less inconvenience for you.

Does Team Stay feel cared for and respected by you? If you are not the right messenger, who is?

4. What's so bad about staying?

Team Move, what do you think will happen if Team Stay prevails? What is the worst-case scenario? What are the physical, financial, social, health, and emotional and spiritual challenges? Is staying *really* so life-threatening? Would staying be financially catastrophic? Are you sure? Did you run the numbers? Is staying a nuisance or an inconvenience for you and others in the family, rather than a real problem for Team Stay?

5. What about a Phase One plan?

Achieving a temporary successful resolution may mean agreeing that staying for a set number of months is a worthwhile first step. What sorts of supports or changes would help that six months or one year work well?

If there are concerns about safety or health, can specific changes be agreed to?

Set up some markers that can be reviewed at the end of the timeframe. For instance, Team Stay agrees to invite neighbors over once a month, go for a walk with someone who walks a dog, declutter one room, or clean out all the drawers in the kitchen or bedroom.

Agree on some specific tasks. If nothing actually happens in the set timeframe, what does that mean? Does inaction come from fear, depression, illness, or the denial of the underlying problem? Does the person need more professional coaching than you, or anyone in the family, can provide?

On the other hand if all the markers are met and the person is feeling better, maybe Team Move has to back off and watch and wait. The action steps tell you that Team Stay is willing to take actions that will generate a positive outcome. Find out about the local and government services and support that could be brought into the home to help your loved one age in place.

6. A more lasting resolution

What is a successful resolution? In whose eyes is it successful?

For Team Move, it's finding a nice place to move into. Nice means what? Affordable, near enough to visit, pleasant, and safe? What are the criteria you can agree on?

For Team Stay, success may be holding on to the place of memories, or to a place that represents having achieved financial stability and some level of success. In addition, the place is familiar. If there is enough money, and the safety issues are addressed, staying makes sense.

7. What if there is no good resolution?

The Phase One plan was not successful and a move still seems impossible. What's next?

It is worth acknowledging that there are difficult people and that dealing with them is like trying to handle a frightened porcupine. If you don't want barbed quills lodged in your skin, go slowly and don't threaten them.

If Team Stay is led by that sort of *porcupine* person who has always been self-centered and negative, you may need to ask a therapist, geriatric care manager, doctor, spiritual leader, or some other professional for help.

Team Stay may belong to the group of people who are self-absorbed, dependent, controlling, fearful, angry, and who have no reason to change their emotional and intellectual patterns. They prefer to operate in their accustomed ways. It is likely that pure reason will not motivate them to see their situation as detrimental. Appealing to their imagination won't work because the desire or ability to dream is shut off.

SUGGESTIONS FROM THERAPISTS:

One technique discussed in *Coping with Your Difficult Older Parent* is empathizing. You may feel furious, frustrated, or guilty, but if you can change your usual response, you may diffuse the situation and start moving to a better outcome.

Here is a brief dialogue between a daughter and her mother who has been refusing to move:

Mother: "What am I going to do with all my things when I move into a small apartment?"

Daughter: "I imagine that it will be hard not taking everything with you, but if you want, I'll help you sort."[1]

By acknowledging the difficulty her mother is facing, the daughter shows she understands and has listened. As a result of that empathy, the mother can hear the offer to help.

Of course, that does not mean that the transition is effortless, without further problems, or that people and situations are not more complex, but it is an example of the daughter's ability to respond without her usual impatience and anger.

No matter the personality and behaviors of older people—whether they act as though they are entitled to preferential treatment, lack empathy, or need continuous praise and attention—stop and consider the baseline of what an older person is experiencing and how aging is impacting them.

Some of the familiar outward changes are wrinkles, age spots, the loss of subtle and easy movement, and slow or unsteady gait. There are sensory changes in tasting, vision, hearing, and mental acuity. There is the uprooted feeling that comes from the loss of loved ones.

Nina Brown, in her book, *Children of the Aging Self-Absorbed,* adds a critical and often overlooked loss that can come with aging: "the awareness of lost dreams or missed opportunities," and the unspoken "fear of becoming irrelevant, minimized, ignored, or overlooked."[2] Those perceptions can intensify self-doubt and worries about legacy and value. Maybe someone will discuss how they feel, or maybe they will have spurts of anger, envy, or sarcasm because they can't express their feelings. They can't get at that underlying nagging pain.

The two key pieces of advice just given are: break away from your old confrontational responses, and imagine being defined solely by your losses and inabilities.

The discourses between Team Move and Team Stay are as varied as the participants, but what they have in common is the need for Team Move to listen.

Team Move may have to conclude that the present house is not the safest place for Mom, Dad, or a loved one, but it is more nurturing than any other setting. Life is not necessarily made better by being made safer. Think about you as a teenager. Think about the heart pumping adventures, even scary risks that you've taken that have enriched your life. Those exhilarating feats might have panicked your parents had they known about them at the time. Is life enriched by being made safer?

You may have to accept that someone on Team Move may become—willingly, or not—the designated caregiver. Caregiving can be a treasured time which allows the parent-child relationship to change into two adults discovering more about each other. It may be a companionable time, or it may turn into a very debilitating assignment. Both the caregiver and person cared for shape the kind of experience it will be. So, if you are the parent, would you want to be like the parents in the stories that follow?

The next section is about adult children who were forced to become caregivers. Carol-Ann and Lee had very difficult parents. Their stories provide insights about how to cope, what not to say, what to do with your anger, and how to heal.

If you've been thrown into the role of caregiver, and if you weren't trained for it, and the person you have to take care of is unusually difficult, what do you do?

As an only child, Carol-Ann Hamilton was the expected

caregiver. What skills or training did she have for the job? She had none, which is true for many who shoulder this responsibility. For thirty years, she worked in Canadian corporations providing leadership development, performance coaching and change management. How did this translate into providing care for her dad?

She says of her father, "If there were a scale for stubbornness that went from 1 to 100, he was about a 500 percent stubborn." After citing the statistic that caregivers have a 63 percent higher death rate than those without those burdensome responsibilities, she admits, "There were many days when I personally felt as though, at fifty-four I could pass away before my dad at eighty-nine. And that's why I'm now on a mission to save fellow caregivers."

As she went through this intense period of her life, she discovered that the skills she had been teaching leaders in corporations could be useful to her as a caregiver.

"One of my first books was *The A to Z Guide to Soul Inspiring Leadership*. And, so, the skills really fall into the realm of communication. My first book in the field was called, *Coping with Un-Cope-Able Parents: Loving Action for Elder Care*. And the second book is called, *Coping with Un-Cope-Able Systems: Advocacy for Elder Care*.

I had to use all of my written and spoken communication skills. I am a life coach, and so, I also had to coach myself through this process. There's a technique called self-management, whereby we manage not just our energy, but also our attitudes and actions, even when we are terribly under stress ourselves.

To try to accomplish anything with the man was an ordeal. I'll give you the example of setting up a joint account status: The purpose was so that, if anything happened to him, I could pay his bills in his stead. And he'd always been used to holding the purse strings. So, trip number one of two, we go to the bank together. Every single bank trip, he was just doing it on his own. He would be accompanied with worn and torn photos from World War II when he used to drive trucks of engine mounts into a local Ontario factory to help build the Lancaster bomber plane.

And there was some part of him that thought he kind of single-handedly won World War II for doing that. And every... every time he went to the bank he had the photos, and the women had to kind of look at them, and appease him.

So, when we were doing the joint account status, I went behind his back so that the women would be all cued up about how difficult this would be to enact, but he knew we were there to set up a joint account status. Anyway, after we duly looked at all of these photos, his pen was literally poised above the signature line and—and then he baulked. And he said, 'Well, does this mean that the government gets all of my money? And does this mean that Carol-Ann has access to my accounts?'

And we kind of said, 'No it doesn't mean the government gets your money. But it does mean that Carol-Ann can perform functions on your bank accounts.' And he said, 'Oh, I'll have none of that.' And he pretty much stormed out of the bank. My dad and I actually got along. But this is, I hope, starting to give you a little example. So, once we were in the cab coming home, he said, 'Oh well.' He knew he'd kind of over-reacted, and so, we did it all over again and we were successful the second time around.

What I'm trying to say is, what makes a parent un-cope-able is that when the child tries to engage in a proactive conversation the un-cope-able parent will make every single thing you need to do, even if it's in their support, a trial.

Whereas a cope-able—suppose, a cooperative—parent says, 'You know what? You're right, and I'm even going to start right now to begin clearing out the house in which I've lived for fifty years. Let's do this together so that I don't leave you the burden, should I pass away.' And Penelope, my answer wouldn't be complete if I didn't also come to realize that what's going on beneath the surface, even of an un-cope-able parent, sometimes may be fear of the unknown. Inevitably we all pass away. And with the unknown beckoning, it may simply be that they're afraid.

For now, I'm going to give you the example of the car keys. My father prides himself on driving these trucks, and so he has always prided himself on his driving skills. And, indeed, he maintained a stellar record. He started as a teen and he continued to drive in his eighties independently, and quite functionally.

When I think about the subject of surrendering the car keys—and by the way, with an un-cope-able parent, never use the verb, 'surrender.'

You can imagine when you put his innate stubbornness together with a point of pride for him and for many seniors, it's the car. It's one of the last vestiges of independence.

When they have to think about, 'Wow I can't just get in the car and go somewhere,' I know how horrific that is.

He had reported to me that cars were starting to bump into his vehicle in local shopping malls. Those cars were parked. But they were bumping into his vehicle. About how kooky is that?

We were heading out to the local grocery store. I was sure that, mistakenly, he had his foot on the accelerator rather than hovering over the brake backing out of the garage. We careened sort of backwards down the street into the base of the neighbor's driveway before he got the car under control.

That stunned both of us. So, there were mounting incidences that I could kind of fight in a roundabout way. And start the conversation by saying, 'So—so you know, Daddy, I was thinking a little bit about what you told me last time about how there are these cars that are bumping into yours in the mall.' And, of course, one needs to keep a deadpan face. 'And, so, you know, I wonder if, because I know you really pride yourself on the condition of your cars and stuff like that, you know, should we should we just, I don't know, start to look at maybe taking a cab to the grocery store sometimes? And then other times we could drive? You know just kind of think about it, because I'm just letting you know, I've been thinking about it, and I'd hate for anything to happen to your car.' Period.

Go on to the next subject. Let it sit for two weeks. And, so, while I'm cooking eggs and it's kind of a comfortable situation, in the kitchen while we're waiting for them to boil and stuff, I sort of sit down and say, 'Daddy, did you have an opportunity to think about my suggestion so that we don't have things happen to your car?'

Maybe he would answer, 'No, I didn't really think about it.' Or he might say, 'I thought about it a little bit.' I'm trying to give you an example of how to approach it gradually."

In so many instances, her method was to gently steer his thinking. She advises that you never tell an aggressive person what to do. She works now to equip others:

"With the coping skills and attitudes that I learned and/or experimented with, I did an A to Z of what doesn't work. I came to my loving action and advocacy through a lot of trial and error.

And what I now know is that there is a tremendous opportunity to heal much of one's family of origin issues, if one will see through this grueling chapter of life. There's an opportunity to learn so very much about oneself in the process, and I would claim to have come out of this journey with a far greater sense of competence, resourcefulness, problem-solving skill, confidence.

And from the bitter place I began this whole process... it was worse with my mother. She and I really did not have a good understanding of one another. And yet, I spoke her eulogy speaking some words that honored the parts of her that I could, that included how courageous she was. That was healing.

When I delivered my dad's eulogy, that was actually quite a milestone. It was so healing that I know that there is tremendous hope for the caregiver, because, honestly, if I can start in a very, very awful place and be speaking to you these authentic words of completion, others can too. And that's also part of why I do what I now do. Both to save the caregiver a fraction of my anguish, and also to provide the possibility that, by mastering some of these skills and attitudes, they too can journey from desperation to, somewhere along the way, inspiration, and finally to hope."

Carol-Ann's bitterness and exhaustion turned into a deeper understanding of herself and of her parents. Her books and her website offer more specific details, but one handy acronym she encourages the caregivers to repeat is *Q.T.I.P.* which is short for, *quit taking it personally*.[3] That's hard to do when a parent is as stubborn as her father was, but *Q.T.I.P* can help in all sorts of situations—not just in caregiving.

Carol-Ann, as an only child, was the expected caregiver, but since Lee had siblings, she was not necessarily destined to be the caregiver for her mother. She was drawn into caregiving way beyond her intentions. The final scene of her experience may puzzle some of you.

Lee's three siblings had different ideas about how to help their mother. Lee recalls:

> "My older brother and older sister felt that my mother had to be very regulated in her expenses. And, at the time, I was doing very well financially, and I didn't want to really put that regulation on her, and I just wanted to give her everything that she needed. But she kept on needing more and more, more attention and wanting me to be around a lot more, which then created more stress because I had a life too.
>
> It started off slowly, but within I'd say a year, I was committing a lot of my time to taking her phone calls, and dealing with the bad things in her marriage. At one point I just had to get help, and I wanted to put her in a home where she could have constant supervision. She went to the hospital one time, and through that period of being in the hospital, I was able to move her things into a really spectacular old age home. When she was out of the hospital, I took her directly to the home. And what happened there is she started demanding attention from the nursing staff just as she was demanding attention from me. However, every time a nurse comes down to your unit, it was on an hourly basis of, you know $60 to $100 an hour. And that escalated greatly to the extent that one month I paid somewhere in the neighborhood of $20,000.
>
> It seemed like every hour they could have a new creative disaster that you could not even possibly think of. There would be a disaster that you would have to attend to. And it was incredible."

For eight years, Lee kept responding to every call from her mother and her second husband whether the phone calls were about trivial or significant issues. Picture Lee in this next scene:

> "When it was all over and done with, I didn't have to take these calls every half-hour or hour, I finally—when everybody had passed on—I walked to the Lake Ontario and took my cellphone and just skipped it out to the water and never got a cellphone again. I just couldn't do it anymore."

Many of you might wonder how, in this era of instant messages, she is conducting her life and her business without owning a cell phone. She answers with conviction:

"Well, we've lived—we lived without it before. ... And it is such a disruptive force in comparison to the good it can do. I mean, at this point, if I get into trouble, everybody has a phone. You can turn around and say, 'Hey can I borrow your phone?' It's better not having a phone. You can actually meet people because you can ask if you can borrow their phone if you need to. I see so many people walking around, even by the pools, with their faces buried in a phone. And I'm looking at the plants and listening to the birds. I'm thinking about thoughts. It's just, it's ridiculous how freeing it is. And I look at everybody they're attached to this phone and it's such a disruptive force. You're doing something and all of a sudden somebody interferes with your life. Are their thoughts and their needs more important than what you're doing? It's a horrible situation to live in."

Lee, like so many other caregivers, just forged ahead without help or training. She says,

"You're trying to clean her up and she goes and tries to scratch you or bite you or punch you or whatever. You just have to deal with that. I don't know if you can learn that lesson in advance. You just sort of say, 'Whoa, that ring really cut me. Let's take those rings off now.'"

Here's how Lee sums up her experience on caregiving and her mother:

"Well you know I—I much prefer not being in it than being in it... I much prefer having my mother living than not living."

As bitter and abrading as the experience of caregiving might be, there are remarkable stories of love and resilience like those of Carol-Ann and Lee.

DIFFICULT PEOPLE—WORSE CASES WITH EMOTIONAL AND FINANCIAL CONSEQUENCES

Carol-Ann's dad and Lee's mom were in the "un-cope-able" group, and by contrast, Angela's dad seems "cope-able." He has many virtues which generally mitigate the impact of his hurtful communications. In each case, these daughters found creative solutions and kept the bond of love.

Sometimes, the parent-child relationship is played out by the older sibling and younger ones. You may have taken on the role of a parent to your siblings, and finally decided, for your own survival, that you had to break the tie. Like many parents who keep support-ing adult children financially, Max funded his siblings. By writing checks to a very difficult sister and brother, he diminished his own retirement savings.

> "I haven't spoken to my brother or sister for seven years. I gave thousands of dollars to take care of them and they just thought they were owed everything because I was successful and they weren't. So, my wife and I don't have as much saved up because you take care of family. That's what I believe. It's our turn now. It's time. We're going to sell this house, add to our nest egg, and move."

Unfortunately, the house is not worth as much as he hoped it would be. Its highest sales price won't make up for Max's generosity and sense of family loyalty. He thought his house was his best, safest asset, but the Great Recession of 2007 has cut into its value. He is struggling with lower values for both his retirement assets and his house. In addition, he *lost* the very people he had made the sacri-fies for.

Family feuds and estrangements can start from anything: an angry word, a misunderstanding, an imagined slight, or just disin-terest. The outcomes might be silence and loss of inheritance.

Cathy summarized her family divisions:

> "I have two sisters. My mother didn't want me to tell them that our father died. My parents and each of the sisters got into feuds over relatively minor issues. They did the same thing with me. One sister was protecting her sons from me because I'm gay. Before she took them out of my life, the kids and I had a great relationship. The other sister cut me out of her life. I don't know why. I have been my mom's sole caregiver all these years. I moved her out of her house to assisted

living and she is pain-free and comfortable. I am grateful that, at ninety-seven, she is still with me."

Even when death shakes people by the shoulders, some people won't forgive and embrace life. That was true in Cathy's family and she became an even more beloved child.

Of course, the primary purpose of the assets of the house and the retirement savings is to support your retirement, but ultimately, they will be disbursed to your heirs. Even though you may not be focusing on your heirs while you are trying to decide if you want to move into a smaller house, a condo, or a retirement community, if you have family members whom you have disowned or want to exclude, consult an attorney so that your wishes are set in the proper legal format.

You may have reached the extreme point of wanting to disown someone because of emotional or physical abuse, because you don't want to be responsible for them financially, or because you refuse to have them inherit from your estate.

Estrangement is tough. Negotiations, therapy, or counseling may not have been attempted, or they may have failed. Families drift apart. Arguments solidify into walls of silence. Individuals focus on just themselves and jettison any effort that might make a relationship work.

Relationships weave us together. Weaving is active and creative. It takes energy and commitment. Some bad relationships can be repaired if there is a will to do that. Other relationships die. Family breakups are dismal and emotionally draining. You can avoid having them drain your financial assets as well by asking your attorney to formalize your wishes with the appropriate legal documents like wills, trusts, and durable powers of attorney.

SUMMARY

Ideally, the decision to move is yours. The transition is easier when the family works together, as we saw in the stories of Elizabeth,

Evon and Howard, and Esther. Other families get through *the move* after shouting, drama and protests. But the sadder story is a move forced on the parents. Those parents might have been spared the bad outcome, had Team Move and Team Stay worked through the seven questions and communicated effectively.

You, the elder, need to be heard, and you, the family and friends, need to listen. Fortunately, most of the stories in this book show people who listened to each other. However, because there are embittered situations, the section on difficult people is included. Even within that group of "un-cope-ables," Carol-Ann and Lee show that, as caregivers, they moved beyond the abuse they endured to a sympathetic understanding of their parents.

Living well and showing respect matters. Creative solutions are possible.

Age should not make you or your preferences irrelevant. What makes you relevant to others? What makes them relevant to you? Taking the time to consider such neglected questions could deepen your appreciation for those in your circle of caring and strengthen your voice among them. Aging has its losses, but also, valuable gains for everyone involved when the quiet courage and small triumphs of another person's life are coaxed out in reminiscences. Seeing how those we love met their disappointments, fears and challenges can make them even more dear to us and can help us be more resilient.

CHAPTER 8

What's New in Housing?

You may have an immediate and extreme reaction to being asked to live someplace other than where you live now. Even a description of another housing choice may irritate you. Well, you're not alone in thinking that some *experiments* in housing are not for you. This push and pull between innovation and tradition is centuries old.

Here is a moment in housing history which provides a broader context for this chapter. The legendary Ansonia Hotel in New York City was part of a variation in the 1870s called the *apartment hotel*, combining the privacy of an apartment and the services of a hotel. "Disapproving critics felt that such apartment hotels were 'unhomelike' and that people who enjoyed being near the bright lights of Broadway might be irresponsible, perhaps immoral." However, they could be appropriate for those who travelled, for

135

young married couples who could not afford furniture and servants, and the *adventuresome*—the *Bohemians*.[1]

Here's another innovation. What do you guess is being described in the following sentence? It accommodates people who "are able to find home, society, recreation—almost everything which goes to distinguish civilized life—without passing from under their own roof."[2] The words *civilized life* suggest that the ad was written long ago. But swapping out those words, the ad could be a description of today's independent living homes. In fact, it was the promotion for Haight House in New York—a modern concept called an *apartment house*. Such buildings allowed New Yorkers to obtain "the ultimate amount of comfort and convenience with minimum effort."[3] This 1901 appeal to ease, convenience, and wonderful amenities in one place is also the current attraction of independent living facilities.

Though you are aware that housing entails environmental, social, and political issues, you may not know that this *experiment* in housing had a significant impact on women. The *apartment house* "allowed women to meet each other and to have access to the city. They [apartment houses] helped break down the notion of a private home being the women's only proper sphere."[4] It was a change from Victorian culture.

What are the new housing options being created now? How might your selection of one of those options change society in the years ahead?

According to Laura L. Carstensen, founding director of the Stanford Center on Longevity, "Americans aged sixty-five to seventy-five are the best educated and healthiest older people yet known."[5] "We need to help people plan for exceptionally long-time horizons, to optimize learning throughout life, and to motivate older people to remain engaged in communities and workforces."[6]

Carstensen is talking about **you**. So, read this chapter with the mindset of being a pioneer or trendsetter. Your feedback as a consumer will shape future housing developments. Whatever age you are, think of yourself as part of the special group Carstensen described above.

New types of housing have proliferated in the last sixty years, but you had no reason to notice. Several of the people I interviewed for this book live near well-advertised independent living facilities, and yet they are unaware of the facilities, and even of the concept of *Independent Living.* That is not very surprising because those people simply never thought about retirement communities. Similarly, unless you need a bungee cord, the fact that such a tie-down exists is not relevant to you. That's how many of us operate. First, we have a need. Then we ask questions. Then we find solutions.

Other than a single-family house, where else can you spend your retirement? A quick way to illustrate the answer is to present a continuum that focuses on two concepts: *services* and *support.* The services range from optional lifestyle choices to *service-enriched,* or *necessary* services. The living arrangements range from you being self-supporting—or independent—to you being fully supported.

A Continuum of Housing Options

	Popular Name and some alternative names. Marketing names are meant to attract your attention. Be sure to clarify what sort of entity you are evaluating.	Buy or rent	Services or amenities
1	Active adult community, age 55+ community, age 62+ community. Concept started about 1960 in USA. Self-supporting	Buy and may have a monthly fee for maintenance of the community areas.	Services are paid out of pocket as needed, just as if you owned your own home.
2	Independent living You are self-supporting, also called independent. It may not have the continuous care described in #3	Buy the unit and pay monthly maintenance fee. Or rent the unit.	All life style services and amenities bundled into the fee, or you select services and only pay for services you want.

3	Independent living May also be part of a Continuing care retirement community, or continued care retirement community (CCRC) which could provide assisted care, memory care, and skilled care. Not all of them offer memory care or skilled care at the same location. Life Plan Community (2015 name change for CCRCs promoted by LeadingAge to focus on younger retirees leading active lives. The focus is on **planning** life not being **cared** for.) Initially, you are self-supporting, although, over time you may need additional services. Ask if the monthly fee changes as the level of care changes. Increased cost is likely if the type of contract you sign is a Fee for service contract, or a Modified contract. If you own a long-term care policy, ask how that policy might reduce your cost of care in that community.	Buy the unit and pay monthly maintenance fee. Or rent the unit.	All lifestyle services, or a la carte selected services.
4	Life Path Communities. These facilities are very similar to the CCRCs in amenities and range of care, but the significant difference is in the contract. The contracts are Extensive Type A contracts that will have little or no increase in cost, even if you need more care. (Fees increase with other types of contracts like Modified contracts and Fee for service contracts). The intent is for you to *age in place*, and not be moved elsewhere, even though your needs for assistance increase. At first, you are self-supporting and full pay, but the contract you sign would allow that, even if your finances are depleted, your care would continue, no matter if your needs changed from independent to assisted, memory care or skilled care. Whether the marketing terms are Life Plan, Life Path or CCRC, read the contract to see if there is a difference in services and promises or just a difference in names.	Buy in and monthly fee, which covers long-term care.	All lifestyle services provided by the contract.
5	In law apartments, granny flats, or separate buildings on the same lot as a one family home, accessory dwelling units =ADU. Spectrum of self-supporting to needing assistance.	Whatever is agreed upon by the family.	Whatever is agreed upon by the family.

6	Cluster housing Multiple housing units built around a common area with an emphasis on land conservation. Many are inter-generational. Generally self-supporting.	Buy	Whatever is agreed on.
7	Cohousing 1972 Denmark What makes this different from Cluster housing is the **intention** to share meals and activities, to be multi-generational.	Buy or rent	Whatever is agreed on
8	Village model—you own your own home or pay rent for your apartment, but your membership fee entitles you to a variety of services. Beacon Hill Village 2002 Volunteers and paid staff arrange for services, such as being driven to appointments, running errands, carpentry, yard cleanups, etc. Spectrum of self-supporting to needing assistance.	Membership fee	Volunteer help and paid help for extra services
9	Shared housing Unrelated adults in the same home, with one needing care and the other as caregiver, or adult foster care provider. Community based services added.	Depends on the agreement	Whatever is agreed on
10	NORC = Naturally Occurring Residential Communities Aging in place where you have lived for a long time. Relies on community based services, such as Wheels on Meals.	Depends on government services	Depends on what community and government services are available
11	Assisted living Private or semi-private rooms. Assistance with daily activities of living (ADLs): incontinence, transferring, bathing, toileting, dressing, eating, etc. *Service-enriched* housing may be part of a CCRC or a Life Care Community. Began 1981, with the Keren Brown Wilson answering her mother's plea. More about that below.	Rent	The monthly fee covers whichever services are needed for ADLs. Services may be priced separately: for reminders to take medicine, help dressing, mobility, etc.

12	Hogewey Village in Weesp, Netherlands where everyone has Dementia, opened in 2009. A daughter, Yvonne van Amerongen, responds to her mother's phone call and works for twenty years to bring about new and better care.	Supported care	Full services
13	Skilled nursing This can be in a stand-alone facility, nursing home, and/ or part of a CCRC. 1954 start date.	May be part of the purchase of a CCRC or a stand-alone nursing home paid by Medicaid for those who qualify.	Full services for ADLs and comprehensive care
14	Hospice care preserves as well as possible the quality of life. It addresses the physical, emotional, spiritual needs of those who are terminally ill. May be part of CCRC, or separate facility, or provided at home.	Paid for in a health care plan provided by a CCRC or Life Path community, or Medicaid or Medicare	Full services provided

As you read thorough that list, you might notice two points. First, some types of facilities are fairly recent *experiments* (Cohousing 1972, Assisted Living 1981, Dementia Village 2009). The dates reflect society's ongoing attempts to figure out what *aging well* could mean. The second noteworthy point is that eight of the fourteen arrangements assume that you are self-supporting or independent.

The Danes are credited with beginning the Cohousing movement in 1972, when an architect designed housing for twenty-seven families.[7] Now, a cohousing complex may be designed and actually built by those expecting to be the residents. The years of development and construction intensify their community bonds. Like-minded people plan the communal meals and activities. They share the responsibilities for the community.[8]

Cluster housing, pocket neighborhoods, shared space, communal living, eco-villages are concepts similar to that of cohousing. Reduced costs and increased social interaction are common elements. One distinction is the degree of what Award winning architect, Grace Kim calls *communitas*, or spirit of community. Having visited more than eighty communities, she said in her TED talk, "How Cohousing Can Make Us Happier (and Live Longer), "...my measure of *communitas* became: How frequently did residents eat together?... I can tell you, those that eat together more frequently exhibit higher levels of *communitas*."[9] That spirit comes from wanting to know and care for each other. That wanting, that intention, creates meaningful community.

Another characteristic shared by the first eight types of housing in the continuum chart is independence. Is that the highest and greatest status for each of us?

New studies from several universities suggest that, although a person may be physically able to live alone, if that person is isolated and lonely, his or her health risks increase. "Lonely people are at greater risk for heart attacks, metastatic cancer, Alzheimer's and other ills."[10] In addition, social isolation "turned up the activity of genes responsible for inflammation and turned down the activity of genes that produce antibodies to fight infection."[11]

In general, independence is highly prized. What does it mean to you? How does it show up in your life?

What follows is a view of independence that you might not have considered. It may be particularly helpful to you if, up until now, merely saying the words *assisted living* would have depressed you. You recoiled because the prospect of needing assistance made you feel a loss of your power—a loss of your independence. Consider what Michelle Woodbrey of *2Sisters Senior Living Advisors*, says about independence:

"I think assisted living communities are an opportunity. And I don't think people view it that way. They look at it as, 'Oh, I'm going to have to do this now because I can't be home alone anymore.' Let me say it this way. No one's independent, unless you're living in the middle of the wilderness and you're hunting your own food. None of us is independent.

I'm not independent. I use my phone to remind me of when to take my medications, when to get up; I have a landscape company; I have a cleaning company come in and clean my house. My daughter's in daycare. I utilize the resources around me to make my life as optimal as I want it to be.

I embrace the things that I can utilize to make me more comfortable and to make my life as easy as possible. The generation that's coming up— they'll embrace that more as well and seize the opportunity that is assisted living, the opportunity to not have to cook—you still can if you want light meals—but to not have to prepare food, to not have to clean your apartment, to not have to change a light bulb if you don't want to, or if you can't reach it. To not have to shovel off your car. To not have to sit and be lonely and wish that you could talk to someone. You don't have to watch TV all day. To not have to worry about how you're going to get to your doctor if it snows.

So, these are all areas of opportunity for people, for life that could be so far beyond anything that they could imagine. And you could actually be more independent by securing services that eliminate anxiety, the fear of being alone, the fear of getting sick, the fear of falling. When those things are eliminated people are in a supportive environment, they are actually able to be a lot more independent than they were otherwise."

Do you think her observations have any merit? In which aspects of your life do you want to stay independent? How will you preserve your independence?

The initial creation of Assisted Living facilities came from a daughter's love for her mother. Dr. Keren Brown Wilson was a college student when her mother suffered a debilitating stroke. At fifty-five she was placed in a nursing home bed, where she spent most of the remaining ten years of her life. She entreated her daughter to take her out of there. Before 1981, there was no other place for someone who was poor and sick to be cared for. Wilson was in graduate school studying Gerontology when her mother said, "Why don't you do something to help people like me?"

Finally, after years of legislative and financial struggles, in 1981,

Dr. Wilson opened Park Place in Portland, Oregon—the first Assisted Living facility.[12] Here, people were residents, not patients. There were doors that locked, so the person could have privacy. There were social activities and medical attention—but equally important, *there was autonomy and respect.*

Another powerful program to help people maintain their autonomy was created for those who could stay at home if only there was some help. The concept is called the *Village Movement.* Maureen Grannan, the Executive Director of Newton at Home in Massachusetts, cited the fact that, in the United States, there are about 230 active programs and another 130 in process. The earliest organization is Beacon Hill Village in Boston, Massachusetts, which opened in 2002.

The mission of these *at home* programs is to provide their members with programs and services so that they can stay in their own homes or apartments. Newton at Home provides services to about 216 members by relying on about 150 faithful volunteers and a few paid staff. It is remarkable that the needed level of volunteers is always at hand. Grannan explains that there are no rules for volunteers for the number of service hours or specific routines. That speaks to a deep commitment in the whole community to the vision of what *at home* means.

The Kendal at Home in Ohio has paid staff rather than volunteers, but as Lynne Giacobbe, the Executive Director, explains:

> "It's still about empowering people and enabling them to live life in the way that they want to, to their fullest ability. And I've learned a lot, I'll tell you that much— it's a journey. It's a difficult journey, and things don't always go the way we want them to. We have to do our best to be able to adapt to the situations we're faced with. And that's what we try to do."

There have been challenging cases where the conventional process of care would have overturned the contract the member had with Kendal at Home. Giacobbe explains one such case:

"I went to see Mary Ann and the doctor; she was still in the hospital, and we were getting ready to transfer her to rehab. And the doctor told me, he shook his finger in my face and he said, 'She will never go home. She will live in that nursing home for the rest of her life.' And I just thought, 'Oh, this can't possibly be. We made a commitment to her. She is going to be so angry.' And she was. She was so upset.

And she was really struggling. And she was angry. She said, 'You know you said I wouldn't have to go to a nursing home.' She joined this program because she wanted to be cared for in her home. So, we put a plan in place, and we went back to the doctor and we said, 'Look, please let us take her home and let us take her home for two weeks. And if in that window of time, we can't manage her care and we can't take care of her in the way in which she needs, we'll bring her back and we're going to pay for her care either way if she's at home or in a nursing home. We're going to be paying for her care.

So, he agreed, and we took her home, and we got the best caregiver we thought we knew to go in and care for her. And this caregiver was a take charge person who was going to make sure that Mary Ann followed all the rules. But it was Mary Ann's home and it was Mary Ann's life, and Mary Ann was not about to allow someone else to make the rules that she would live under in her own home.

And so, it didn't go well. We had to get another caregiver, and another caregiver, and another caregiver until we got the right fit. And we probably went through four caregivers until we got the right two. And they rotated and they lived in her home with her for almost two years until she died. But she never went back to that nursing home.

What's really interesting is adult children and their interaction. They'll call us. 'You need to make my mother stop driving.' Oh, okay we can't do that. They'll call us, they want us to clean out all the food that they don't want them to eat. 'Get it out of the house so they quit eating ice cream, or they quit eating candy bars.' 'They shouldn't be doing this.' 'She should be exercising every day. Make sure the caregiver's taking them to the gym and they're swimming or exercising.'

You know we can't make them do the things that they don't want to do. It's understanding that, just because people are older, it doesn't mean that now somebody else gets to be in charge of their lives. And I think that's how we see caring for someone—it's taking charge. Making the decisions for them. Perhaps, because they can't ambulate very well, now we take away their ability to make the decisions, and I think that's not right. We still have to allow them to have choices. We might not always agree with their decisions, but as long as the decision will not harm someone else or harm the individual, ultimately, it's their decision to make.

You know we all make decisions that we probably should have made differently and nobody's telling us we can't do whatever it is. We're grownups; we make our own choices. It is a learning experience for all of us. But just because we need care now doesn't make us a child."

Each of us, if we felt vulnerable, would be strengthened by having such a determined and strong advocate as Lynne Giacobbe. It may be a hard principle to accept: we need to allow people who are in our care to make *bad* decisions.

Perhaps, neither considering an alternate view of independence nor knowing about the creation of a whole new categories of care changes your attitude about assisted living or needing care. My purpose in adding these ideas is to ask you not to reject solutions, but to see that housing alternatives are developing and that you can be part of shaping what's coming. If cohousing, with its multigenerational emphasis, suits you, contact places like *cohousing.org* to find out what homes are near you or how to start such a community. You are a pioneer. Your opinion and choices matter.

Where on the housing continuum do you fit? The next questions may clarify what's right for you.

Put a check mark next to all the things that you want to have in your new home, or wish you had in your current home:

- ☐ No stairs to come into the house
- ☐ No stairs inside the house
- ☐ Full kitchen rather than a kitchenette
- ☐ Washer/dryer placed near the kitchen
- ☐ Open floor plan with living room, dining area
- ☐ Patio or balcony or easy access to outdoors
- ☐ Good closet and storage spaces

If you checked most of these as desirable, an Independent Living, Continuing Care Retirement Community, Life Plan Community, a ranch home, or apartment could be the right setting for you.

For the next list, put a check mark next to the activities that you want to continue to do:

- ☐ dusting and vacuuming
- ☐ waxing or polishing floors
- ☐ preparing meals in your own kitchen
- ☐ shopping for food to prepare meals
- ☐ mowing the lawn, maintaining a garden
- ☐ washing windows, putting in screen/or storm windows
- ☐ maintaining and fixing your car
- ☐ making repairs inside your home
- ☐ driving to local events, appointments, dry cleaners, etc.
- ☐ taking care of pets (cat, dog, etc.)
- ☐ laundering and ironing clothes

If you checked off more than five of these, you probably want to stay in your home. If you checked off fewer than five, you may be happier in a setting that took over the work. You're closer to moving to a CCRC, Independent Living, or Assisted Living.

Check off which of these is important to you:

- ☐ neighbors who have some of the same interests you have
- ☐ someone who arranges for transportation and tickets for concerts, museums, or sporting events
- ☐ easy access to cultivating new hobbies or taking classes
- ☐ knowing that maintenance people are readily available at no extra cost
- ☐ a wide variety of clubs or groups to join
- ☐ convenient exercise classes—a gym and pool in the same facility

☐ knowing that medical staff is on call and can reach you quickly

If these attract you, and you checked off most of them, then you might be happy in residences in the categories of Independent Living, CCRC, Life Plan Communities and Assisted Living.

What if your aches and pains and medical conditions are altering what you can do, and you need help with daily activities? A nursing home is only one of many settings that could work for you. Other residential choices are Assisted Living, Naturally Occurring Residential Communities (NORC), the Village Model, Shared Housing, Cluster Housing, Accessory Dwelling Units (ADU), or granny flats. Additional supportive services or care services can be brought into any of the settings.

If your medical issues become complex, then a skilled nursing facility might provide the safest, most attentive, and medically effective care. However, other settings like the Village model have been very creative about helping people stay at home even when their medical conditions were very challenging. Lynne Giacobbe's story about Mary Ann is one good example.

HIDDEN GEMS

There are many good choices represented in the housing continuum. There are hidden gems among them. What if finding one of those hidden gems could add money, time, energy, or all three to your lifestyle? Would it be worth looking for such a gem?

If your answer is yes, then start your imaginative search by looking at where you live now. It's the baseline against which you'll measure every other choice. Ideally, where you live now pleases you. It has things that are attractive and important to you. It's familiar. It's set up to suit you. You're comfortable.

Jotting down your answers to the questions that follow will help you stabilize your thoughts and remind you about the decision process that brought you into your current house. You may want to run away from the *Move-Stay* debate, so not writing an answer or giving vague and non-committal responses may feel safe. That is understandable, but not helpful. So, do your best. Remember the point of the exercise is to find a place you like even better than where you are now. A place that could save you time, energy and/or money.

Can you remember what attracted you to the particular house you are now living in? What was it?

_____

_____

Were you enthusiastic about buying this particular house at the time of purchase, or were you settling for the best of so-so choices?

_____

_____

How many other houses did you look at before you decided on this one?

_____

For how many months did you *try on* houses before you bought this one?

_____

What about your current house makes it very special to you? Can you list five things?

1.
2.
3.
4.
5.

Was it easy to list five things that make the house special to you? Yes?

_____

Could you list twelve things? Yes?

Even though you really like your house, there may be things that are unsatisfactory. What's wrong with it? What would you like to be different?

If money and patience were limitless, what five changes would you make and why would you make them?

1.
2.
3.
4.
5.

Would it be easy to list more changes and improvements?

Bravo for answering the questions! You've just sketched out some of the pluses and minuses of your current house. You ignore these objective good and bad points as you rush around to get things done, but by pausing to evaluate your home, you are preparing your mind to compare what you have now with what a hidden gem could offer.

ODD

Would you agree that there is something *odd* about how we make a decision to buy a house? By *odd*, I mean that logic gives out and something else takes over. You do the arithmetic on the projected utility bills, real estate taxes, and mortgage—it's all neat and logical data, but then, something else takes over that says to you, "This is the place."

What other decisions started out logically, and then morphed into a more emotional answer?

This same *odd* phenomenon may show up again as you look at the variety of other homes available to you.

PERMISSION FOR YOU TO ASK, "WHAT IF...?"

"What if...?" opens your mind to new possibilities: to an imaginative leap. The leap will seem natural when you get to it because you'll arrive at that point by taking clear, logical steps. Suddenly, you'll realize that *odd* thing has happened. You've leapt from logic to a new reality. Give permission to your clever self to explore. It's that part of you that has pulled you out of other messy problems that seemed to have no clear or easy answers. Imagine "What if...?" Here are the steps:

Step one: What if, for the next sixty-six days, you allowed yourself to consider where else you might live? This is not a binding referendum. It is just an imaginative thought experiment. Why do it? For fun, for continuing to be independent, for not getting stale, and for allowing the unexpected (a *good* kind of unexpected) outcome. You can keep the experiment to yourself or share it with whomever you want. You can invite another person to participate.

Step two: Cultivate the mindset of the hidden gem experiment. Be open to a fortunate outcome. Here's an example of being open to that hidden gem mindset. Your friend has come across a great sale on something he or she knows you've been pricing. Your friend calls you with the news. You check it out and probably buy the item.

Suppose your friend had found a retirement community that he or she thought was very special, how would you react?

_____

_____

Would you visit the place to evaluate it for yourself?

_____

_____

Hidden gems are like that. They are things that you would be happy to take advantage of, and things you would share with a good friend.

Step three: Look at the lists you wrote a few minutes ago. You noted some pleasures and some improvements for your current house. What if there was a place that already had those good features? What if the new place did not need any repair or renovation? What if it was *just right as it is*?

Just right as it is—what would that look like? Even if you don't consider yourself an artist, can you sketch the floor plan of the place that you are imagining? Can you describe it in words? Can you find a picture of it in a magazine or online?

How many rooms does it have? How do they connect to one another? What is most important to you? Can you list five things in order of importance that would make this place you are imagining just right as it is?

1.
2.
3.
4.
5.

Step four: What if living *there* cost less than living where you live now? Would that lower cost mean you had extra money for things you really enjoy? How would you spend the surplus?

The hidden gem has made you feel *richer* or more financially secure.

Step five: What if living *there* made the details of everyday life easier? What if you could capture time, meaning that you did not have to spend hours on shopping for food, preparing meals and cleaning up after? You weren't hauling the laundry and garbage and doing all of the cleaning, maintenance, and repairs? What would you enjoy doing instead of those and other routine tasks?

Step six: What if there were a lot of like-minded people around who were easy to talk with and who enjoyed some of the same pastimes that you liked? You want to talk with them. It isn't a strain. It feels comfortable.

How would interacting with those compatible people on a daily basis be different from your current social activity?

Step seven: If having more money, more free time, and more fun sounds attractive to you, then write out on a piece of paper or an index card, a post-it note, or the back of an envelope, **"More money, more time, more fun."**

Put that statement somewhere where you'll see it during the day, and at night before you fall asleep. Why? Because this is a thought experiment that rests on you focusing on potential change.

Step eight: Take action. Check your newspaper, talk to your friends, ask a librarian, or search on the internet for retirement residences near you. In your search engine, you could start with age 55, 62 or 65. Type in, "*55+Retirement communities* + (your state or zip code)." Another search could be, "*CCRC* + (your zip code), or, "*Assisted living* + (your zip code)." The same inquiry can be made for any of the categories in the housing chart.

Browse through the list and select one place that attracts your attention. Is there a phone number to request more information? Can you fill in a form on their website for more information?

Be aware that, if you are calling a phone number from a list in your internet search, your phone call may be routed to a third-party service whose representative is trained to ask you questions about what kind of facility you are looking for. That person may be attempting to match you up with one of the places on his or her list of providers. Other services may include both properties that pay them a fee to be on the list and those that don't. As long as they are listening to what you really want and offer recommendations, that could be fine for your first foray. However, if you already know which place you want to tour, insist on connecting with the marketing director at that property. Don't be worried about a sales push. You are in control. You can always say, "No, thanks, that's not what I want."

Step nine: Take the tour. Go to one of the events for prospective residents, a luncheon, wine tasting, BBQ, etc. Meet people. Ask questions. Take a few notes. Have a good time. Try three to seven different places. The more places you visit, the more important it is to write down your impressions, so the residences don't become one big blur.

For each place you visit, use this format, or make up your own:

NOTES ON MY VISIT
Where I visited_____Date_____
Type of event Tour___ Luncheon____ Other_____
Contact person_____Phone #_____
Email_____
What I liked: 1.   2.   3.   4.   5.
Who I spoke with—Residents?
Staff? Other guests?
What did they say?

What I didn't like:

1.

2.

3.

4.

5.

Specific unit I saw was #___independent_____or assisted_____

Studio____ One Bedroom____ Two Bedroom____

Size–square feet_____

What do I see out of the window(s)?

How many windows are there?

Microwave and small refrigerator or full kitchen

Available now_____ How long of a waiting list?_____

Buy in lump sum $_____ Monthly fees $_____

If a lump sum, is there a return of principal to my beneficiaries?

Includes: one meal_____three meals_____

Linen service_____Light housekeeping_____

Laundry service_____or washer and dryer in or near my unit____

Parking space(s) 1____ 2____ in garage? ____ outside?_____

Cost or no cost for heat?_____ electric_____ water____

Internet____ transportation for medical appointments____

Activities and clubs available that I would like:

1.

2.

3.

4.

5.

Did the food in the dining room smell inviting?

| The facility smells clean_____ |
| Fresh flowers and plants_____ |
| Do they allow pets? |
| Did it feel welcoming? |
| Is the overall look of the place appealing to me? |
| Is there an events calendar with the sorts of entertainment I like? |
| What I want to ask:

1 If my health changes, do my monthly fees increase?

2 Would I be moved to another unit if I entered as independent and then needed assistance or memory care?

3 What happens if I run out of money? |
| Overall impression:

□ Really like it □ Maybe □ No way |

Did you find your hidden gem?

If not, do you need more time to think about your experiences? Should you visit more places? Are you willing to keep looking? Are you giving the "What if...?" experiment an honest try? After all, it's your well-being that's at stake.

SUMMARY

This chapter starts with a few snapshots of historic buildings. It invites you to see yourself as a pioneer in the evolving housing market. It asks you to be aware of what you like and don't like not only about your house, but also about how you are living.

Then it asks you to take a bold step: Engage the "What if...?" mindset for sixty-six days. Allow yourself to think that, *maybe*, there is someplace else to live that would be even more satisfying.

Of the people I've interviewed, many found their hidden gem after just a few visits. No matter how many places you explore, your hidden gem will be the one that satisfies your list of logical criteria and then pulls you closer with that *odd* factor we discussed earlier. It says, "This is the place." In this regard, you're like thousands of high school seniors who have checked the courses, activities, and social life of colleges, then toured the campuses and finally turned to a parent, and said something like: "This is it. I like this place."

It's not surprising. So many major decisions in life are like that— part logic and part that *odd* pull.

You've made many serious decisions in your life, and you will successfully make this decision about staying in your home, or moving to the hidden gem you've found.

Remember that your opinion matters. As you saw in the continuum chart, many types of residential choices are relatively recent. Even the apartment house which we take for granted was a new social experiment in the early 1900s.

So, when you give honest feedback to the places you visit, you are shaping the future. All of you, as visitors giving your feedback, may alter plans of builders and city planners because you are voting with your dollars. They will hear you.

How will residences change in an environment of less available land, more demand on natural resources, increased population and more seniors? People from many disciplines are working on answers. From a baseline of 2012, the census estimates are that, by 2050, the population of those over sixty-five is likely to double. Those over sixty-five might be 20 percent of the people in our country.

With the possibility of a long life, how will you live out your retirement years? Will it be in a community of active friends, who encourage you to do more and cultivate more interests? In which setting will you find *your* community?

CHAPTER 9

You Moved Where? Offbeat and Idiosyncratic Housing

Creative housing solutions are blossoming everywhere. The overview in the last chapter didn't include all the clever ways that people are rethinking *home* and tailoring it to their needs. Here are just a few more. Some retirees have found places to live that are less expensive than both their current homes and the independent living communities they have visited. These solutions may intrigue you and liven up your idea of retirement, or they may seem so bizarre that the traditional choices of the last chapter now look very attractive.

Home is partly a structure and partly a way of living.

The tiny house movement exemplifies an approach that simplifies life, because instead of living in an average home with about 2,600 square feet (sf), the tiny house may be 168 sf to 400 sf. According to Ryan Mitchell, Managing Editor and Owner of *The*

Tiny Life website, 68 percent of tiny house people have no mortgage, more money saved than others in their category, a desire for self-sufficiency and have made a commitment to the environment.[1]

Currently in Miami, Florida, micro-unit apartments of 350 sf are being sold for $300,000 and up. Picture two parking spaces side by side. That's the living space that some people are choosing so that they can live in locations that they think are very desirable.[2]

The limited space forces you to think about what you value the most. You keep that and get rid of the rest. If you pride yourself on being able to multitask, then you might feel that you and your house are aligned. You'll be happy to see the space in your tiny house serve many purposes

Does living closer to your values intrigue you? Does getting rid of the excess feel liberating? For over two years, Henry David Thoreau lived at Walden Pond in a house that was 10' by 15', 150 sf. Why did he live there? He writes in *Walden*:

> "I went to the woods because I wished to live deliberately, to front only the essential facts of life, and see if I could not learn what it had to teach, and not, when I came to die, discover that I had not lived.... I wanted to live deep and suck out all the marrow of life, to live so sturdily and Spartan-like as to put to rout all that was not life..."[3]

Do you think he is very extreme? Another version of unencumbered living is followed by the four million people who drop onto couchsurfing. Some of them are retirees who travel from futon, to couch, to bedroom provided by hosts around the world. There are websites that help hosts and travelers find each other.[4]

If meeting people so spontaneously seems too adventurous for you, then take your suitcase and board a cruise ship. The cabin might measure over a thousand square feet, and you will be pampered by the ship's attentive staff. For how many years of your retirement would you be willing to fend for yourself, making your own housing arrangement between one cruise ending and another lifting anchor?[5]

If you like the water, why not try a houseboat? It can stay at one dock or travel around. About 2,500 houseboats line the canals in Amsterdam. They provide permanent housing for some, and hotel rooms or bed and breakfast for others. Houseboats are popular near cities like Los Angeles and Sydney, where house prices and real estate taxes are high. Buy a houseboat and cut your expenses.

If being rocked by a boat is not your kind of lullaby, what about living in a hotel? Your hotel room or suite may not be painted your favorite color, but the bed linens and bath towels can be changed daily; the housekeeping staff takes care of changing light bulbs and scrubbing the tub. An extraordinary chef may be preparing meals that can be delivered to your room.

If taking a glimpse at those retirement settings makes you wonder "What were they thinking?," then the next section may be more satisfying because you'll hear how people more on your wavelength made their decisions. Their choices are less conventional, but, for them, very successful. The place of their retirement is not astonishing, but how they came to that decision may add scope to your own decision-making process, and may even encourage you to follow in their footsteps.

I'll sketch a few facts about Janette and Bruce, and then I invite you to imagine what retirement decision they made. Bruce was a district sales manager with thirty sales people reporting to him. He served on committees in various social organizations of their city. Janette was a district manager for a worldwide corporation. They lived in a 3,400 square foot well-furnished home where they had raised their three children. At retirement, did they stay in that lovely house? You're right if you said "no," but where did they go? Your guess is that they...?

Their children and grandchildren were in Arkansas, Wisconsin and Virginia. Though they wanted to visit their families and spend time with them, Janette explained:

> "I did not want to do that inside their homes because every group that we get to visit or every partnership has a different way of doing their things, and different rhythms to their life. When they get up, when they lay down, that kind of thing; the food they want to eat, the way they want to set things up. Everybody has different patterns. It's fine to be company in somebody's place for a day, but after a while it's just awkward for everybody. But if you have your own place that you can just be near to them, then you can go back and go spend time. That's what I told Bruce that I wanted to do and we began by looking at the idea of downsizing ourselves into a physically smaller house.
>
> But we originate out of Arkansas and it didn't take us very long to realize that when you leave a place in Arkansas in the summer months, if you leave it for very long at all you're going to have to have someone else tend to it."

They considered buying a smaller house more strategically located, so they could visit their families more easily, but Bruce was the one who said that wouldn't work because the "reality of leaving a place behind in the summer is somebody's got to maintain it and guard it. You still have to worry about the grass being mowed." So, they didn't buy a smaller house.

The solution had to fit these criteria: they wanted the freedom from worrying about an unoccupied house; they wanted longer visits with their families without intruding on their lifestyles; and they wanted to travel all over America. A recreational vehicle, an RV, became their secret plan. They told only their children about the RV adventure because they didn't want to be embarrassed in front of their friends who would have thought it a pretty *extreme* idea. They wanted to do their research in private and away from the comments of others, whether well intentioned or skeptical. It struck even Janette and Bruce as a bold and unexpected solution. Bruce made it clear:

"Keep in mind, neither of us had ever spent a night in a travel trailer. We didn't know what was involved in the decision. We started then looking at full-timers and what they thought.

Janette: We started buying books that were available. We read every book that we could come up with and we started reading blogs online of other people who were doing it. And I started reading books aloud to him all the time. And we just began investigating. We went to RV shows and looked at different setups and what was available to us. It was about a two-year process. We registered ourselves for an educational seminar, Living the RV Dream."

They bought a fifth wheel, which is a travel trailer towed by a truck. They parked it in their driveway and they started moving their stuff into it. Then they put their house on the market. They lived in the RV, which allowed the house to be a pristine show-place for potential buyers. Staying in the RV for those months also allowed them to get used to the daily maintenance and rhythms of the RV, all 400 sf of it.

To clear out their home, the children came and loaded up their cars with what mattered to them.

"Everything special had been removed. So, we had a living estate sale and sold almost all of the stuff in our house. It was very successful. There was very, very little left in the house. Some clothes were left, because those don't sell really well, so we donated them. In the end, it was all done so we hooked up to our fifth wheel and pulled out."

They enjoy the freedom of their new lifestyle. Bruce comments on one component of that freedom:

"We just live in a fifth wheel rather than in a brick and mortar house. It just depends on what you're tied to. If you're tied to your house, if you're married to your house and lots of people are married to their house, or if you're married to the town you're living in, then you're not going to like what we're doing."

Janette adds:

"There is a long time as you travel that it's just with your spouse or you're partner if you're not friends or buddies you wouldn't last in this, because that's who you're going to spend your day with."

They let go of the house and the stuff in the house and furnished their lives with each other and nature. Bruce made another crucial observation about the change in his life and his peace with it.

He reflected on questions familiar to many retirees: Am I my job title? Am I a leadership position in an organization? Who am I? What should I let go of? What's valuable to me? Bruce identifies the change in his life as liberating. He is experiencing a release from social and work-related titles that circumscribed his identity:

"One of the things that I didn't realize about my life, in addition to my job, I was on the board at the college, I was on the board at the museum. I was an officer in the Rotary Club. I was at the Chamber of Commerce. There was something every day that I was involved in. I watched my brother who's retired; he's not really retired because if you call him, he'll say, 'Well I've got this oil conservation meeting' or 'I've got this...,' he's hooked up in the community so tight. That's a great thing to be, but I'm glad I'm loose from all that now, because if I do want to jump in the RV and run out to Lake Placid or wherever, that's what I'm going to go do."

He used to be like his brother but he has found a way to let go and hold on.

"'Oh, I've got to do that.' Well, the reality is somebody will replace me on the board. They brought this perspective to your board, and so that's a good thing. So I can watch newspaper articles with interest and see the direction that they're going and it doesn't mean that I'm not interested and care about all that, but you know it is just somebody else setting those directions now."

Janette admitted that obligations constrained them.

"Years ago when we had our nose to the grindstone, we wanted to ride on the boat on the river, but we had never gotten up and done it because we had too many responsibilities. If we rented a place, we'd rent for three or four days or maybe a week at the most. And made sure to lay out what needed to be done while we were gone.

Now we're looking back more philosophically, and I think there is a change in the fact that we see more and enjoy what we're looking at now, because we're not looking over our shoulders and worrying about stuff behind...Does that make sense?"

The RV freed them not only from a tie to the land, but also from certain habitual social obligations. At this time in their lives, they are traveling the country, meeting all kinds of lively people, spending a winter in the desert in California, and building memories.

"We are every bit as happy as we ever were before. I don't think it's happier, but it's as happy."

Bruce recalled,

"I used to work with a man—every time I'd see him and say 'How are you doing', he'd say 'I'm just proud to be here.' I guess that is the way we are, just proud to be here."

Janette and Bruce underscore the idea that the quality of your retirement may be enhanced by where you live in retirement. They consider this an adventure, a radical choice, but a happy one.

Janette and Bruce were motivated to explore new places, but Erin was longing for the familiar. She called to tell her mom, Leigh, how homesick and isolated she felt. That phone call lead ultimately to four generations living under one roof. Erin and Bruce were living in New York with their baby, and Erin explained why she wanted to come home:

"I thought it would be a wonderful thing to move back to Wisconsin, which I knew and I loved. I particularly loved Waukesha because I grew up there, my parish was there, my family, my brothers, my friends were all there. Mom said that she would talk with my dad and call us back."

Leigh called back, "We have the room. You just come. We'll figure it out." Erin and Bruce had no jobs. Leigh said, "We will figure that all out."

They did make it work, because the details of daily life were flexible, as Leigh explained, "We didn't feel obligated to be home for every meal; they didn't feel obligated to be like 'Hey, tonight let's do this.' 'Oh, I got a go here.' Nobody really took a hardship."

What wasn't flexible were the underlying principles of pitching in, respect for each other, sharing the same values, priorities, and the wordless recognition that Leigh was the matriarch.

The next step to becoming a four-generation household was Leigh's very blunt way of dealing with her mother's refusal to move out of the house she had lived in for years. Leigh just took over:

> "My mother, who lived in Antigo, Wisconsin started not doing very well. She was eighty-seven at that time. I'd been up there numerous times and on one trip, I said, 'Mom, just come. Just come to Waukesha.' She said that didn't want to move out of her home. Finally, I said, 'Mom, you can make your home anywhere. How many old ladies have a family that wants them? Come on. We have the room.'"

Leigh's mother, called Grandma Goggy by the rest of the family, voiced her objections and brought up the very common roadblocks to moving: How could she manage the physical move? What would happen to all the stuff in the house?

Grandma Goggy felt as though the whole move was her responsibility.

Leigh assured her,

> "'You don't need to do anything. I'm bringing everybody up. We're packing, we're selling, whatever.' She lived in a senior citizen's apartment. 'You just basically sit in this chair. We'll get it done.' So, we all went up there, Cliff and Bruce and all five of us kids, and we packed everything up and then the crowning moment. Mom looks out the window and she sees the van. We had a full-size GMC van at that time and she says, 'Honey, I'm just not going to be comfortable in the back

seat.' My husband, Cliff, asked her, 'Well, what is your most comfortable chair?' She answered, 'I love my La-Z-Boy.' Cliff said, 'You'll be just fine.' He took the backseat out of the van and put it in the truck, put the La-Z-Boy in. And tied it all down so it was secure. It was some sight. My mother went to Erin's old bedroom. My mother loved, loved, loved that room. She did. It had two windows that looked out on the yard, and within like a day she was settled. That was all good ."

Despite Grandma Goggy's reluctance to move, the change enhanced her life. She now had a *job* taking care of Erin and Bruce's baby. However, the story gets better. Leigh said,

"Then the interesting thing that happened is my mother found out from the doctor that she would have to go to a senior citizen program during the day. The doctor is a very smart man. He told her, 'Everybody needs to have their own life. Catherine, you need to make a life for yourself. This is an excellent program. You're going to like it. There are a lot of people there your age. You need something to do.' So, my mother, of course, did not want to do that but because the doctor told her, it was very acceptable. She said, 'Well, I'll give it a try.' We had a plan in the morning. The first couple of weeks I think we dropped her off in the morning and then I picked her up every day on the way home from work at 3:30. So, the first day, I asked her, 'How did it go?' She said, 'Well, it was fine. I was very busy. I had to help the nurses. There are some people there that need extra care.' My mother was a baby nurse and I said, 'Well, without a doubt, Mom.' She said, 'It was really nice. I think they're happy to have me.'"

Grandma Goggy's adaptability is impressive as is the perspective of her wise doctor: "Everyone needs to have their own life." The rhythms of life went on. Erin and Bruce had more children and moved to another house. Grandma Goggy died at 96. Leigh and Cliff retired. At that point Leigh and Cliff proposed a joint venture. This time people weren't moving into their house; instead they all would be looking for a house that they could buy together and that would be a second version of four generations under one roof.

Erin recalls that friends asked her whether the new family house was going to have a separate mother-in-law suite for her parents. She replied, "Absolutely not. When we gather together, we want this to be the place for everybody."

Leigh was aware that their health might change, and she said matter-of-factly about this next multi-generational house: "This may only last a certain amount of time and then we'll move on and do our own thing and if that day comes, we'll all be okay." Through searching and luck, they found the right house for them. They've been there since 2005.

Erin was eager for them to move into one big house because

> "the relationships that my children have forged with my parents have been wonderful and I feel lucky for them just as I felt really lucky that I was able to have that time with my grandmother. We had only moved three and a half blocks away. So, I got to see Grandma Goggy almost every day and that brought a lot of joy to my life as well. Someday my parents will get to an age when we don't know if this will all fly and all work, but in the meantime it's really been a gift and it's worked famously. There is an understanding, the general understanding of their combined reality and then along with our individual realities."

What Erin just said about the respect for the general and individual realities is critical for families, organizations, communities, and all the groups we form.

Could four generations of your family live together harmoniously? If that seems like a stretch, how about two generations? What if that should happen by accident, and not by the sort of design that Leigh and Erin planned for? How would you feel about sleeping on the floor in your mother's house? Then getting up, achy, not very rested, and running off to your full-time job? This rugged routine might come under the heading of "What I did for love." Caregivers are known to make extraordinary sacrifices to care for a loved one, and also fulfill the duties of a full-time job. They hardly notice what it's costing in terms of their health. You may not set out to be the caregiver, but circumstances may pull you into the role.

Here's why Judy, a veterinarian, and her husband, Hugh, an architect, found themselves sleeping on a sofa and the floor in the home of Judy's mom and dad.

Sally gives us the background:

> My husband [Richard] was having a lot of difficulty at that time. He had been in the hospital. His medication was not correct. He has been diagnosed with Lewy Body Dementia. It's a type of Parkinson's. And he was having a lot of difficulty, and could not sleep at night for many, many months. Then finally, Judy and Hugh [our daughter and son-in-law] were trying to help me because my husband weighs 220 and I weigh 118, and as a result, I was having a lot of trouble trying to take care of him. And he was almost wheelchair bound at one point. And so, then I was paying people to come in and help me at night, because he couldn't sleep at night—with this particular thing that he had he would have like night terrors. That was very difficult. So then, Judy and Hugh were also coming and staying sometimes at night. But, of course, this is difficult for them because they had nine or ten dogs at home that they needed to take care of and they had their own house to take care of, and it was just getting very, very difficult.
>
> Judy: We were camping out. My dad was in a hospital bed in their living room so that mom could get some sleep and we would go over and spend the night. Hugh was on the sofa, I was on the floor, and nobody was getting any sleep. Our dogs were home by themselves. I said, you know we just, I'm sorry, I'm not sleeping on your living room floor for the rest of my life, I can't do this and I'm trying to go to work.

How did they get to this critical point?
Were Judy and Hugh inattentive?

Judy: Frankly I think that we should have made this decision to move in together probably about three years sooner. But I will tell you that my parents, being proud and independent, and my mother being the stubborn little thing that she is, probably it wouldn't have worked.

Hugh and I, for the past few years, had made it a point to take dinner to them, because my mom got to the point where she was like, I just don't want to cook anymore. I don't blame her. I don't want to cook anymore, so thank God for Hugh.

But at least twice a week we were trying our best to bring them dinner and sit and chat with them, and kind of keep tabs on how things were going. But again, as Hugh always says, when you go visit, people put on their best party pants, and everything on the surface looks great. By the time we found out that they were really struggling, they were really, really struggling. And we only found out because they both had had a really bad day and didn't sleep. Neither of them had been sleeping because Richard couldn't sleep, literally for probably two years.

I called and found out that Mom had gotten hit in the head on a windy day with the trunk of the car, and it just, it sent her over the edge. It was kind of like the straw that broke the camel's back. I called, and she answered the phone in tears. My dad was screaming in the background that you need to come here right now.

You do not want to get to that point, you know. So, we were on the road, we turned around, drove immediately to their house. We got there twenty minutes later. Everybody was upset. And at that point, I looked at Hugh and I said, 'We're not leaving.' So, I sent him home to take care of the dogs, bring back some clothes. Other than running home to take care of our dogs, we pretty much didn't leave.

You don't want to wait until that point. You want to try to see things coming. You know I would say to older people, start talking to other people, see the future. Talk to the people at church, in your circle of friends. How are you coping with this? Can you afford to hire caregivers? Who takes you to your doctor's appointments? Who monitors your medications? That was one of the biggest problems that we discovered.

Dad would say, 'I don't like that medicine, I'm not going to take it.' Or I think... my Mom would say, 'Well I got this over the counter. Let me give you this.' Nobody was keeping track of what he really needed or didn't need, what was working, what wasn't working, what was interacting with something else. Luckily, I have a medical background.

Plan A was the immediate solution of camping out and sleeping on the floor.

Judy: So, then we came up with the next idea [Plan B]. The real estate market was pretty bad and we had bought our house at the top of the market so if we sold it we knew we were going to get killed.

Instead we thought maybe someone could rent our house. So, we pro-posed to my parents, 'How about if we find someone to rent our house. We'll move into your house. We're going to have to figure out what to do with all the animals.' And then Mom said, flat out, 'Absolutely not, I will not allow you to do that.' And I said, 'Really? You won't let me live in your guest room, but I can camp on your living room floor?'

Hugh: Judy and I had been together long enough, that while we don't read each other's minds, the question of our all sharing one house was in the back of both of our minds. Also, the positive answer I think was in the back of both of our minds. And it took us really perhaps a split second to say, 'Yes, this is the right thing to do.' [Plan C] It's worked out perfectly.

Plan C: They decided to sell their own house, take the financial loss, and look for a house the four of them could share.

Judy: When Hugh and I finally found the perfect house, we agreed that there's no way Mom can say no to this. So, behind Dad's back, we snuck Mom out of the house to take her to see the two proper-ties that we had picked. She liked them both, but she really loved the one that we ended up buying, because it's in Woodstown, which is the town where she grew up. It's where I grew up. We've been in this area forever. The harder sell we thought, was going to be Dad. So, I remember we were sitting in their living room, and he was sitting in his chair, and he was having a pretty good day. And I said, 'So, Dad, how much do you like your house that you're living in? He goes, 'Oh, I hate this house.' I said, 'What?' He said, 'Oh I've never liked this house.'

Sally looked shocked by that. He clarified that it was the decora-tive details he didn't like.

Judy: The new house wasn't completely wheelchair accessible, even though it was advertised as such. So, we had to do a little fina-gling to get my Dad in. But he saw it and he liked it and he thought it would bc good.

Why did you want to see this house before you moved into it?

Richard: I think that's a natural reaction. Anybody would want to see where they were moving into, the living conditions.

Sally's response to the two families moving to one house:

Sally: I think sooner or later we would have had to do something, because we knew that this was coming on for actually two, or three years. But I didn't know if we were going to have to go to assisted living. I would have never come right out and asked Judy, 'Can we come live with you?' I would never do that.

Why wouldn't you have asked?

Sally: Because I would feel like it's intruding into their privacy. I would never be the one to suggest doing that rather than doing that I would have probably taken my husband to an assisted living, and went there with him, even though I feel physically that I'm not ready for something like that. But that's probably what we would have done. So, I feel very fortunate that it's worked out this way, and that they've been willing to have us and put up with us. There's a lot of children who just aren't that close with their parents and would not be willing to do this.

Since you were moving into one house, how did you manage all the stuff that was in each of your homes?

Judy: The concerns for us: one, getting the other houses cleaned out and sold, and trying to do it quickly. That was just an incredibly huge undertaking because they'd been in the same place for nineteen years and she hadn't thrown out a file or a piece of paper in nineteen years.

Other things that we had to consider were the privacy issues, but this house has worked out incredibly well for that. The animal issues— we have eight small dogs, and a couple of them are blind and deaf. My dad uses a wheelchair and a walker. And we also have four cats... My parents have never lived with cats, and my dad's not a big fan of cats.

There was the concern of the animals tripping him up with his walker or his wheelchair. That has ended up being a nonissue.

They had bought beautiful, beautiful furniture, fifty years ago, that still is pristine and looks brand new. And, of course, they had a whole houseful. And Mom wanted to bring everything with her. I don't care that much about our furniture, and we didn't have anything that we were that attached to, but there were a couple of things. We have this extra room, and I said, 'Well, Mom, it's your choice. You can have a formal living room, or you can have a dining room. You can't have both.'

She made her choice and she chose the dining room. She was very sad giving up her beautiful living room furniture, but there was no other living room for it to go in because we have a big great room that we all share. Our design style is pretty similar.

My mom got the dining room and she got her bedroom. We got our big office and library where Hugh and I do our two businesses. My mom has her own business, well, their business, but my mom pretty much runs it now. And so that's in the corner of the family room.

But it was kind of okay, you get to decorate these rooms, and we get to decorate these rooms, and then the other bedrooms—who cares? We had to really downsize, and between their incredibly full house of furniture and our full house of furniture, we gave away a houseful of furniture.

Any regrets about giving up prized collectibles?

Judy: Mom is shaking her head "no", which is a good thing because she had a lot of antique collections that had to go. And people don't collect antiques anymore, so we found that their value was almost nothing and that was pretty sad. My mom had to choose which collections meant the most to her that would fit in the house, and that's what she brought....Some of the collections—she just brought a few pieces of them that were the most sentimental. We did the same thing.

But, you know, it's like with anyone downsizing, you just figure out what's important and what's not, and frankly, if we had to move into something that was a quarter the size of this house, I could downsize more. Nothing material is that important to me. We got to bring our miniature horses here, which for my mom has been her best therapy. She likes all the animals.

They all agreed that life was richer for them because they were together.

Sally: With the four of us, even if all of us aren't here all the time, Richard just feels much more secure than he did when it was just the two of us living in a big house. I don't think that we've really had any real obstacles. It seems like it's worked out very, very well.

Hugh, how has your relationship with your in-laws changed?

Hugh: Actually, I think we've become much, much closer. I think that we are learning a lot about each other's habits and idiosyncrasies, and I think that's all been a good thing. Because, you know, when you just go to someone's house for a visit, you're always sort of on your best behavior, but when you're in the same place 24/7, you become more cognizant of your actions and reactions. I think that's all been a good thing. I think that it's actually brought Judy and me even closer together because we enjoy working together on different projects.

As an architect, Hugh has been thinking about housing for multi-generational households.

Hugh: There's a great value in their being able to live together, not only for support, but also for entertainment, for companionship and all of those types of things. It's something that has always occurred in European countries where homes are built to be multigenerational. That's the way it used to be here in the United States, probably as far back as the nineteenth century, but, for whatever reason, after World War II, we got away from that and became maybe perhaps too independent from our family.

We learn so much from people of different generations. You know I learn a lot about what things were like back in the '40s, the '50s, and early '60s from Judy's parents, just like Sally has learned how to do things on Facebook, and how to work her cell phone from her granddaughter. So, when the generations are together, then I think there's more of an opportunity to share and learn.

Any other advantages to making it one household?

Richard: It's a way to conserve capital.

His remark captures his business background. When he was sixty, he started a tool company that continues to bring in revenue.

It was an outgrowth of his work as a national sales manager and vice president of a tooling company.

Richard: My abilities have deteriorated; my wife handles the business. It's additional working capital because you can't just rely on your savings and Social Security.

Judy: It is a way to decrease expenses, for sure. We bought a bigger house. The expenses here are more than either one of our houses were individually. My parents are fortunate because my dad was a planner and did a phenomenal job saving for retirement. But you know, when you look at it, if you have to hire care givers who move in, it's going to cost $180,000 for six months. I don't care how much money you have, you're going to run out pretty fast unless you just were phenomenally successful. You know either that or you're going to be sitting in the dark by yourself with no one to care for you.

It's so hard, I mean, I don't know how much earlier I could have convinced my mom to open the conversation. It was hard for Hugh and me to open the conversation, partly because we did worry about giving up our autonomy.

Prior to moving in with them, we were on the road a lot for my speaking nationally and showcasing my veterinarian books. We were probably on the road more than we were home. We literally took about a year off from that, and we are just now starting to go out again. You know, last year we went to the Caribbean for the month of February. This year we would not have considered doing that.

So, when we travel now, we kind of try to keep it to a week. We really try to keep it to more like two or three days, because we figure things can't hopefully go too awry and one of my technicians comes and stays overnight so that they have somebody here. They have a couple of women that do come in and help if my mom needs to run errands, then they can come sit with my dad.

Are architects designing homes that are making it possible for people to stay home?

Hugh: Actually, yes. There is a huge movement because of the aging population, the baby boomers, and that sort of thing, to make homes more accessible, or even adaptable. I do a lot of work also with Habitat for Humanity. Any home that I design, I think about hallway width, I think door width, I think about certain things that can be added to the home easily, so that as a person's health needs change, the homes can be updated and upgraded to work.

If we took Rich and Sally's, for instance, the doorways, particularly in the bedrooms, were very narrow and it was difficult to get the wheelchair through the doors. The hallways were narrow. So, getting around with some sort of wheelchair or walker became more and more difficult. So, yeah, I think designers are thinking more about it. But so many of the folks live in the homes that were built 20, 30 and 40 years ago and it's very, very difficult to retrofit those homes so they work.

It is expensive and when you are on a fixed income, when you're retired, if you don't have the luxury of a savings plan that allows you to do some of those kinds of things, then it becomes almost impossible and that's why I think people get trapped and accidents can occur. And things can deteriorate very rapidly.

What advice do you give to people who are in their seventies or older about moving out of their homes?

Richard: Get out now.

Hugh: Keep an open mind.

Sally: Really, you really have to think about it. A lot of people think about it too late. By the time you reach seventy, you probably should be thinking about it pretty seriously. It's about the care. How convenient is it if you're not going to be able to get around the way you were? My husband had stopped driving. He decided that he didn't feel he was safe to drive anymore, so I was doing all the driving. That's something you have to think about. You know it's just a really big decision to decide what you're going to do but you've got to have an A and a B plan, I guess.

Well, I think that's really, really hard to do, to plan ahead. But when you see a medical problem coming, and a lot of the times you can see it coming down the road, then I think you just have to face it, that you're going to have to do something and so you really have to think about what you're going to do. I had really thought originally what we would do is have somebody come in and live with us or stay with me and help me all the time. But that becomes extremely expensive, because if you're paying somebody to come in twenty-four hours a day, the minimum you'd have to pay them is like $20 to $30 an hour.

I mean, it just eats up the money so fast. I think Judy mentioned that one of her clients had said that in six months they used $180,000 just paying people to be there twenty-four hours. And that, that's really difficult.

Judy: You have to look at the finances. In recent years, my dad never mowed their lawn or done their lawn care, any of that kind of stuff, because he just doesn't like to do it and he could afford to pay someone else. But for someone who's been doing all that, there is going to come a point when you can no longer paint the trim, or mow the lawn, or do the gardening, or take out the weeds, or shovel the snow. Is your financial situation going to allow you to hire the army of people that is now going to have to start doing that, or do you have friends or neighbors who are going to start doing that for you? You want to try to see things coming. I would say to older people, start talking to other people, see the future.

Moving in together did change our relations. It did bring us all closer together. So, you know while everybody's afraid to broach the subject, you never know when you open that conversation what you're going to find at the other end.

For this family, the outcomes from all their conversations and changes are closer relationships, shared expenses, and more security. Personalities and flexibility, respect and sensitivity matter. These four people have cleared a path for happiness while dodging the cats, small horses, dogs, wheelchair, walker, and worries about health and mortality.

The experience of these individuals seems to support what Leigh said to, Grandma Goggy, "...you can make your home anywhere."

Do you agree? Do you say, "Well, maybe if it's the right place?"

These stories are about more than the move from one type of house to another. They are about the mix of motivations, values, character, creativity and practical steps that make successful transitions possible. It's fine to test out Plan A, Plan B, and Plan C. It's worth giving yourself time, but as Sally said,

"A lot of people think about it too late. By the time you reach seventy, you probably should be thinking about it pretty seriously. It's about the care, if you're going to need a lot more care."

In these particular stories about Janette and Bruce, Leigh with her four-generation family, and Sally, Richard, horses, cats, dogs, Judy and Hugh—we see that their loving choices expanded and enriched their lives.

SUMMARY

This chapter started with a sketch of some retirement choices that may seem either impractical and odd, or a new idea worth a try. Since many of you are looking for somewhat more traditional choices, I introduced you to several families who found solutions for either their dreams, or their problems. Had you asked any of them ten years earlier than their big moves whether they thought they would make the decision to live in an RV or move into one big house, they probably would have said, "No." When they started thinking about the future, they had a glimmer of an idea, but no specific result in mind. They moved forward and let the ideas develop. You can do that, too. What's important is that you are involved in the process and that the outcome fits you. Isn't it better for you to make the decisions rather than having them made by an accident, illness or your misaligned finances?

CHAPTER 10

From "I'm Not Ready!"
to "It's Time."

W hat are you saying to yourself about staying in your home or moving? Do any of these statements resonate for you: "I'm not ready yet." "We knew we had to make a change." "It's time."

This chapter presents stories of how other people came to make their decisions. Their circumstances may be very much like yours. Their words may make you feel more confident.

"Where should I live during retirement?" is not one question. It is a question packed full of many other queries, emotions and health concerns. It seems straight forward, objective and easily answered by checking the internet for real estate, but in reality, it's a question which requires that you disentangle strands of fears, facts, and finances.

You may have bought and sold other houses, but this time it's different. When you bought your first house, a major determining factor was how the mortgage amount related to what you earned. Now, where you choose to live in retirement is related to how long your savings will last, how long you may live, and how healthy you will be. Unknowns.

Since this housing decision is different from other real estate purchases, I urge you to engage, with your active imagination, the stories of those who have travelled the road you are about to travel. They've faced the same unknowns you're facing.

Helen feels very strongly about making the decision to move, and she wants you to take heart and not be overwhelmed. Here is what Helen explains about her situation:

"We lived in a big house for over thirty years. But my husband developed Alzheimer's, so we had to make some decisions. That's what forced us to move. In normal situations people say they are not ready yet, because they look around them and they have their friends and they have a working situation, often retired, and they don't want to leave that. But the preference is to leave when you still have the energy to clean out that house and just to start a new period of your life.

People think of moving into an old age home, which mostly these senior communities are not. When you move in and you meet new friends, you join new groups, you have new activities, and it's really another stage of life. So, you should have the energy to do that.

But it was a big house. Not tremendously large but four bedrooms and it was on an acre of ground, and we had lived there for over thirty years. My husband did not want to move initially, but once he became ill, something had to be done because we wanted to move near Danny and Jackie, to be nearer the children.

We decided to sell the house. We moved into an over fifty-five development initially, but it was obvious that wasn't going to work either. So, first I joined a support group for Alzheimer's, and then, within the support group, they recommended places to move. Now I live in what is called a CCRC, continuing care community, retirement community.

It's the perfect arrangement, because you move in and it's like moving into an apartment building. You have your own apartment and it's independent living. Many people move in and still work, still keep their jobs on the outside. And you have to understand that that's possible. The possibility for me was that because it was a continuing care community, there was a Dementia ward in this arrangement. So, Richard could move directly into there while I moved into the independent living. Because, by that time, it was a necessary arrangement. As difficult as it was, that's the way it happened. People move in with spouses that are not quite healthy, and you know that that's coming, and it's a lot easier when it's in the same building because he lived here for three years, and those three years I could get to him every day no matter what the weather. I didn't have to worry about driving. He was in a safe place. It really was a sort of a lifesaving arrangement for me.

The people who live here are wonderful. I've never had so many friends."

Helen and Richard had to move twice because, though they knew about an over fifty-five development, they had not investigated what Helen calls their *perfect arrangement,* the CCRC. It was a hidden gem. Had they known about the CCRC first, they could have saved effort, time and money.

Helen has been enjoying her new home for over eleven years. Even though some of her friends visit and see that she is doing so well, she says

"They think that once they come here it's a rocking chair arrangement and it's far from it. You just don't wait until it's that, when that's all it is for you. I took up painting, and again, I never painted before. I've become quite successful. It's something that developed here. When you're in your house, you have people on the block, you have people in the next town—here I have 250 people. I never had so many friends."

Since dinner is included in the monthly fee, Helen pointed out another benefit. There is no extra charge for meeting your friends for dinner every night.

"And what happens, too, is that your American Express or whatever you use, when you're home, you often go out to dinner with friends and that adds up. But here you meet your friends for dinner every night."

Another bonus is that she has learned to appreciate wines, new tastes which were not part of her life before.

How did Helen decide on this particular CCRC?

> "The interesting thing is that people have to be willing to come in and be part of the new place they're in. It's like going to college. You go in and you get a feeling for the place you're in. Now there were a few CCRC's in this area, and people would go into one or the other, depending where they're comfortable. They'll go and have dinner a few times, and something appeals to them. I know it did to me. I was comfortable here. I liked the formality or lack of formality in this place. I am comfortable here. So, this was the place where I finally decided to come."

She is a little frustrated with people who don't understand that the process is, at bottom, really that simple. Helen says,

> "As long as I've been trying to get people to understand that it's really the way it works, I still hear from people, 'I am not ready yet.'"

Yes, for Helen, sorting out the stuff in the house and leaving her home was both physically and emotionally difficult and she added:

> "When you're giving up everything, it's very hard. So, I understand these people, but they have to understand that there's a new life coming; there are new things you can enjoy. You don't totally have to spend your life looking backwards. So, it's very hard to convince people."

Now at eighty-seven, Helen is as passionate as ever about urging people to move when they are feeling well, can deal with the tasks and emotions of moving, and can embrace the new life that is coming.

A diagnosis of Alzheimer's made it clear to Helen and Richard that something had to be done, and within the year they moved out of the house they loved.

Alice and Chris had a different motivation.

> "We got sick of the house and we got sick of taking care of it. We owned the house. It was very vertical, had a lot of stairs. It was

becoming more difficult, because the laundry room was in the base-ment. I have to say, though, over the years we had developed a working group of people who did different things for us—landscapers, snow removers, fix-it people, carpenters, and others. We had our own team. But still and all the house was a nuisance.

And then, the property next door to us was purchased by a developer and what had been a tiny ranch house next to us, disappeared in a day. It became a McMansion or whatever you want to call it. The trees were all cut down, so the temperature in our house went up twenty degrees and there was no shade left. It was really amazing what happens when developers get their way in a neighborhood and cities."

They decided to move and were saved from the two-step move that Helen and Richard made by recognizing one of the drawbacks of a condo. Alice explained that they went to see a condo in a new development at the lakeshore,

"We actually put a deposit down, and then we thought, 'This isn't what we want. This is just going to be other people making decisions about what needs to be done instead of us. And we're going to be stuck with the same level of liability, but without the same autonomy.'"

Alice made a very significant observation about a key differ-ence between a condo community and their new independent living residence:

"We have a lot of friends who live in condos and condo board stories are unbelievable. There are people like that here, too, who don't fit well with the community, who have personality problems, mental health problems, but you know what, the staff takes care of it. It's not my problem. Whereas my friends who live in condos, deal with people who have behavioral problems, and there's nobody to set limits with them. I see that here when we all get together, and we talk about this stuff. You know there's a social worker here. There's someone in charge of activities, there is this, there is that. There are medical services. They deal with it."

About the time that Alice and Chris had decided against taking the condo, both sets of parents needed medical attention.

> "We did the best we could to keep our parents in the community and to take care of them. We saw what happened when people needed specialized services, long term care, support services. The last few years were extremely difficult. I was supervising care that I brought in 24/7. The expense was outrageous, and everything was fragmented."

Chris and Alice knew what they didn't want. They didn't want their house any more, and they didn't want to find themselves piecing together fragments of medical care. What did they want? A friend of theirs suggested that they look at independent living places. They did. They walked in to what was going to be their future home and simply fell in love with the place.

> "We started working through the finances and all that stuff, and we realized that we could swing it."

What other criteria did they use for deciding on their next home?

> "We would never have considered a place that wasn't a CCRC because once you move to a place like this, why would you think about having to move again, you know what I mean? It doesn't make any sense.
> The predictability of the financial situation was also important to us; the way services would be delivered; whether they would nickel and dime us to death. In other words, is the monthly fee comprehensive or are there all these add-ons? What were the annual increases? It depends also on the arrangement that you make. How you buy in. How much you put down. What type of long-term care contract you make with them. What happens when you do need the services? How would the fees change?
> And then I would say the feel of the place, the intangible stuff. If you walk in, do you like it, or do you not like it? Were people friendly?"

Alice, who is about seventy, has a very chipper answer when friends make a comment like "Isn't where you live a place for old people?"

"Oh, we hear that a lot. Our friends have said, 'Well do you really want to be with all those old people?' and we would say, 'Well, you know we hope to be one eventually.' We both really, really loved our grandparents. I mean some of it is just amusing. Like whenever I go out, if I were to go out now down to the elevator, probably two or three people would say to me, 'Do you think you're dressed warm enough?' I mean, suddenly I've become a kid again, do you know what I mean? It's very sweet.

I'm just not bothered by the whole thing of 'that's for old people.'

A lot of people here will tell you that they wished they had come earlier, because they could have taken more advantage of it. The fitness center, all the activities, the trips, the lectures, all that kind of stuff. They really didn't think it through well enough. As you get older, it's harder and harder to get out at night. There are programs here every night; movies, lectures, live music. The music's unbelievable. There's a lot of enrichment and you don't have to be so much of a self-starter. It's right here."

Alice wants to pass on this perspective to you, the reader:

"If I had to say what I think is very, very important – it's not to make long-term decisions in a crisis. I think it's tremendously important to try to get your life in order when you're well. And you're not in the throes of a health crisis or some other kind of crisis, because that's not the time when good decisions get made.

Sometimes people don't want to do that. People do not want to talk about things that worry them before they have to. Making big life decisions is best done when you're not preoccupied with anxiety or impaired by feelings."

People often say about moving from their homes, *"I'm not ready yet."* Alice offered this insight to explain what she thinks the statement means:

"I think they mean that they're not frail yet, or that they don't feel that they need support services or care, but that's my point. Because when that does happen, you don't have the options. For one thing, here they're not going to give you a life care contract if you've got multiple health problems because you're not a good risk."

But the problem is that they're 100 percent wrong. Because when they think it's time, it's already past time.

Also, it's very hard to adapt to a new environment when you're not well, or when you're not intact. The whole thing of transfer trauma, the less well you are, the less well you're going to adapt to a change in environment, it's very, very hard and it's not going to be good for you."

The next couple was not initially pulling in the same direction the way Alice and Chris were. Marty wanted to stay in their home and Audrey wanted to move. However, he is a thoughtful and caring person, and he began to see the situation from another perspective. Marty and Audrey explain how they made the decision to move from the Berkshires to Canton, Massachusetts. When Audrey was ill, their daughter was driving six hours for each round trip to visit them. Since she was working full time, she needed her parents to move closer to her so she could be helpful to them.

Audrey: We were resistant, especially my husband.
Marty: I fit the person who stayed too long in the house.

I loved the area and I loved the house. I didn't want to give up my lifestyle there to come to an unknown old age home. I'm very honest with you. I didn't know what to expect and I was happy with my life the way it was. Then I came to the realization that I wasn't the only one that was affected. I had a wife to consider, who I knew, from what she told me, she would never live in the house alone. Never.

It would be unfair for her to walk into the house in a desolated area with two acres of wooded grounds. Most people are there for the weekends and in the winter time everybody is basically away. We were living there full time. I came to the realization you have to do the right thing. I'm sorry we didn't do it a few years ago.

Audrey: We were one of those people who keep saying, like our friends, 'Oh, we'll consider it when we're ready.' I don't know what the term, 'when you're ready,' means. 'When are you ready?' That's the term everybody uses. We're not ready for this environment. Their concept is different. They don't see this kind of environment. They see the environment that their parents maybe were in, a nursing home and things like that.

Marty: Yeah, those memories are your introduction to this type of life. Not how it is today, but what you remember as to how it was then. And basically, it stays with you in some way.

We came here to Orchard Cove not knowing what the future would bring us here. The sheer beauty of the entire place is very pleasant.

Marty and Audrey, in their late eighties, are fit and active. Are they old? How do they define *old*? What was their reaction to seeing so many residents using walkers? Some people have a negative view of age and walkers. Marty's and Audrey's answers show us the mindset of those who are aging successfully and happily.

Marty: I'm sure Audrey would agree with me. Seriously, 'old' is not in my vocabulary and I don't feel old. I don't feel inferior. I know that there are things that I can't do that I did twenty, twenty-five, or thirty years ago. I know that. But that doesn't stop me from trying. I can still get out on the golf course. I still work out in the gym. Maybe not as strenuously, but 'old' really is not in my vocabulary. Maybe a book is old, seriously.

Audrey: Well the only thing I would add to it, though, the first night we were here, we went to something in the ballroom and we didn't realize the women came out one walker after another. A parade of walkers. Women using walkers. And we looked at each other and we said, 'Are we in the right place?' Because the concept was everybody here is needy, needy...and we were pretty active.

But as time went on, there were still a lot of women with walkers, but my thinking has changed. I don't see the walker as a sign of infirmity. I see the walkers now as a sign of independence. It allows these women to have greater mobility. There are long corridors here. If their apartment is over in the residential area, and they want to go to something here, if they have a walker, they feel secure holding on to that walker, their balance is better. They are less likely to fall so that mobility gives them greater independence. I see it now more as a sign of independence. There are people here in their late eighties and nineties. I think they would be very limited in where they could go. These women with the walkers can go here, they can go to any one of the restaurants, without help. The hallways do not have any railings to hold on to. After you talk to the people, the women, they're so bright, and they're so interesting. They have such interesting backgrounds you don't even notice the walkers anymore.

Marty: Yes. I mean a walker to me is an extension, one step up from a cane. I know a cane, I think of it like a walking stick. Any one of us may fall. They're free to go into the restaurants. They're seated. And then the walkers disappear. They're not in the restaurant. So, you're sitting as you would sit in any other restaurant. People are sitting in chairs. They're not sitting in wheelchairs at the table. There's no sign of the walkers. The walkers are put away. And when they're ready to leave, when they're finished with their meal, they automatically appear, and they leave, and that's it.

Well, I would say the time to move to a place like this is when you're well, when you're healthy, when you can do things, when you can participate in the environment...not waiting until you need a lot of help.

Audrey: That's too late because you don't get to enjoy it. Move here when you're well and mobile, interested in things and able to participate so that you really can get the richness of the environment.

Marty: Well, I would say what Audrey has said, and I would add that getting here and developing friends helps your recovery if you become ill. It's amazing the support that you get from the people who are here. Friends you build up over the course of many, many years. But the acquaintances that you make here are so interested in you.

Marty's last comment about friends speeding up your recovery is supported by many research studies that assert "Social relationships have as much impact on physical health as blood pressure, smoking, physical activity and obesity."[1]

Some people refuse to discuss leaving their homes. Others say what Audrey quoted, "I'm not ready yet." They are in the group that is responding more emotionally than logically. That bias can lead them to a decision that does not serve them well. However, being more logical than emotional can also lead to a misstep, an 'Oops' factor. Next is Betsy's honest and gutsy story. Hopefully, it will not comfort procrastinators, or those who refuse to look seriously at the *Move-Stay* dilemma. Instead, Betsy will show you the need to acknowledge and balance your emotional and logical motivations.

In her early seventies, Betsy is healthy and active in her community. She is an only child, so her devoted circle of friends has become her expanded family. Having been responsible for her ninety-year-old aunt who was in assisted living, Betsy was aware that she did not want that sort of obligation to fall on her friends. Even though she is very capable and self-sufficient now, she's realistic and knows that, like her aunt's health, hers could falter. So, she researched a variety of retirement communities, even staying for a few days at some of them to get a feel for the place.

She interviewed residents.

> "The couples said while neither of us has a medical issue at the moment, we felt that we might eventually, and each of the spouses said, 'I wanted to make sure that my spouse would be, if I died or went into a nursing home or assisted living, taken care of. My wife wouldn't have to sell the house by herself and everything.'
>
> When I talked to the single people some said, 'I was tired of cooking. And I was tired of doing lawn work or raking the leaves or worrying about ice on the roof.' Some of the recently widowed would say, 'I was finding that weekends were very hard. I wanted a community.' Some said, 'Well, I'm in independent living, but I'm in touch with my friends. I leave during the day. I drive my car. I come back here at night. And I have two communities, the community here and the community near where I used to live.'"

That last concept was appealing to Betsy because she did not have to give up what she had in town and could add another group of friends at her new home.

After visiting various communities, she found a model she liked—an individual cottage that looked out into the woods. She thought that would suit her better than an apartment in the main building. She was excited. She made a down payment and had an architect draw up modifications. She was moving ahead with a solution that addressed the problem as she posed it: If I am solely responsible for myself, and I am living alone in a big house and my health fails, how will I get daily care? If I live in a cottage in a continuing care retirement community, if, and when I need more care, it will be right there. In the meantime, I will enjoy this charming cottage and all the activities. Betsy was very well aware that our view of being perpetually healthy can be undermined by a sudden and untimely diagnosis. So, she felt that her decision to move sooner rather than later was a protective and prudent solution.

She had the appropriate professionals review her financial portfolio, the retirement facility's contract, and overall financial stability of the organization.

> "Well, I was beginning to feel this isn't a lot of fun. And I thought, come on, Betsy, big decisions don't always have to be fun. This shouldn't be so hard, I was saying to myself. Then I put my house on the market, and that was traumatic to see the sign go up on the front yard. A neighbor stopped me, saying, 'Betsy, I hear you're leaving. Oh, that's awful. You know, we loved having you here, and the boys have enjoyed seeing you.' I didn't want anybody to know I was going to a retirement community but my comment to her said through my tears, and you can quote this: 'But the people there aren't all on walkers.' That must have bothered me more deeply than I realized."

Another person reminded Betsy of something she had said earlier in the process.

> "I think I'd be embarrassed to have my friends come to the dining room to see all those walkers."

If Betsy had spoken with Audrey and Marty, might she have seen the walkers as the *pseudo-sports car* of the CCRC, instead of signs of limitation? Had her experience with older people been as loving and close as those of Alice and Chris with their parents and grandparents would *old* have been a less threatening and more favorable concept? If she could have responded to her friends' rejection of aging with Alice's remark "Our friends have said, 'Well do you really want to be with all those old people' and we would say, 'Well, you know we hope to be one eventually.'"

Betsy did not see aging the way Alice did, though they were about the same age. She took the house off the market and canceled the contract with the CCRC.

> "People said to me, 'Oh, I bet you were relieved with the decision,' and I was not relieved with the decision. Which was a bit of a surprise. I think more than anything, I was flustered by the fact that I am a pretty logical thinker and I guess there was something else operating there that I didn't give credence to. So, I guess planning can be a real plus. But it can be a negative if one doesn't give credence to one's gut feelings."

Betsy was embarrassed to change her mind and to admit that her usual and successful logical process led her to the wrong decision. She had steamrolled over her emotions, and not allowed them to be part of her calculations.

There is nothing in the medical books that indicates we die of embarrassment, though we may want to shut ourselves away from facing friends. However, at the heart of Betsy's story is courage, honesty and intellectual independence. She did not go through with a plan just to save face. She allowed herself to correct her course for now, and that is admirable.

She wants to pass on this idea to you: "Go and visit and stay overnight. And ask to speak with people that are sort of in your own situation. And listen to them." If you're looking forward to the next chapter in your life, then that's a good decision for you.

Betsy drew comfort by returning to the familiar society of her neighborhood, but Ruth flourished by moving away from a town where she was so well known. If everyone knows you, and knows your long marriage ended because your unfaithful spouse found *the love of his life*, you might want to meet new friends who don't associate you with those ungracious facts. Ruth explains further:

"The house was too big, and I didn't need the location, and where was I going to go? I mean, some people at age sixty-nine might have gone to a condo for twenty years or so. Or ten or fifteen. But I decided I only wanted to make one move. And even if I were in a condo, it's still the same problem about getting in people's houses. I've been in the wheelchair since 2005. But I've had MS since '93. And it affected mainly my walking, and I sort of went downhill very, very slowly. I had the cane, the walker, you know, the manual wheelchair and now I'm in the power wheelchair. I was only working twenty hours a week, I was working five days a week. Yeah, luckily it didn't affect my fingers, didn't affect my brain. My eyes were affected at first, but they recovered. So, I was very lucky in that respect."

Ruth says of her move to Orchard Cove,

"I really wanted to begin a new life, and I mean I view the day I moved in as the first day of the rest of my life. The day I came here, they were hanging for the first time the resident's art. The resident's art is good enough to be displayed instead of spending a lot of money on famous artists. It's just a whole different way of thinking about things."

Ruth explored other choices before she made her decision. She was particularly aware of another residence in the same general area, because her ninety-two year-old mother lives there. That facility went through a bankruptcy

"and they've come out the other side now, but, you know, I just see little things that are still a problem there. My mother has a stove with the controls in the back and I'm asking, what were they thinking?"

It is a riskier placement for controls. Consider what could happen if you were wearing a loose-fitting robe, and you were to reach over a burner that was on. The sleeve could catch fire. It's significant because her mom cooks.

"My mother is a very sort of antisocial person. She's still cooking for herself. She never liked the food there. My father died shortly after they moved here, from Florida. She used to go out food shopping and come home, prepare her meals. Now, she has a walker and she has to have the food delivered. But I'm the oldest of five, and her refrigerator still looks like she has five kids. She knows her neighbors right around this small circle that she lives near. She certainly knows what's going on in the community, but she doesn't do a thing. She just stays there all day and she has her routines, and she's happy."

Ruth's sketch of how her mother is living shows that even people who want very limited contact with a community can be happy in a CCRC. However, Ruth is very social and offers this trenchant insight:

"I like the people that I've met, and it's really opened my eyes as to what you can be like when you're in your nineties as long as your mind stays good. There's a woman here who is ninety-nine and her mind is still sharp. She's very politically involved, and there's a woman around the corner from me, she will be a hundred. You would never guess she's a hundred. She reads books, she tells me about them. They're interesting people to be with. Somebody said, 'Oh well, you're going to be (now I'm seventy) with these ninety-year olds, why would you ever want to do that?' They're living really good lives in their nineties.

My mother's ninety-two. She's very, very sharp. She keeps up on politics. I mean, she reads, she knows everything that's going on. There is no age that you're old. It just depends. I would say you're old if you don't have your ability to think and interact the way you used to. Otherwise it's just a number. Here you just can't tell how old anybody is."

Ruth offers a few more stories that illustrate how people she knows well have made their housing decisions.

"Well, my sister is sixty-seven, and she is adding on. She lives in Newton, in a colonial. She's adding on the first-floor a master suite with a garage. She wants to stay there. For now, she's fine and she actually has neighbors she knows, and it's a multi-aged community. So, she might be okay there. But I know, one of my friends from New Jersey, when a lot of her friends moved to an Erickson community, she didn't go and that was fine for a while, but now the friends that were around her, the ones who didn't go, they've died. Half the ones up in the community have died, and she's left there by herself. She's very lonely. She has 24-hour care now in her house. But she's not happy. So, I don't want to see that happen to anybody.

It's better to be able to look at places and decide where you might want to be while you're in good shape and you have a say in it, then when all of a sudden you need assisted living, and you haven't looked at any place. People are living longer than they ever did."

Like Ruth, Helene and Larry found that their health issues steered them to a new home. When they first retired, they were a very social, busy, and healthy couple, and as Larry remembered

"We went through the fairly normal question about where are we going to retire to. One of the things you always think about; well, let's retire to the sun; let's go somewhere where it's warm. We thought about Arizona, or Florida in the winter, and staying in the Berkshires for the summer. We actually went out on hunting expeditions. We went out to Arizona, looked around, saw some places we thought would be suitable. Did the same thing on the West Coast of Florida. And we finally came to the conclusion that that wasn't going to work, and it wasn't going to work for one simple reason. We have twelve grandchildren. Two of our children live in New Jersey, two of our children live here in Massachusetts. Helene did not like the idea of being separated from the kids for long periods of time, so, in spite of the fact that I said, 'Okay you can fly up once a month,' or something like that, we decided that was not the way to go."

Their children and grandchildren lived in, or near Massachusetts, which made all the attractive places they found during their hunting expedition ultimately undesirable. Shortly, after they firmed up that decision, the shocker was that each of them was diagnosed with an autoimmune disease that interferes with their ability to walk. Larry was falling down stairs because his legs would suddenly go out from under him. Helene was diagnosed with a neuropathy. Another factor which was pushing them to move was the setup of their house

Helene: To walk from our garage door to the mailbox in the winter, we couldn't do it. It was icy. We just had to make a decision. We couldn't stay there.

Larry: We were contemplating getting somebody into the house.

Helene: It's lonely doing that. It's like you feel sick. I never envisioned, and this is something that I think a lot of people feel, I never envisioned I would be in a senior care. It didn't enter my mind. I really mean that. I don't know why. I was healthy, my stats were the best. Nothing was wrong, I mean nothing.

Coming to live in a continuing care retirement community was as startling to them as were their life changing health diagnoses. Their happy, healthy, active lives changed suddenly. It was hard to believe. Helene sums up her approach to their new life in a simple expression that is a mixture of acceptance and setting new expectations; "I have an expression, 'here we be.' And that's what you got to get used to, 'here we be.'"

For Helene and Larry, the move to the CCRC seemed best, despite their wanting to stay in their home, even with the expense of bringing in caregivers. Helene's perceptive remark goes beyond the issue of cost: "*It's lonely doing that. It's like you feel sick.*"

Hiring caregivers may seem like an obvious and practical solution, but there can be psychological costs. As Dee points out, round the clock care solves one problem and creates another.

"My husband, who was confined to a wheelchair—at that time it was for ten years, still had his faculties. When I came home one night from work, because I worked then, and I still do, he was going to bed at 6:00 p.m., because he had nothing else to do. During the day, he really didn't have any communication. That's when the lightbulb went off in my head that said my husband is losing his social skills."

Dee makes it clear that a caregiver solves the problems related to the activities of daily living. The body is cared for, but not the person's intellectual and social needs.

Without telling her husband or children, she started visiting retirement communities. She wanted an environment that would engage her husband and keep them close to the theatre, opera and museums. Dee found what she wanted, a CCRC in the center of Philadelphia called The Watermark.

"It was the best decision, one of the best decisions I've ever made in my life. And we should have moved here five years sooner. But when I made that decision, and, of course, I told my husband, and our caregiver that we're moving, and they said, 'No, we're not. I'm not moving.' And I looked at both of them and I said, 'Then you'll live here alone because I'm moving.'"

Her husband was resistant to the move because...

"Number one, he was, for ten years, really not being very social. What would he say? What would he do in a strange environment? He did have a fear that if we were at the Watermark he would see less of me. That I would be out too much. So, I assured him, I said, 'No worry, no worry.' But he adjusted very quickly and really enjoyed it. He did say to me, after about three or four months, he said, 'You were smart, this was right.'"

Dee continued:

"I had to also convince my children, because they did not want me to move here. They said, 'Mom you don't fit in. There is no one in that community that looks like you. No one wears six-inch high heels; no one wears leather leggings; no one has any relationship to you or your world.' I came from the world of glamor."

She and her husband owned a well-known beauty salon and employed ninety people in the beauty business. Dee, who is now eighty-five and still works, remembers entering The Watermark

"When I did walk through the lobby here, the first time, in my leather leggings and my six-inch boots, they looked at me like I was an alien. Inside I was giggling. I looked and I said to myself, 'They'll get used to me.' And they have."

Health issues pushed Helen and Richard, Helene and Larry, and

Dee to move to a retirement community. The next couple, Glennie and Joe, are a variation on that pattern.

Glennie explains that they had been looking at places.

> "We lived on the river and had two acres of land, and it was the house that we lived in the longest in our marriage because we had many moves. My husband was working with Dupont and we had eleven major moves. He understood that it was more than I would be capable of taking care of. He also knew that two or three hours a week of cutting the grass is more than I wanted to spend."

They put their names on a waiting list, but the timetable was altered:

> "When I found out that Joe had a terminal illness, we talked about it, and I contacted the home and just said to move me up on the list to as soon as the next place that met my needs would be available. So, I was able to get in within a year of his death. And then when the time came to make a decision, my daughter Sarah and her husband went with me to look at several places and helped me make the decision. The one thing that I knew was that I did not want to continue to live in the country. I felt that life is too short to spend my time cutting grass and taking care of the waterfront."

Twelve years ago—

> "When I first moved in to Cedar Fields I was still hiking and taking two or three bicycle trips a week. But that all has faded into the background. I'm eighty-seven. As I've gotten older, somehow or another my body seems to have gotten older faster than I have. Well, old is relative. And I think old is an attitude more than a year. And that's why I say my body is older than I am, because my body is showing its age in some ways, and I'm not willing to give up living my life and doing the things that I love."

Glennie's observation that our bodies and spirits are on different timetables is succinctly and vigorously expressed. Like the people I've interviewed, you are probably nodding in agreement with

Glennie's disarming wit: "somehow or another, my body seems to have gotten older faster than I have."

Want to stay young, or sharp mentally? Try playing Bridge. With this pastime, you may be doing more than entertaining yourself and enjoying a social time with friends, you may be improving brain.

Similar claims have been made for sports and the arts.[2] Though scientists may not yet be able to show us the direct connection between certain activities and staving off mental decline, talking with an avid Bridge player like Ed seems to support the argument that the challenge of duplicate Bridge at the Master's level does liven up the brain.[3] Ed is now eighty-seven. He and his wife wanted to be challenged.

> "We got to play at very high levels, and above ourselves. That was always what we wanted to do. We wanted to play against people better than we."

Less than eighteen months ago, Ed's wife of sixty-one years died of a massive brain hemorrhage.

> "At first of course, I felt sorry for myself, and stuff like that. So, where many men get depressed for quite a while, it lasted a very, very short time with me. Then the other thing is that I had this Bridge thing. I had a ton of partners ready to play with me when she passed away."

By nature an optimistic person, Ed credits his love of Bridge and his family for his being alert and interested in events.

About four years ago, as a couple they began to explore options of where to live during retirement, and the one mistake they wanted to avoid was settling someplace that was five and a half hours away from their children. That was a strain they had to deal with when his mother-in-law chose a place that was so far away.

> "Oh, we started thinking about finding a place once we started to face mortality and stuff. I encouraged my kids, who live within this general area, to do some looking also. They found places and I had appointments to see some of those places. When I really made the

decision to come here, it was about April of this past year. I came here for my first interviews and I said, 'That's all; I'm not looking anyplace else'. I cancelled any other appointments. I was so convinced—just simple things. There was such obvious warmth in this place. I said, 'Why do I have to look elsewhere, this is really the place.'

I downloaded plans for the apartments and all that sort of thing. I did a lot of work. I've looked into the things. I called some people. There was no question in my mind."

What does Ed say to someone who is refusing to consider a change?

"You got to have a good outlook to start with— shape up. Yeah, don't fence yourself in. Keep an open mind. Talk to people who've done it. As a matter-of-fact, I have a friend that I just called recently. I understand his wife is having some serious problems, and he's thinking about a place like this."

Yes, sickness is a motivator, and, also a problem. Tom said,

"I know for sure that you have to make this change before you need it. That's the hard part."

Barbara, his wife, added,

"This is a terribly hard decision and one that we should make plans mentally, and one that we are happy not to think about."

Tom's progressive disease will reduce his mobility. They don't know how much time they have to find a right solution. So, they will experiment by going to live for three or four months in another part of the country near one of their children. They are attracted to being closer to the antics and laughter of their grandchildren. Will that feel comfortable, or will they find more happiness staying where they are among the wide circle of friends that they have cultivated over the past thirty years? Two good choices. Nonetheless, Barbara summarizes the choices as a trade-off. They will, in time, choose one path. It's a dilemma that Robert Frost captures in his poem, "The Road Not Taken," "...sorry I could not travel both/And be one traveler..."

SUMMARY

Which people did you relate to? Did any of their comments stay with you? The perspectives came from couples, singles, lovers of exercise, of city life, from those with and without children, from those who always loved to play cards, to someone who just learned to paint. Your circumstances don't need to be exactly like theirs to gain something from their experiences. Their motivations are diverse: wanting to be closer to family, getting rid of the burdens of caring for a house, wanting an environment that is safer and closer to medical care, cultivating new interests, new relationships, and getting rid of the time wasters like preparing meals and maintaining a property. They see their new home as a new adventure. What do you see?

CHAPTER 11

What to Do with All This Stuff?

A.C.E.–How to move

Moving to a new home takes **Awareness** and **Confidence** and **Effort**. It's you're **A.C.E.** to play. You are **Aware** that you are not your *stuff*. Separating from the *stuff* does not threaten your body, though it may pull on your heartstrings. Because you are **Aware** that your memory makes an item valuable to you, you can be freed from having to take the physical item with you. It is already in you, traveling with you wherever you go. You can't lose it. No one can take that away.

It takes **Confidence** to sort everything into categories: donate, gift to specific loved ones, sell, recycle, reuse, repurpose, and discard. You need **Confidence** to know what to take with you and what to part with. The **Confidence** comes from knowing yourself and what is practically and emotionally necessary.

It is an understatement to say that the move takes **Effort** that's both physical and emotional. You'll handle hundreds of pieces of paper, clothing, household items, books, knickknacks, and gadgets. Is the item valuable in the marketplace, or only in your mind? Is it only because you have that physical item that you remember a special person or event? Instead of packing that item and moving it to your new home, could you take a picture of it, and write a paragraph explaining its significance, then add the write up to a scrap book or life/memory book? It's your commentary that will make the item a valuable reminder to you in later years. For one of your relatives whose hobby is genealogy, wouldn't that entry be a great find? It's an insight into you. Objects can help us share memories. Have you ever wished that you had asked your parents, or grandparents, or siblings, or friends—why something was special to them? Even after many years of living with someone, how much do you know the person? How little did you ask at the time?

How can we capture the meaning and reduce the clutter?

Beth, whose husband had recently died, was moving to an independent living residence and wanted to take her husband's favorite chair to her new home. When he was sitting there, he always seemed so relaxed and content, which made her feel peaceful, too. It was a very big recliner chair. Where would it fit in her living room? She had hired Felicia Reynolds, whose company, *Spotted Salamander Organizing & Design*, helps people organize, de-clutter and redesign their living quarters. Felicia looked at the floor plan of the new apartment and the size of the chair. It would be out of proportion in the new living room. It would feel like it was taking up a quarter of the living room. Felicia offered this idea:

> "Why don't you curl up in it and I'll take your picture, and then you'll have the picture of you and the chair and the memory, and you don't have to keep the actual chair?"

That appealed to Beth. However, each situation is different, and Felicia explains that if another woman had said,

> "'This chair belonged to my husband. I know that it's beat to death. I know that I can't keep it, that I don't even like it. It's just that it was his.' Then I might say, 'You know what, if you're going to throw it away anyway, let's slice off a piece of the leather and you can keep that as a mouse pad, or throw it over the arm of your chair, or make a placemat, whatever. But you'll have that little piece of it.' And she responds, 'Oh, that's a good idea.'"

Here is another creative solution that you might adapt for your purposes. After a death, you might have the task of clearing out all your loved one's clothing. Clothes can be a poignant reminder of the person you love and hard to part with. Felicia relates one of her solutions for a client:

> "Her father had passed away. He was an accountant who wore a nice, crisp cotton shirt to work every day. In this case, since my sister makes quilts, I put her in touch with my sister, and we shipped all the shirts out there. And my sister sent back a quilt. When the client saw it she burst into tears. She was thrilled, she's still thrilled. It's so much nicer than a closet full of dusty shirts."

PLAYING YOUR A.C.E.:

The actual move from one home to another has five parts to it.

1. Sorting

How to sort the stuff? Suppose as you sort you are putting things in piles. You can name those piles whatever you want. Those category names help you decide what to do with the hundreds of items. Here are some suggestions. Judy Cohen, a business coach, who recently moved into a smaller home, started her sort by asking about each item: "Do I love it, want it, need it?" One *yes*, meant she would keep it. Otherwise the item went into one of the many discard piles. Tricia Sinn of *Sinn Design Build* offers names for the discard piles: give to a specific person or organization, throw out, keep, don't know what to do, so store for a year. Others might add: sell, recycle and repurpose piles.

Mary Jo and Mary, both with long careers in nursing, have a practical bent. They say, "Don't wait to move before you discard things." Mary Jo's timeline for holding on to stuff has continued to shorten.

> Mary Jo: You know I used to say if I haven't used it in two years, let it go. And then I got down to a season and then I got it to if I don't use it now, I'm not going to use it tomorrow. And that's helped a lot. How much do you really need this? Is there somebody else who needs it more?
>
> It's hard I think for people to deal with downsizing. You have to start separating yourself from the things that you have lived with. And I think a lot of people have trouble with that. Our feeling was, if we have relatives who want something, give it to them now, unless you need it in your life whether that be a piece of furniture or a picture or whatever just start giving things away. We're more inclined to give away rather than sell. So, we find somebody who needs a couch and we give it to them.

Charlotte and Ed are also generous about giving stuff away, but not as quickly as Mary Jo and Mary. The very thought of going through twenty-five years of stuff was overwhelming. They wanted to sell their house and move closer to where their sons lived, so they hired a painter to spruce up the house. The house looked so much nicer, they decided to stay. A few years passed, and they realized it was harder for them to make the three-day drive to visit their sons, so they spoke to a Realtor®. He advised them to get rid of the clutter. They did what he said. That effort made the house feel so roomy, and so much more comfortable that they stayed, but they missed their family. The Stuff was between them and their family. They acknowledged it and stopped sidestepping the Stuff. They knew that they couldn't do it alone, so, they hired a specialist in organizing who sat with them and helped them sort everything. It took months. They finally moved and are happier being near their family.

The big pieces

What will you take with you? How big is the new place? Yes, square footage is important for the big pieces of furniture. Once you know the dimensions of the new place and the floor plan, it is easy to measure the chairs, tables, sofa, beds, etc., and determine what will fit in what spot. That can be done last after the small stuff is sorted into piles that you may have named: gift, donate, sell, throw out, move with you, store for a year, recycle, repurpose.

Invite the family to help

Michelle Woodbrey of *2Sisters Senior Living Advisors* suggests that you invite your children to go through the house with you and take the items that they want. Alternatively, you might offer certain friends or nieces and nephews that opportunity. In either case, you will be reducing the items in the house, and enjoying the sweet pleasure of gifting right now to those you love.

Brace yourself for the reality that your circle of family and friends may not want your treasures. That can be hard on you emotionally. Just as you may want your house to be sold to someone who will love it as you did, you may wish that your family wanted your workshop tools or crystal, your photography equipment or fine china, or whatever it is that has been important to you. Your loved ones may have plenty of their own things and their tastes may be very different from yours. That someone does not want to give house space to something you care about does not mean they don't care about you.

Awareness

Again, you are not your stuff. Would you rather the next generation love and accept you and your values, or that they become the curators of your stuff?

Time Table

The sorting and de-cluttering are important actions. If you have a set date to move in to your new residence, you can parcel out the tasks so you will meet your deadline. How do you know what your pace is, and how much you can get through? Begin. Take one corner of one room or one closet. See how much you can sort through in how much time. If it helps, make a simple log: "date, time, task, my observation." Example: "Today I worked for four hours and I sorted the linen closet and the hall closet. Feel good. Did it." After a number of days, you'll be able to guess how much time the next section of the house might take.

A note to would be procrastinators: consider hiring a professional organizer or senior move manager,[1] or ask someone with emotional distance from your turmoil to keep you on pace. If you are on a waiting list that estimates your move in date is indefinite—maybe nine months, maybe eighteen months—don't postpone the sorting. The unit you want could be available much sooner than you expected. Is there any disadvantage to being prepared ahead of time?

Even if you have not found the right new home yet, or if you have decided you will never move, start sorting and de-cluttering. It will make you feel more independent and in control. Do you want to burden your children, friends, trustees, or executor with the task of going through an undifferentiated mass of stuff without knowing what is trivial and what is significant? At an estate sale, both the house and its contents could go to the lowest bidder. What you treasure could become part of a fire sale, if the house and its contents need to be sold quickly. Is that the outcome you would prefer? In your most thoughtful frame of mind, you are likely to say, "No, I want to sell my heirlooms at the best price and live on the proceeds," or "I want my loved ones to receive these items as gifts if they want them." If that is how you feel, you are taking control of the situation. Ask for help and proceed with the sorting.

The sorting takes time. Which do you have more of: pieces of furniture, or everything else, which includes: mugs, plates, glasses, gadgets, old tax returns, insurance contracts, tools, sports equipment, receipts, sheets, pillow cases, clothes, photos, books, mementos, and on and on. The *everything else* category is time consuming. You evaluate each document, old letter, card, and piece of clothing. Some of these call up memories of relationships and events. Stirring up the past can slow you down, make you laugh recalling past antics, or depress you and throw you off course.

Feel. Think. Relive. Reclaim. Enjoy. Forgive. Share memories. Those memories are important parts of your life just as the next days are when new memories will be created. If the sorting process helps you recover memories and reintegrate them into the **story of you**, then it is a time of discovery and deepening. Whatever your age, you are growing in understanding and insights. You might be able to let go of an old anger. You might be able to mend fences. You might savor some of your accomplishments and victories. You are becoming more fully *you*. You might have been approaching the task of sorting as a depressing, mechanical, and dreadful waste of time. However, you may find that if it's approached with good heart, it is a gift you give yourself of yourself. It really isn't about the stuff. It's about you.

However, if you are getting stuck in the past in a way that is not healthy for you, and if you have a deadline for the move, then work with a family member or trusted friend to keep you on pace.

To build your **Confidence** about your decisions, keep a small voice recorder with you, and as you handle significant treasures, record why that item is important, and maybe name the person to whom you would like to give that item. It doesn't matter if you intend to gift it now, or as a bequest.

In addition to asking for a friend's help, you can hire a house organizer, or senior move manager. These professionals understand the complexity of emotions you may be experiencing, and they know how to help you stay focused on the task of sorting while respecting your **Effort**. Their knowledge of local places to sell, recycle, repurpose, donate or dispose of your stuff will reduce your anxiety and encourage your sense of purpose. Their services may also include actually moving your things out of the house and to their next destination. As a result, cartons of things will be moving out of the house. Seeing that happen can make you feel that you are making great progress.

2. Selling your home

Value of the house

Will your house have a sign that says: "For sale by owner," or will you hire a Realtor® to sell your house? Either way, it will make sense to interview three or more Realtors® and have a comparative market analysis prepared. You want your asking price to reflect the current market. Ask the Realtors® how quickly houses like yours are selling. Is it months, or days? This timeframe is especially vital if the proceeds from the sale of your house will fund the purchase of your new home. Retirement communities can be paid for as rentals with a first month, last month and activity fee; other communities, especially independent living ones, are ordinarily buy ins.

Funding the new home

Could there be a gap in time? Suppose that the retirement community requires your down payment by a certain date. Where will that money come from if your house has not sold? Will you liquidate an investment portfolio? Could you apply for a loan using your investment portfolio as collateral? Do you have a sufficient home equity line that you can draw on? Will you look for a bridge loan which is designed precisely for this transition?

Receipts and cost basis for tax preparation

Ask the Realtor® and your tax preparer what information you

need to document for next year's taxes. Label a big envelope: "House Basis and Deductions." Put in receipts for donations, major renovations or improvements. As you go through old tax returns, save any information about renovations that can help you reduce the potential capital gains tax on the sale of your house.[2]

3. Measuring and Placing

When you have a floor plan of your new home, you can measure your furniture and decide what fits where. Just because it fits doesn't necessarily mean it looks good placed that way. For many of us, it's hard to imagine what a new space will feel like and look like until the furniture is placed. Ask for help from someone you know who has an eye for interior design; ask if someone at the new residence can provide guidance or find out if the home organizer or senior move manager has a talent for interior design.

How much wall space is there for hanging pictures, art, etc.? How much closet space will you have for clothes, kitchen gadgets, towels, and linens? Where will the plants be set out? Where will you display the pretty and significant mementos? Does your new residence have storage space outside your unit? Maybe the best news is that it doesn't. Would you actually use whatever you put in storage? Or is the storage unit a time capsule? It stores layers of things that you assigned to the pile called "I don't know what to do with it; keep it for a year."

4. The Move itself

Your Realtor®, friends, or residential community may have a list of movers that are trustworthy, careful and reliable. You can also ask for recommendations for movers from neighbors, senior centers, and other trusted sources.

Will you do some of the packing and labeling of boxes so you know what is in each box and what must be unpacked first? Who will you hire if you want to do very little of the packing?

Who will be there on the day you move to open boxes, situate furniture, hang pictures, fill dresser drawers? Will the same organizer or senior move manager help? Can family and friends help? The retirement community may offer help, too.

Party time

How about a party once your space is settled? You have made a major change. You've shown spirit and courage. This move is something to celebrate. It is a commencement, just as a graduation is. It is a new chapter in your life. You've A.C.E-ed this test of life.

Michelle Woodbrey of *2Sisters Senior Living Advisors* recalls one of the best compliments she had from a client:

> "I worked with so many people over the years, as an activities director, and they often told me, 'I wish I had made this decision sooner. I was so resistant to leaving my home, and I was so worried about all the things that I was going to be giving up. I didn't realize the things that I would be gaining.' And in fact, the best compliment that I ever received was a resident telling me that I helped 'open a chapter to a book that she thought was over.'"

5. Redirect the mail

Make sure people can find you. Who has to be notified that you will move by such and such a date? Make a list or write each name on an index card. Keep the list or pack of index cards handy. You might need to notify that same group about a change in phone number. What or who should you notify? Include: post office, doctor(s), dentist, accountant, lawyer, veterinarian, gardeners, phone, gas, electric, cable, Medicare, Social Security, Veteran's Administration, banks, companies handling your investments and insurances, loans related to school, car, boat, hospital fees, credit card companies, clubs, houses of worship, Department of Motor Vehicles, IRS, State income tax department, local real estate tax authority, subscriptions for newspapers, magazines, theatre, and concerts, etc..

Though you may not be eager to have the bills follow you, it is better that they find you than that you pay late fees, or have your insurance canceled for non-payment.

SUMMARY

Thoreau's 150 sf house, a college dorm room, a room in a nursing home, a monk or nun's cell, a summer cottage, a studio apartment, a five-bedroom Colonial—all have in common, no matter the size of the space, the imprint of the resident. Things collect. Things are gifts, or items you spent money on, or spent time making. In our society, it is easy to accumulate lots of stuff. Like layers in an archeological dig, the things in your space may represent different periods in your life. They piled up over time.

So, if and when you decide to move, be patient with yourself. Ask for help. There are five steps to the move, but the most critical step is likely to be the first one, the sorting. It is in this sorting that you are revisiting your experiences, your values, your relationships and your sense of self. It is a gift you give yourself of yourself.

CHAPTER 12

Summary: Your Home Sweet Home Decision Guide

How well you live during your retirement depends in part on where you live in retirement. The central question is "Do I stay, or do I move? The chapters leading to this one have rotated that question as if it were a diamond. With each turn, we looked at another facet carefully, though we can't comment on all the refractions. *Move-Stay* has four main facets:

You: Who are you? What do you want to do with your days? What do you value? Your A.C.E., as you sort your stuff, is that you rediscover something about *you*. Is that what you've experienced as you looked through the mix of clutter and treasures? How do you take the past into the future successfully so that it enriches and does not constrict the new adventure? That process is fundamental to your well-being, whether you stay or move.

Your house: Is your house still the right place for you? Does your house support how you want to live? Does it make your life livelier and safer? Should it be remodeled so that you can stay? Can you afford to maintain the market value of your house **and** your life-style? What does your house cost you in Dollars, Mind Share, and Physical Energy? Are you paying more to maintain your house than you would pay to live in a retirement community? Of the many types of living arrangements, which can nurture you better in the years to come?

Your money: Will your money last? How have you reduced your exposure to risk? Have you considered how risks to your portfolio can compromise your being able to afford your house? If there were a *perfect storm* of both a downturn in your portfolio and a decline in your health, would the safety nets you put in place minimize that damage?

Your vision: Can you look forward? Do you mostly look back? Can you imagine another way to organize your days that would be better for you? How many different communities are you part of? What are your affinity groups: alma mater, sports teams, hobbies, spiritual communities, ethnic groups, artists, musicians, charities, social justice organizations, gardeners, etc.?

How many people do you interact with near your house, in your town, in your city, or beyond your city? At the big party in Chapter 6, where people were confiding how they figured out whether they should stay or move, you were connecting with people all over the United States. Did you hear anything that shaped your decision? The people at that party, and all the other people who've shared their stories with you, are one of your affinity groups or communities. They are a natural fit for this period of your life—for the *Move-Stay* debate.

Some explain how the whole family worked harmoniously to find a solution, and some show us what happens when parents are difficult, when couples disagree, and when death and illness disrupt your plans. The interviewees were earnest and thoughtful because they wanted to help you. They will feel gratified if they did.

What outcomes do you want? What does your decision say about who you are? What is your legacy? There will be more about this later in this chapter.

THE *MOVE-STAY* QUESTION—ON THE VERGE OF AN ANSWER...

The *Move-Stay* question and its four facets look very orderly, but you may feel unsettled. You are almost at a decision, but need one more run-through of the ideas.

Your Home Sweet Home **Decision Guide** aims to pull together in one place the facets of the questions that have appeared in earlier chapters. Seeing the facets in one place, you may be able to isolate what is holding you back, or you may realize with surprise that you are ready to move forward.

Your Home Sweet Home **Decision Guide** sets out a fresh approach. Sometimes, simply asking a question in a different way can open up another avenue of thought and get us *unstuck*. If, after you complete this chapter, you feel that you are leaning more than fifty-one percent in one direction, then it is just a matter of working out the physical details like how to fix the house, or deal with all The Stuff. Haven't you made other important decisions without being 100 percent sure that your course of action would lead to the ideal or most desired results? In ten years, in twenty years, how likely is it that your financial, physical and emotional well-being will be exactly as it is now? If you could get in a time machine and see you in the future, what would you do now to create good outcomes for that older person? What will best nurture and support you? Where you live is a key part of that answer.

Your Home Sweet Home **Decision Guide has two versions.** The first one is a **narrative** version that will invite you to express yourself in a few sentences. The second version, a **chart**, is directive. If you've circled most of the items in column Stay, then it seems you've made your decision.

NARRATIVE VERSION

Complete *Your Home Sweet Home* **Decision Guide: Narrative Version** at your pace in a few hours or a week or more. Allow your imagination, not just your calculator, to work on the material. Writing your answers or recording them is critical to catching whatever is flitting through your mind. You are catching yourself in the process of making a decision.

Getting ready

Sit in your kitchen or wherever you do your best thinking. Remove the distractions of radio and television. It's possible that petting a cat or dog that's nearby, or that's curled up on your lap will contribute to your calm completion of this assessment.

If two of you are making the decision to stay or move, complete this guide independently. Then compare notes, which might generate some very useful conversations.

If you are single and the decision is just yours, you may feel like there are two people inside your head. One refusing to move and the other attracted to a change. If that's so, you are like being part of a couple, but there is no one outside of you to debate with.

What's the question? What are we solving for?

Why move? What problem would moving solve? Alternatively, you could frame the question this way: In what setting will I, or will we, continue to thrive independently? The crucial words are *thrive independently*. If *thrive* means to be the most alive with your loves, interests, values and talents, then is it cultivated by being in a physical space (this home and no other), or is it dependent on the inner peace that comes from eliminating distractions and encumbrances?

Adding the word *independently* to *thrive* means paradoxically accepting whatever assistance is needed to remove obstacles and limitations, and making sure you are using your time and energy on what makes you thrive.

As Geralyn said earlier, "When people say I can do it, I can do it. Well, yes, you can do it, but you're spending a lot of time and energy, and someone else can do it for you. Give them the joy of doing it for you."

Your house: why do you like it?

Heart. What is it **specifically** about your current home that makes you smile? Is it something structural about the house? The furnishings? Is it the current neighbors? Is it memories? Write down whatever it is:

_____

_____

_____

What could be replicated in another home?

_____

_____

_____

Your house: how do you use it? Should you remodel?

1. Use. List the rooms in the house, including the basement and attic. Next to each, write: use it daily, use it once a week, pass through it, rarely use it. Your summary might look like this:

Room list (all the rooms with whatever name you give them).	Daily use	Once a week	Pass through	Rarely use

Could you live in a house that had just the rooms you use daily?

What if your real estate taxes and heating/cooling only had to cover the space used daily? Would your expenses be lower?

2. Adaptations: For you to stay in your home for ten or more years, what changes would have to be made? For instance, if the washer and clothes dryer are in the basement, should the laundry be relocated? Should closet space be redesigned to make things easier to reach?

List the items you'd like to change or must change to accommodate changes in you. Cost for the change? By when should those changes be made?

The change	The approximate cost	Do now/do in five years

Estimated total cost $_____

Can you comfortably spend that amount to make the changes? If not, what are your options?

Would the cost of those repairs reduce the amount you have monthly for customary living expenses?

Your money: What are you spending on the house?

3. Cash Flow: If you have already completed *Your Home Sweet Home* Cost Analysis. (Appendix B and discussion in Chapter 3), you will be able to answer the following questions quickly. If you haven't, complete the cash flow analysis later. Just forge ahead with the Decision Guide and answer what follows as well as you can. Guess now and verify later.

On a monthly basis: what does the house cost in

Dollars $_____,

Mind Share: Amount of time I'm thinking about what needs to get done for the house: hours a day_____

Physical Energy: Hours I/we spend working on the house, cleaning it, and maintaining it: hours a day_____

4. What's left for other living expenses after you pay for the operating costs, repairs, and maintenance of your house?

You may want to stay where you are, but does your budget allow for that?

My (our) monthly income $_____

Minus the monthly house costs, repairs, and maintenance $_____

Equals what's left for other expenses $_____

What is needed for other monthly living expenses $_____

Are you cutting back on luxuries, niceties, necessities, travel, or fun because the house repairs or maintenance are using up more of your monthly income? Yes___No___ Uncertain___

If you answer yes, what are you cutting back on (e.g. eating out less, shorter, or less expensive vacations)?

_____

_____

Are you not maintaining the house in tip-top shape because there isn't enough money? For example: I continue to defer painting the outside, etc.

_____

_____

Your money: how is your retirement account doing?

5. Assets

What's the total of all your investable assets? $_____

How much income do those assets provide to maintain your lifestyle? $_____

How much more income could they produce? $_____

How much additional income do you receive from Social Security or Pension or other sources? $_____

6. What's the current **market value of your house?** _____

If you sold your house and added the proceeds to your total assets, how many months of living expenses could you cover?_____

What would be left in your total investable assets if you had to pay $97,455 for one year in a nursing home?[1]

Investable assets $_____minus $97,455 = $_____

Would that reduction in assets lower your available income? Yes__No__

Your house: could you live someplace that lowered costs and increased your sense of well-being?

8. Searching for your hidden gem:

You may have already completed the search for a hidden gem when you read Chapter 8, if not, here's a reminder. Make a list of at least three retirement places to tour.

How to find places to visit? See what ads are running in your local newspaper. Ask for research help from the town librarian, the local senior center, or one of the many services like www.seniorliving.org, www.mylifesite.net, www.seniorhomes.com, www.senioradvisor.com, www.aplaceformom.com, or www.caring.com that can match you up with residences for you to review.

Additionally, you can search on the internet in many ways. You could write in the search bar:

55+ communities near [put in your zip code or the zip code near where you would like to live] or

CCRC + [zip code] or

Assisted living + [zip code] or

Retirement communities + [the name of a state]

9. Lunchtime. Go to lunch or attend one or more events held by a retirement community that seems attractive to you. Visit and tour at least three places. Take your spouse, significant other, or a friend or two with you. After each tour, write notes about what was attractive and what wasn't comfortable. You may locate a hidden gem that changes your life.

10. Comparing the places you visit

To avoid blurry recollections, it's smart to make notes to yourself the same day that you visit the community. Appendix F has an easy chart for capturing some of the details: **Notes on your visit**.

11. Compare costs of your house to the hidden gem

Compare the cost of the residence you liked best to the cost of your current home. Use the *Your Home Sweet Home* Comparison Analysis in Appendix C. Which residence is more cost effective?

Could you live less expensively in one of the hidden gems? _____

You: what runs you?

12. Your heart. Who are you? What nurtures you to be the part of yourself that you most admire?

Finish each of these sentences:

- "For me, another day of life is _____ "
- "I describe a good day as a day in which I _____ _____ "
- How many days a week are like the good day you just described? _____
- "For me, being independent means _____ _____ "
- "Regardless of my age, I want the people I care about to think of me as _____ _____ "
- "What I want for myself in the coming years is _____ _____ "
- "What I want to become is_____ _____ "
- Are you growing? _____ _____
- If you are not growing, when did you stop? Why?
- _____ _____
- "My biggest worries for the coming years are _____ _____ "

- "The way I am living now, I am like... _____
  _____ "

- "I think what would make me feel more alive, more like myself, and at my best is _____
  _____
  _____ "

- The reasons I don't want to move are:

1.
2.
3.
4.
5.

Would moving into the new place add more life to your life? Would adapting the house be better for you? It is your decision. The narrative version of *Your Home Sweet Home* Decision Guide that you just filled in gives you the chance to express your thoughts and explain yourself to yourself. It collects key numbers about daily use, adaptations, income, costs, and assets. It reviews how to search for alternative residences. Critical data is in one place so that you can evaluate the interconnecting parts.

The next version is more directive. Circle a number of ideas in one column and your decision is made. Done.

YOUR HOME SWEET HOME DECISION GUIDE: CHART VERSION

Stay home or Move to your hidden gem

The columns are *Stay home* or *Move to your hidden gem*. The strong sentiments and facts pulling you in one direction or another are summarized. It isn't intended to list every thought. But if something really important to you is missing, add it to the mix. This is not a score card with specific points for each item in each column. It is, rather, an overview to help you see in bolder strokes the significant issues that contribute to this decision. It is precisely because you are full of nuances and many things matter to you that the chart moves away from your complexity and narrows down to the main issues. Take a pencil with a good eraser and circle the items that resonate with you. Which column reflects what you are thinking?

Ultimately, where you live in retirement will affect how well you live during retirement. What are the right trade-offs for you? It might be a challenge to your imagination to keep in mind two of you: *You*, as you are right now, and *you*, as you might be in the years ahead.

As you are now, if you and your house have passed the financial, physical, and social tests in the preceding chapters, then you might feel confident about staying. The hard part is imagining how your situation might change and admitting that those changes could be a reason to move **now.** Even if you agree that you should move, unless you know about attractive alternatives, you will settle for what you know and have now. So, to be fair to yourself, you should search for and evaluate alternative settings before you commit to staying where you are.

If you cannot imagine a satisfying alternative to whatever is in the *Stay Home* column, then you have made your decision. If, however, you have circled more choices in the *Move to Your Hidden Gem* column, then you're preparing to a move. Move.

Question	Stay	Move
Question: Heart. *What about the house makes you smile?*	*Stay Home* Physical layout Architecture Unique location	*Move to Your Hidden Gem* Memories Neighbors who could visit you wherever you live Furnishings
Question: Use of space	All rooms regularly used 90% or more	More space than I use.

Question	Stay	Move
Question: Adaptations	I have plenty of money to make all the changes.	If I make the changes, I will deplete my retirement assets and reduce my regular standard of living.
Question: Cash Flow	Now, I have surplus income every month, even after house emergency repairs and maintenance. I may not have a surplus if the cost of living rises or my investments don't do well, but I will still be able to cover my costs.	Repairs and good maintenance would reduce my regular income. I defer maintenance. Or, I would rather spend any extra money on travel and entertainment.
Question: Cash Flow: measured by Dollars, Mind Share and Physical Energy	I like taking on projects to beautify my home and I enjoy engaging in the regular details of maintaining it.	It would be a relief to not have to worry about all the housework, the repairs, and constant maintenance.
Question: Assets	I can cover long-term care for several years and my regular living expenses will not be reduced.	Long-term care for more than one year would deplete my assets. If I sold the house and entered a CCRC, that could remove my worry about LTC.
Question: Lunchtime	I refuse to visit any other residences. or Where I am living is the cheapest place I can live. I completed the *Your Home Sweet Home* Cost Analysis and I followed up with the comparison analysis for three other places.	I found a gem of a place that I like and can afford. In total, it costs less in Dollars, Mind Share and Physical Energy than where I live now. Selling my house will increase my income, and I can spend more money on what I really enjoy.
Question: Your heart	Where I live, and how I am living now is helping me become the best of who I can be. Here's **why**….	It's my turn to have more of what I want. I will have the time, the money, and the encouragement from like-minded people to expand my interests. I will grow. Someone will be right there for me if I get sick.

If you circled more items in the column *Stay Home,* you want to stay, and it seems that the finances are on your side. If you decide to stay where you are now, how have you answered the very last question: Your heart. "Where I live, and how I am living now is helping me become the best of who I can be. Here's why..." Is the **Why** compelling, satisfying, and authentically you? If so, then you have backed up your position convincingly. Enjoy your home. Continue to cultivate the friendships and activities that have been part of your life for many years.

However, if after you answer **Why**, you see ambiguity or flabbiness in your statement, you might want to reconsider your decision. Have you allowed yourself to address both your hopes and your fears? Maybe staying in your home is a decision that can work for a few years. If something shifts, you can always reconsider your decision.

If you circled most of the statements in the *Move to Your Hidden Gem* column, you have decided to move. You are accepting a new adventure. You see that there is more to life than what you have already experienced. You are not confining yourself to the happenstance of being in just one neighborhood. A retirement residence can be like a college campus in that it draws people from many different states who have had a variety of life experiences to share. There are new people to meet and more things to explore. Residential settings like those discussed in *What's New in Housing?* Chapter 8 and *You Live Where?* Chapter 9 can maximize both your independence and your curiosity. By clearing away the less productive uses of your time, you can focus on what matters most—you growing into your full potential.

Wherever you live, take to heart what Oliver Wendell Holmes Sr. said—"Many people die with their music still in them." Anthony M. Coniaris adds a different image: "The tragedy for most of us is that we die before we are fully born. We die with so much unlived life in us. We have a hundred acres of possibilities and only about one-half acre under cultivation."[2]

YOUR WHY? YOUR LEGACY

What motivates you? Who are you? What is your legacy?

We are familiar with the concept *keeping up with the Joneses*, which reminds us that we often buy things or do things that we see others around us are buying or doing. We often say that young people are being influenced by peer pressure to act in ways that will make them acceptable to their group.

Each of these concepts underscores that we respond to our social environment to some degree, even if we think we are not touched by marketing and trends. We are social beings who are interdependent and connected. For instance, in a traffic jam, no man or woman is an island. We are directly affected by everyone else. In other settings, we see crowds of people choosing whatever is popular in the width of neckties, the hemlines of dresses, the trendiest hairstyles, and must have electronics. Polls are continually highlighting what masses of us agree and disagree about.

The most introverted and reclusive people and the most creative and gregarious ones respond to a social context.

I emphasize this because the decision you make about staying or moving—your **Why**—creates a social connection. It stirs ripples. Your decision is not about just you, your parents, and your immigrant great-grandparents. It is about everyone who knows you. Your decision matters more than you may appreciate.

You have the challenge, we each have the challenge, of leaving a legacy of a life well-lived. That is a life that shows you have made choices that demanded courage, love, integrity, and imagination. You made choices, not because you had all the facts, but because you weighed whatever information you had and risked making a decision. You did not run away. You've maintained your independence each time you thought through your options and acted, instead of hiding and waiting for an accident, illness, or some exterior force to determine your course of action.

People who are retired, look old, or seem out of step don't want to be overlooked or pushed aside as irrelevant or ignored. But when they abdicate their role in making difficult decisions, or won't voice their opinions, they are inadvertently putting someone else in charge of their lives, and they start becoming irrelevant.

In your circle of family, friends, neighbors and casual associates, what you do matters. It teaches; it expands what is possible. "If they could move into a new home and feel revitalized, we can too." "If she can take up oil painting in her eighties, I can pursue a new hobby." "If he can still play tennis in his nineties, I can too." "If he's in his eighties and collecting Master points in Bridge, that says to me my brain can be sharp too." "If she's in her nineties and writing poetry and teaching, there's no limit on growing."

What a fine legacy you prepare for others when you inspire them to say, "I can do that." By continuing to grow into the best of your-self, you sing your song, and share it. You are not the one who dies with your music still in you.

Where you choose to live in retirement is not at its core a real estate decision; it is a decision to live life as fully as you can. That is why it is a crucial decision. Whether you stay or move, let it be *your* choice. Put your energy and creativity into it.

SUMMARY

Although the conflict between two primary retirement assets— your house and your retirement income—is the crux of this book, the resolution of the conflict includes, but goes beyond simply strengthening your portfolio and fortifying your house for your comfort and safety. I am urging you to focus on the quality of your life. Your decision should give you more scope for happiness, more freedom in time, and more income for what you want. Your ability to live fully and well matters not just to you, but to those who know you and love you. Choose to live as fully as you can no matter your physical or financial condition.

You are not a house, nor are you a portfolio of assets. You are more valuable than anything that can be owned. Choose an environment that nurtures the best of you. That teenager who wanted adventures is still in you. Your life experience gives you the discernment to value the past, and, also, the spunk to say **yes** to new-fangled stuff. You've lived through enough ups and downs to say, "I can do this!"—whatever *this* is. Your family, friends, and I will be cheering you on. You are vibrant and relevant because of your commitment to living with energy, love, insight, and courage. We celebrate you.

APPENDIX A

Maintenance List

The maintenance tasks for your house may differ from this basic list, but what is important is that you check off which of these you take care of yourself and which ones you have someone else do for you. Add whatever additional projects are routine for you. Maintenance costs will probably average out over five years to be between 1% and 3% annually of the initial value of your house according to John Riha. He explains that budgeting between $5,000 and $15,000 a year for a house that you bought for $500,000 will help you prepare for a range of expenses.[1]

Maintenance tasks	My job	I hire someone
Landscaping/planting		
Weeding/mowing		
Cleaning and repairing gutters and downspouts		
Pruning trees away from electric wires and roof		

Maintenance tasks	My job	I hire someone
Pest and insect control—rodents, ants, mosquitoes, etc.		
Pool, hot tub, spa—filters and right balance of chemicals		
Garage—clean out toxic chemicals. Test garage door auto-reverse function		
Roof – leaks?		
Chimney repointing, flashing		
Chimney flues cleaned		
Attic—any signs of moisture or damage to insulation		
Shingles or siding—repair?		
Porch and deck painted or weatherized. Brackets—corroded?		
Masonry—cracked? Crumbling?		
Driveway—concrete or blacktop surface intact?		
Stairs and railings firm and in good repair?		
Windows cleaned		
Windows caulked, locking well, weather stripping		
Storm windows on and off		
Shutters painted or repaired		
Trim painted		
Storm doors and screen doors-- intact and closing properly		
Doors—weather stripping? Locks in good repair?		
Screens for windows—no holes or rips		
Heating and cooling systems tune ups		
Furnace filters and air filters changed/clean air ducts		
Humidifiers—repair? Replace?		
Dehumidifiers—repair? Replace?		
Toxic chemicals and paints—store or dispose of safely		
Fences—paint, repair		
Water filtration system		

Maintenance tasks	My job	I hire someone
Irrigation system—flush out before freezing temperatures		
Cleanout main water drain		
Test sump pump		
Appliances repairs—new parts, clean coils of refrigerator		
Clothes dryer vents cleaned		
Degrease stove hood and vents		
Caulk and repair ceramic tiles—floors, shower and caulk around sinks and tubs		
Test replace GFCI outlets		
Electric cords frayed/right gauge for the appliance		
Security system—back up battery in good condition		
Septic tank pumped out		
Faucets—leaking?		
Kitchen sink—disposal, tighten connections, clean		
Clean shower and sink drains		
Toilets—running?		
Water heater—drain until clear of sediment. Test pressure relief valve to prevent corrosion, then leaks		
Water softening/water filtration system—check filters and chemicals		
Clean floors and rugs		
Fire extinguisher(s) fully charged		

APPENDIX B

Your Home Sweet Home Cost Analysis

Your Name:			
Date:	Dollars	Mind Share (Time Thinking About a Problem and Resolving It):	Physical Energy:
What Does Your House Cost?	**Dollars Monthly**	**Mind Share**	**Your Physical Energy**
Mortgage			
Home equity loan/line			
Real estate taxes			
Water/sewer			
Garbage collection			
Homeowner's insurance			
Heating			

What Does Your House Cost?	Dollars Monthly	Mind Share	Your Physical Energy
Heating annual tune-up			
Air conditioning tune-up			
A/C filters/duct cleaning			
Interior painting			
Exterior painting			
Chimney cleaning/flashing			
Repointing brick work			
Driveway sealer/repair			
Garage door maintenance			
Snow removal			
Landscaping/leaf cleaning			
Electricity			
Repairs plumbing/electrical/ roof			
Appliance maintenance/ repairs/new			
Furniture/decorating			
Cleaning drapes/carpets/ floors			
Alarm or security system			
House cleaning service			
Fence repair/maintenance			
Gutters cleaned/repaired			
Window cleaning			
Pest control			
Other: detectors, smoke, CO_2, radon			
Total House Expenses			
	$0.00	**Hours**	**Hours**

What You Need	Dollars Monthly	Mind Share	Your Physical Energy
Food to be prepared at home			
Eating out			
Wine/liquor other beverages			
Telephone—land line /cell phone(s)			
Cable			
Internet			
Laundry/dry cleaning			
Medical insurance			
Medicare A/B			
Medicare D			
Medicare C			
Medical Co-pays/ deductibles			
Medicine and over the counter			
Other medical expenses			
Dental exams and care			
Vision exams and eye glasses/contacts			
Hearing exams and hearing aids			
Clothing—the basics			
Personal grooming/haircuts			
Personal care—other			
Life insurance			
Long-term care insurance			
Income tax preparation			
Updating legal documents			

Time correcting billing or other mistakes			
Annual fees for credit cards			
Other			
Other			
Total Needs	**$**	**Hours**	**Hours**
What You Want	**Dollars Monthly**	**Mind Share**	**Your Physical Energy**
Entertainment			
Vacations			
Education			
Sports and sporting events			
Car payment			
Car insurance			
Car maintenance			
Car excise tax			
Driver's license			
Highway tolls			
Car parking			
Car wash/detailing			
Clothing—discretionary			
Gifts			
Charity			
Magazine/newspaper subscriptions			
Club or association memberships			
Gym/fitness coach			
Professional licenses			
Other loans			

Other payment plans			
Pets—vet			
Pets—food and grooming			
Hobbies			
Electronic gadgets upgraded			
Other— family events e.g., weddings, family reunions, funerals			
Other			
Other			
Other			
Total Wants	**$**	**Hours**	**Hours**
What Items Push Me to Spend Too Much?	**Dollars Monthly**	**Mind Share**	**Your Physical Energy**
1			
2			
3			
4			
Totals			
	Monthly		
House	$		
Needs	$		
Wants	$		
Total Expenses	**$**	**Hours**	**Hours**
Income Sources			
Social Security for Me	$		
Social Security for Partner	$		
Pension for Me	$		
Pension for Partner	$		

Income from Retirement Plans	$		
Income from Retirement Plans	$		
Income/rental/royalties	$		
Other Income	$		
Total Gross Income	$		
Federal Tax	$		
State Tax	$		
City Tax	$		
Net Income	$		
What Percent of Net Income			
Pays for House			
Pays for Needs			
Pays for Wants			
Balances			
Credit Card Balances End of Last Year			
Credit Card Balances Now			
Investment Balances End of Last Year			
Investment Balances Now			
Other Comments or Questions:			

Your Home Sweet Home
Comparison Analysis

Comparison of costs for your current home and the hidden gem

	Current Home		Hidden Gem	
	Monthly	Annually	Monthly	Annually
Service fee/maintenance fee				
Mortgage/ condo fee				
Home equity loan/line				
Real estate taxes				
Water/sewer				
Electricity				
Garbage collection				
Homeowner's insurance				
Heating/cooling cost				
Heating annual tune-up				

	Current Home		Hidden Gem	
	Monthly	Annually	Monthly	Annually
Air conditioning tune-up				
A/C filters/duct cleaning				
Interior painting				
Exterior painting				
Chimney cleaning				
Roof loose or missing shingles/leaks				
Repointing brick work				
Driveway sealer/repair				
Repair holes, deep cracks in sidewalk				
Garage door maintenance				
Snow removal				
Landscaping/leaf cleaning/ mowing				
Trees cut back from gutters, cables, wires, house				
Electrical/frayed or old cords on lamps, appliances				
Test/replace GFCI outlets				
Alarm/security system				
Plumbing/faucets leaking				
Appliance maintenance/ repairs				
Furniture/decorating				
Cleaning carpets				
Cleaning or refinishing floors				
Cleaning drapes or window treatments				
House Cleaning Service				
Caulking windows				
Repair/clean screens				

	Current Home		Hidden Gem	
	Monthly	Annually	Monthly	Annually
Degrease stove exhaust fan and hood				
Cleaning clothes dryer vents				
Drain hot water heater				
Repair or replace weather-stripping				
Humidifiers or dehumidifiers—clean				
Masonry cracked, crumbling				
Fence repair/maintenance				
Gutters cleaned/repaired				
Window cleaning				
Pest control				
Storm damage repairs				
Smoke detectors, carbon monoxide test/batteries				
Recycle/ store properly toxic chemicals, paints				
Septic tank/pumped				
Cleanout the main water drain—tree roots, debris, etc.				
Deck wash/check loose posts				
Other				
Other				
Total House Expenses				

Safety Checklist—Your Body and Your House

S afety starts with **You**—assessing your body. Before you think about having a chair lift installed, talk with your doctor(s). Is there a physical therapy program, or exercise routine that will strengthen your body and your balance?

Balance, leg strength, and flexibility are critical for your safety.

I offer the following websites only as examples of programs that you might find as you search online. Be sure to review whatever program interests you with a professional who knows your health profile. The goal is to find something you are willing to do and will do consistently. Ah, yes, hard if you are not enthusiastic about exercise.

- https://www.silversneakers.com/blog/
  daily-exercises-older-adults

- https://health.usnews.com/health-news/health-wellness/articles/2016-01-29/8-best-equipment-free-strength-exercises-for-older-adults
- http://agingresearch.buffalo.edu/hssat

When did you last have your eyes examined? Are medicines causing dizziness? Are you eating nutritious food in appropriate portions?

When did you last have your hearing tested? Michael Schmit, BC-HIS, owner of *At Home Hearing Healthcare* in Billerica, Massachusetts, explains that people tend to ignore or downplay hearing problems because hearing loss is not painful the way a broken bone might be. However, he wants us to be aware of research that shows that seniors with hearing loss are significantly more likely to develop dementia and experience depression and anxiety. Hearing loss may isolate an individual socially, and also decrease his or her ability to respond to smoke detector alarms, or the sound of a faucet that was left running.

Start with **You**, and then follow one of the lists that checks for safety in your house.

In addition to the cautions cited in the text, learn more from *Living Safely, Aging Well: A Guide to Preventing Injuries at Home* by Dorothy A. Drago.[1] It's a clear and helpful resource for understanding the changes that age brings, and the sorts of frequent accidents experienced by those over 65. Drago provides many examples of potential dangers. Here is one example that makes eating both dangerous and less enjoyable. The loss of taste can make it hard to detect spoiled food and could lead to food poisoning.

There are many checklists online. Search for home safety checklist for older adults, seniors, or elders. Here are two:

- http://www.seniorcitizensguide.com/articles/services/Homesafety.html
- https://www.caregiverstress.com/senior-safety/making-home-safer/interactive-safety-guide/

Soiree Recipes. What Tasty Food Are They Eating at the Soiree in Chapter 6?

O dd to have recipes in this book? Not really. The questions and worries expressed by people I have cared about for decades gave rise to this book. They are friends, not abstract statistics; they are people whose feelings, finances, and family lives were woven into my advice. Yes, we shared meals as well as business meetings. I view you in the same holistic way, though we have not met. The Soiree and the recipes are my way of saying that I see you as a person with complexities who is making a crucial decision about where to live. You are not a house, nor a bank account. You are full of memories, hopes, worries, talents, fears, and courage. You want to make the right decision that addresses you as a complete person. All the people I know enjoy good food, so welcome to the Soiree.

These recipes are party favorites at my home because people like *comfort food* that tastes good. The quantities can be multiplied to serve more guests. The emphasis is on easy, not fancy entertaining. It's about making people feel welcomed and cared for. Of course, you have your own favorites and I would be delighted if you wanted to share them with me. Send them to penelope@wealthychoices.com. They might be posted with other recipes on www.WealthyChoices. com/Your Home Sweet Home/Soiree Recipes.

STARTERS:

Hummus is an easy and healthy vegan, gluten-free dip made with chickpeas or cannellini beans. Dip sliced carrots, cucumbers, pita bread or crackers.

- One 15 oz can of chickpeas, or cannellini beans
- ¼ cup of tahini
- 4 tablespoons of lemon juice— generally that's two lemons
- 2 or 3 cloves of garlic which if minced would be about 2 teaspoons worth
- ¼ teaspoon salt
- ¼ cup of the liquid from the can of beans

Drain a can of beans over a bowl so that you can keep the liquid. (Using canned beans is faster. Yes, you can soak beans overnight if you prefer.)

Put the garlic in the food processor, unless you prefer to mince it by hand. Add the beans, salt, liquid, and lemon juice. Mix to puree consistency, then add the tahini. Done. Refrigerate or dig in. It keeps for days.

Hummus in a Wrap

My friend, Maria, uses the same Hummus mixture, not for a dip but to make a sandwich or mini-appetizer. Choose your favorite wrap or flatbread, whether round or rectangular. Gluten-free wraps are available. I prefer to make the hummus and tabbouleh myself to get the tastes I like, but if you buy hummus and tabbouleh already prepared, you can assemble this in a few minutes. Put the flatbread or wrap on a cutting board. Spread the hummus to within a half inch of the edge of the wrap. Top it with a layer of tabbouleh. Roll the wrap up. Cut into 3-inch segments. Add a toothpick to hold it together.

Make these close to when you want to serve them—say, within 30 minutes. If the hummus and tabbouleh are very moist, the bread might get soggy.

To make a simple tabbouleh, put a cup of bulgur wheat in 2 ¼ cups of water with ½ teaspoon of salt. Bring it to a boil. Then lower the heat, cover the pot and let it simmer for about 15 minutes, until the water is absorbed. Let it cool.

Dice half a cucumber and one plum tomato. Mix them into the cooked and cooled wheat. Add about 2 tablespoons of chopped-up fresh parsley. Use half as much, if you only have dried parsley.

Mushroom Cups

- A muffin pan with 12 cups will hold toast that you'll fill with a mushroom mixture.
- One loaf of sandwich bread. Thin white is easier to fit into the muffin cups.
- 4 oz. butter
- 1 pound of sliced mushrooms—any type
- 6 slices of bacon
- Medium onion diced
- ¼ cup heavy cream
- ½ teaspoon salt
- 2 plum or small tomatoes cut into small pieces.

Trim the crusts from the bread. (Save them for bread crumbs.) Flatten the slices with a rolling pin. Melt the butter and coat the muffin cups. Fit the bread into the cups. Bake at 350° F until golden toast. Depending on how your oven heats up, the browning may take about 8 minutes. Remove from the oven. Brush the bread with melted butter.

Cut the bacon into one-inch pieces and put it in a frying pan, cooking it until is just about crisp. Drain on a paper towel. Remove all but a tablespoon of the bacon fat. Mince the onion. Cook it in the pan until golden. Take the onion out. Add the mushrooms and cook them until they are soft. Add more butter if the pan is too dry. The mushrooms will give out liquid. Add the heavy cream and salt. Add the bacon and onions. Mix well. Fill the toast cups. Garnish with the tomatoes.

Baked Crab Rangoon

- 8 oz. of cream cheese
- 8 oz. of crabmeat. Check for tiny pieces of shell or use imitation crabmeat.
- 2 cloves of garlic minced
- 1 teaspoon of Worcestershire sauce
- 1 teaspoon soy sauce
- 2 scallions or ⅓ cup of diced onion
- Prepared wonton skins or wraps. You can make your own if you would like.

Mix all the ingredients. Set out three wonton skins at a time. Put a scant tablespoon of filling on each. Moisten the edges with a little water. Bring up the corners to the center. Press together. Set on a jelly roll sheet that you've coated with oil or lined with parchment paper.

Bake at 475° F until golden brown about 15 minutes. These can be deep-fried but that process adds calories, time and mess. Instead just spray a little oil on the wonton packets as they sit on the jelly roll sheet before you bake them.

Water Chestnuts Dressed in a Chili Sauce and Bacon

- 1 lb. bacon
- 1 can of whole, not sliced, water chestnuts
- ⅓ cup dark brown sugar
- ⅓ cup mayonnaise
- ⅓ cup chili sauce

Cook the bacon partially so that much of the fat is rendered. It should not be as crisp as you'd like to eat with your eggs. It needs to be soft enough to wrap around the water chestnuts. Drain it on paper towels. Mix together all the ingredients except the water chestnuts and bacon.

Line a jelly roll pan with foil. Otherwise this is a messy clean up. Wrap each chestnut with bacon. Secure with a toothpick. Set on the prepared baking sheet. Spoon the sauce over the water chestnuts and bake at 350° F for 20 to 30 minutes or until the bacon is crispier.

Artichoke and Spinach Squares

- 8 oz. whole milk mozzarella, cut into small pieces or shredded
- ¾ cup grated Parmesan cheese
- 5 large eggs
- 1 can of artichoke hearts (14 oz.) cut into small pieces
- ½ cup scallion, white and green, or 1 medium onion diced and cooked for 5-10 minutes until golden.
- 12 oz. baby spinach
- 1 teaspoon each of garlic powder, salt, and oregano

Butter a 9 x 13 pan. Set the oven to 350° F. Mix all the ingredients. Pour into the pan. Cook until a butter knife comes out clean, about 40 minutes. Cut into squares.

NEED A FORK TO EAT THESE:

Crustless Ham and Cheese Quiche

It is easy to experiment with this egg-based mixture. This one is for a 9 x 13 pan, but you can double it for a lasagna size dish. Preheat the oven to 450° F.

- 8 oz. of sliced gruyere cheese or cheddar
- 6 oz. heavy cream
- 6 oz. baked ham, bacon, or Canadian bacon
- 4 eggs
- ½ teaspoon salt
- 1 tablespoon of butter
- 2 medium onions, diced
- ⅓ cup Parmesan cheese

Brown the onion in butter. Mix the cream, eggs, salt and onion together.

Cover the bottom of the 9 x 13 pan with cheese slices. Top them with meat slices.

Pour the egg mixture over the cheese and meat slowly so that the cheese and meat pieces are not moved to one spot by the tidal wave of liquid. Sprinkle with Parmesan cheese. Bake at 450° F for about ten minutes. Lower to 325° F for 30 to 40 minutes.

Test for doneness with a butter knife. If you insert it and it comes out clean, the quiche is cooked.

Vegetarian Version of the Crustless Quiche

Instead of meat, add 8 oz. of mushrooms. Cook them with the onions.

To add a crust to the quiche, use an electric mixer to beat until smooth 4 oz. cream cheese and 4 oz. butter. Add in 8 oz. flour, ¼ teaspoon salt, ¼ teaspoon baking powder. It's a soft dough. If it is too soft to roll out into a rectangle for a 9 x 13 pan, refrigerate it for an hour. Roll it out to fit the pan, then continue with scattering the cheese and meat or mushrooms in the bottom of the 9 x 13 pan. Pour in the egg mixture. Cook as above.

Cut into twelve pieces and serve.

String Beans and Lamb Stew

This is a one pot dish that needs a few hours to cook. It can be prepared ahead and heated just before serving.

- 3 lbs. lamb stew meat or shoulder chops
- 2 lbs. fresh string beans
- 3 chopped onions sliced
- 1 cup tomato sauce
- Half a bunch of fresh dill and half of parsley chopped
- 1 teaspoon of salt, pepper to your taste
- 3 tablespoons butter or olive oil
- 1 cup water

In a pot or casserole deep enough to fit the string beans and lamb, melt butter or oil, add the onions. Cook the onions until soft. Cut the meat and string beans into bite-sized pieces so that you don't need a knife to cut the food while you are walking around and talking to your friends at the soiree. (If you are serving this dish for a sit-down dinner, cut the meat into larger piece and leave the string beans whole.) Put the stew meat into the pot. Brown it. Mix the tomato sauce with water, parsley, dill, salt, pepper, and string beans. Add to the pot with the lamb and onions. Bring it to a boil. Then lower the heat and cook covered for about two hours or until the meat is tender. Serve with orzo or rice.

Meatball Soup

- 32 oz. of beef stock
- 2 lbs. of either ground beef or lamb
- ½ cup of raw rice

- 1 teaspoon salt
- 1 ½ large onions
- 2 eggs

Cook the onions in the pot with some butter until they are soft. In a bowl, mix the soft onions with the meat, rice, salt, and eggs. Roll into meatballs (walnut-sized). In the meantime, bring the stock to a boil. Drop the meatballs into the stock. Lower the heat after five minutes. Cook for an hour on lower heat until the meat is tender. Enjoy with your favorite crusty bread.

Chicken and Cucumber Salad

- 4 cups each of cooked chicken and diced cucumber
- Mix 1 cup mayonnaise, ¼ cup milk, ¼ cup white vinegar, or rice vinegar
- Add to the mayonnaise mixture, 1 teaspoon each of curry powder and salt.
- Mix in the chicken and cucumber. Refrigerate for two hours or serve at room temperature.

Pasta and Broccoli with Peanut Sauce

You can adapt this dish by using noodles or pasta that is gluten-free, or you can enjoy the broccoli with the sauce and no pasta. I've used a variety of noodles and pasta shapes—penne, ziti, small shells. It all tastes good, though experts on pasta and noodles might have a different view on what is appropriate.

Make the peanut sauce first.

- ½ cup creamy peanut butter
- 1 tablespoon minced garlic
- ¼ cup soy sauce.
- ¼ cup water
- 1 tablespoon rice vinegar
- 1 teaspoon sugar

- 1 teaspoon Asian chili paste (optional)
- Mix the ingredients in a blender until smooth. Set aside.

The ratio of broccoli to pasta is up to you. If you love vegetables increase the broccoli from 8 oz. to 16 oz. Cut it into small pieces. You will need 6 oz. of pasta or noodles

Cook the pasta according to the package directions. About two minutes before the timer sounds, add the broccoli. In about two minutes, it will look bright green. If you like it well cooked, add it to the pasta earlier.

Before you drain the pasta and broccoli, save 2 cups of the water. Drain it. Put it in a serving dish. Mix in the peanut sauce. If it stands too long, the pasta will absorb the sauce which is why you have the water handy. Add a little at a time to moisten the mixture.

Chicken Baked in Filo Packets

These can be made bite-sized or meal-sized. Chicken tenders can be used for the appetizer and chicken breast for the meal serving. Alternatively, if you are patient, you can cut the breast meat into small pieces for the appetizer.

You'll need one package of filo (which you will find in the freezer section of many supermarkets). Defrost it overnight in the refrigerator. Stores specializing in Greek or Middle Eastern food often have it fresh not frozen. It's easier to work with. There will be around 20 sheets of filo in the box.

- 10 skinless, boneless chicken breast halves, or about 20 chicken tenders
- 1 ½ cup mayonnaise
- 1 cup of chopped scallions or onions, but if you use onions, cook them in butter until they are golden brown.
- ⅓ cup fresh lemon juice about 3 lemons
- 2 cloves garlic minced (yes, you can add more, or omit the garlic)

- 3 sticks unsalted butter
- ½ cup grated Parmesan cheese

First, prepare the sauce by combining the mayonnaise, garlic, scallions, and lemon juice.

For the chicken tenders, salt and pepper both sides. Cut into appetizer-sized pieces.

If you are using breast halves, pound them between two pieces of wax paper so they are thinner. Salt and pepper both sides.

Melt the butter. Have a pastry brush ready.

Open the filo and lay it out. Cover it with wax paper and a damp towel. Move one sheet at a time to the work surface; butter it. For the bite size servings, fold the sheet in half. Cut that in half (either horizontally or vertically). Put one piece of chicken on each filo sheet about 2 inches from one of the edges. Cover the chicken with sauce. Fold the filo over the chicken and roll it. Tuck the ends into the center, continue rolling the packet. The filo is a packet holding the chicken. Any shape you make is fine. Butter the filo all around. Set the packet in a baking pan which you have buttered.

If you are using the half breast, take one sheet of filo to the work surface, butter it. Lay another sheet on that. Place the chicken. Add the sauce. Make a packet.

Butter all the packets once they are in the pan and sprinkle with Parmesan cheese.

Cook for about 20 minutes at 375° F for the smaller pieces and 25 to 30 for the larger ones. An instant read thermometer will say 165°.

Because ovens heat and cook differently, after the filo looks golden, take one packet out. Cut into it. If the chicken is cooked, then you have determined what the right timing is for your oven.

Shrimp in Butter and Garlic

- 2 lbs. raw shrimp, deveined and shelled
- 3 cloves garlic, minced
- 1 teaspoon salt

- 1 small onion diced
- 1-2 sticks butter (4 oz. to 8 oz.)
- ¼ cup white wine
- Juice of half a lemon

In a frying pan or heavy pot, melt the butter. Add the onion and cook for 3 minutes. Add the garlic and cook 1 minute. Add the lemon juice, seasonings, and wine. Cook for another 3 minutes. Add the shrimp and cook until pink. Serve with rice, or serve with toothpicks if it is an appetizer.

Sweet Coconut Bread (no yeast, no kneading)

This bread has a firm texture and keeps well. Make one large or two smaller loaves.

- 1 ½ cups canned coconut milk
- 1 ½ tablespoons white vinegar
- 2 tablespoons of either oil or apple butter
- ½ cup dark brown sugar
- 4 cups all-purpose flour
- 1 ½ teaspoon salt
- ½ teaspoon baking powder
- 1 teaspoon baking soda
- 1 cup flaked coconut
- ¾ cup walnuts (optional)

Add the vinegar to the coconut milk. Let it stand for five minutes. It will look like it's curdled.

In a mixing bowl, combine the sugar, flour, salt, baking powder, and baking soda. Mix. Add half the milk and oil or apple butter and mix. Then add the walnuts and the remainder of the milk and beat for 3 minutes in a stand electric mixer. The dough is very sticky.

Either grease the cookie sheet with butter or cover it with parchment paper. Shape one large or two smaller round loaves. Use your oiled hands to shape the loaves. You may need a dough scraper to pull the dough out of the mixer.

Preheat your oven to 375° F. Bake 45 minutes for one large round and 30 minutes for two small ones. They are baked when an instant read thermometer registers 180° or higher and the thermometer probe comes out clean without dough sticking to it.

Nancy's New York Date Nut Bread

There's a two-step process: soaking the dates first in a pot, then mixing them with the flour mixture which you prepare in a separate bowl.

- ¾ cup chopped walnuts (make sure that there are no pieces of shell)
- 1 cup chopped and pitted dates. Many supermarkets carry these already prepared with a light coating of sugar.
- 1 ½ teaspoon baking soda
- ½ teaspoon salt
- ¼ cup (½ stick unsalted butter)
- ¾ cup boiling water

Combine all the ingredients just listed in a pot that will allow the dates and nuts to be submerged. Cover and let stand for 15 minutes.

In a bowl, mix 1 cup sugar, 1 ½ cups flour, 2 eggs, and ½ teaspoon vanilla extract.

Pour the date mixture into the flour mixture. Mix until blended.

Butter a loaf pan well (9 x 5 x 3). Pour in the batter. Bake at 350° for 45 minutes to an hour. A cake tester should come out clean and an instant read thermometer will read 180° to 200°. Let cool on a rack. After 15 minutes, turn it out of the pan and let it cool for two hours before cutting it. IF you like cream cheese, this is a good bread to smear it on. Freezes well.

Ravani—it's a sweet cake that is gluten-free.

- 1 lb. unsalted butter
- 3 ½ cups rice flour (24 oz bag is available in the International isle in many supermarkets)
- 2 ½ cups sugar
- 13 eggs, separated
- ¼ teaspoon almond extract
- ½ teaspoon cream of tartar
- 2 teaspoons of sugar
- 1 teaspoon baking powder
- For the syrup: 2 cups sugar and one cup water, 8 drops of lemon juice ½ teaspoon vanilla, a sprinkle of cinnamon

Beat eggs whites. As they begin to form peaks, add ¼ teaspoon almond extract and ½ teaspoon cream of tartar and 2 teaspoons of sugar. Continue to beat until there's no liquid.

In another bowl, cream the butter and sugar. Add the egg yolks.

Add to the flour, 1 teaspoon baking powder. Add the flour to the butter-sugar-yolk mixture. Fold the egg whites into the mixture. Pour into an ungreased 9 x 13 pan. Cook at 350° F for about 30- 40 minutes. It could take 60 mins. Once the cake has completely cooled. Cut in diamonds and pour on warmed syrup. Make a simple syrup: 2 cups sugar, one cup water about eight drops of lemon juice. Bring to a boil, then lower the heat and simmer for 5 minutes. Sprinkle a little cinnamon and stir in ½ teaspoon of vanilla extract. If you put the whole pan in the sink, then pour the syrup over it, you won't have to worry about making a mess with any syrup running off the edges. Makes about 26 pieces.

College Comfort Bars—You mix this in one pot. It's a quick preparation and very welcome to chocolate lovers.

- 2 sticks salted butter
- 1 lb. brown sugar either dark or light

- 4 eggs
- 1 teaspoon vanilla extract
- ½ teaspoon salt
- 1 teaspoon baking powder
- 2 cups plus one tablespoon all-purpose flour
- 1 cup flaked coconut
- 1 cup chopped walnuts (optional)
- 12 oz. chocolate bits

Melt the butter and sugar in a pot large enough to mix all the ingredients. Cool to avoid cooking the eggs. Mix in the eggs and vanilla. Add in everything but the chocolate bits. Blend. Pour into a well-greased 9 x 13 pan. Bake at 325° F and check at 30 minutes. If the cake tester comes out wet, it might need another ten minutes.

As soon as you take the pan out and put it on a rack, sprinkle the chocolate bits on top. The heat should be enough to soften them. With a spatula, smooth the chocolate to make an icing.

Apple cake—It's vegan and can be made gluten free with rice flour. If you are cutting back on oil in your diet, substitute apple butter for the oil and line the pan with parchment paper instead of greasing the pan.

- 4 cups chopped apples. Chunky not diced. About 4 apples peeled and chopped. (I use 3 or 4 different apples but choose what you like.)
- 1 ½ cups light or dark brown sugar (can use white sugar)
- 1 cup apple butter or scant cup canola oil
- 3 cups flour
- 1 teaspoon baking powder
- 2 teaspoon baking soda
- 1 teaspoon scant salt
- 1 ½ teaspoon cinnamon
- ¼ teaspoon ground clove (sometimes I omit this)

- 1 teaspoon vanilla
- 1 cup raisins (optional)
- 1 cup walnuts chopped (optional)

Put the apples and sugar in a big pot. Cook until the sugar melts. Don't boil the apples. Let cool a little.

Mix the apple butter or canola oil and vanilla in the pot.

Mix all the dry ingredients in a bowl, then add them into the pot. Mix. It will be thick.

Pour into prepared pan—either parchment paper or oil.

Bake at 350° F for about 40 minutes.

Sprinkle very lightly with sugar when it comes out of the oven or make a sugar glaze: 1 cup of confectioner's sugar, 1 teaspoon vanilla extract and 3-4 tablespoons of water or apple juice, just enough to make it spreadable.

To make this recipe gluten-free, use

- 3 cups rice flour instead of all-purpose flour
- a full cup of oil, or increase the apple butter by 2 tablespoons
- ½ tsp ground clove (optional)

Finding Your Hidden Gem

Use this format—**Notes on my visit**, or make up your own **for each place you visit.**

Notes on my visit
Where I visited_____Date_____
Type of event Tour___ Luncheon____ Other_____
Contact person_____Phone #_____
Email_____
What I liked:
1.
2.
3.
4.
5.

Who I spoke with—Residents? Staff? Other guests? What did they say?
What I didn't like: 1. 2. 3. 4. 5.
Specific unit I saw was #___independent___ or assisted_____ Studio__ One Bedroom___ Two Bedroom___ Size—square feet_____
What do I see out of the window(s)?
How many windows?
Microwave and small refrigerator or full kitchen_____
Available now_____ How long a waiting list?_____
Buy in lump sum $_____ Monthly fees $_____ If a lump sum, is there a return of principal to my beneficiaries?
Includes: one meal_____three meals_____ Linen service_____Light housekeeping_____ Laundry service_____or washer and dryer in or near my unit___
Parking space(s) 1___ 2___ in garage? ____ outside? _____
Cost or No cost for heat?_____ electric_____ water____ Internet___ transportation for medical appointments___

Activities and clubs available that I would like:
1.
2.
3.
4.
5.
Did the food in the dining room smell inviting?
The facility smells clean_____
Fresh flowers and plants_____
Do they allow pets?
Did it feel welcoming?
Is the overall look of the place appealing to me?
Is there an events calendar with the sorts of entertainment I like?
What I want to ask: 1. If my health changes, do my monthly fees increase? 2. Would I be moved to another unit if I entered as independent and then needed assistance or memory care? 3. What happens if I run out of money?
Overall impression: □ Really like it □ Maybe □ No way

WHAT TO DO NEXT IF YOU'RE READY TO MOVE IN?

You recall that the **Continuum of Housing Options** in Chapter 8 lists many settings which offer either independent or assisted living. The names differ, but the questions you ask will be similar. You want to know what the services, activities, and costs are. What should you ask?

Your computer and local librarian will help you source many articles and books that offer guidance. Here are two articles:

- https://www.caring.com/articles/
  choosing-senior-independent-living
- Homeability.com/assisted-living-25-questions-
  to-ask-before-you-move/

Yes, there are many details, but that would also be true if you were planning to buy a new single-family home. If you've made yourself dizzy with checklists, remember what you heard in Chapters 6, 8, 9, and 10 from those who have already moved: "Will this setting nurture you and help you live as well as you can?" That is the key.

When you say, "I like this place. I can see myself here," then go over the finances of the facility, inquire about its reputation and corporate structure. Ask an accountant who is familiar with these sorts of properties to review the financials. Alternatively, learn how to understand the numbers yourself:

- https://www.oranjccrc.org/ORANJ/wp-content/uploads
  /2017/03/2017FinanceGuide.pdf

The document just referenced was written for residents who are members of the finance committee at their CCRC. It is a teacherly document. It does not expect you or those other residents to start with knowledge about how CCRC's manage their finances. It will give you a working knowledge of the key metrics.

In addition, for the legal angle, look at the checklist from Elder Law Attorneys https://www.elderlawanswers.com/checklist-choosing -an-assisted-living-or-continuing-care-facility-12147. You might want to hire an attorney to read the residence's contract and explain whatever is unclear to you.

ENDNOTES

CHAPTER 1: RETIREMENT—WHAT DO YOU WANT IT TO BE?

1   Robert Holzmann, Joseph E. Stiglitz, with Louise Fox, Estelle James, and Peter R. Orszag, *New Ideas about Old Age Security: Toward Sustainable Pension Systems in the 21st Century* (Washington, DC: World Bank, 2001), 452. https://openknowledge.worldbank.org/handle/10986/13857.

2   Nari Rhee and Ilana Boivie, "The Continuing Retirement Savings Crisis," The National Institute on Retirement Security (March 2015), 1. https://www.nirsonline.org/wp-content/uploads/2017/07/final_rsc_2015.pdf

3   David Wagner, *The Poor House: America's Forgotten Institution* (Lanham, MD: Rowman & Littlefield, 2005), 10.

4   Larry Dewitt, "The Age of Social Security," *Retirement Revolution Series: It's Never Too Late,* https://interactive.wttw.com/a/main.taf-p=46,7,4,2.html.

5   Abe Bortz, "Lecture on the History of Social Security," Special Study #1, p. 16. https://www.ssa.gov/history/bortz.html.

6 "Unemployment Statistics during the Great Depression," *United States History*, http://www.u-s-history.com/pages/h1528.html.

7 "Presidential Statement Signing the Social Security Act," *The United States Social Security Administration* (August 14, 1935), https://www.ssa.gov/history/fdrsignstate.html.

Franklin D. Roosevelt, "Message to Congress on the Objectives and Accomplishments of the Administration," (June 8, 1934), *The American Presidency Project,* http://www.presidency.ucsb.edu/ws/index.php?pid=14690: "Security was attained in the early days through the interdependence of members of families upon each other and of the families within a small community upon each other. The complexities of great communities of organized industry make less real the simple means of security. Therefore, we are compelled to employ the active interest of the nation as a whole through government in order to encourage a greater security for each individual who composes it. This seeking for a greater measure of welfare and happiness does not indicate a change in values. It is rather a return to values lost in the course of our economic development and expansion."

8 "Policy Basics: Top Ten Facts about Social Security," *Center on Budget and Policy Priorities,* Fact #7. https://www.cbpp.org/research/social-security/policy-basics-top-ten-facts-about-social-security.

9 There were earlier patents on a game like Monopoly, and one of them was by Lizzie Magie in 1904 for the game, The Landlord Game, "with the object of demonstrating how rents enrich the property owners and impoverish tenants." She wanted to make the ideas of the economist, Henry George, concrete. https://thesocietypages.org/socimages/2010/08/16/toys-as-socialization-agents-monopoly-vs-the-landlords-game/.

CHAPTER 2: IS YOUR HOUSE STILL THE RIGHT PLACE FOR YOU?

1 "Home in Retirement: More Freedom, New Choices," *Merrill Lynch Bank of America Corporation, Age Wave,* http://agewave.com/what-we-do/landmark-research-and-consulting/research-studies/home-in-retirement-more-freedom-new-choices/.

2 Lisa J. Dettling and Joanne W. Hsu, "Returning to the Nest: Debt and Parental Co-residence Among Young Adults," quoted in Kathleen Coxwell, "Boomers Have a Retirement Problem: Boomerang Kids—An Adult Child

Living at Home," *New Retirement,* https://www.newretirement.com/retirement/boomers-have-a-retirement-problem-boomerang-kids-an-adult-child-living-at-home/.

3   "Home and Recreational Safety," *Centers for Disease Control and Prevention, US Department of Health and Human Services,* https://www.cdc.gov/homeandrecreationalsafety/falls/adultfalls.html.

4   "A Time to Give Thanks, and Secure Throw Rugs," *Fall Prevention Center of Excellence,* http://stopfalls.org/a-time-to-give-thanks-and-secure-throw-rugs/.

5   Jaqueline Mitchell, "Move it, or Lose it," *TuftsNow* (August 26, 2014). http://now.tufts.edu/articles/move-it-or-lose-it.

6   Jim Norman, "In U.S., Women, Poor, Urbanites Most Fearful of Walking Alone," *Gallup News* (November 10, 2015). http://news.gallup.com/poll/186563/women-poor-urbanites-fearful-walking-alone.aspx.

Chapter 3: Would You Be Just As Happy if Your House Cost You Less?

1   "Median and Average Prices of New Homes Sold in the United States," *United States Census Bureau,* https://www.census.gov/const/uspriceann.pdf.

2   "CPI Inflation Calculator," *Bureau of Labor Statistics, United States Department of Labor,* https://www.bls.gov/data/inflation_calculator.htm.

3   John P. Harding, Stuart S. Rosenthal, C.F. Sirmans, "Depreciation of housing capital, maintenance, and price inflation: Estimates form a repeat sales model," *Journal of Urban Economics* 61 (2007), 213-214, 197. https://www.sciencedirect.com/science/article/pii/S0094119006000763: "Deeply entrenched folklore has also long held that owning a home is one of the most effective investments a family can make. Our estimates indicate that after controlling for depreciation and maintenance, homeownership was basically a breakeven investment for the typical homeowner over the 1983 to 2001 period. This result is well below what advocates of homeownership might hope for. Using data from the American Housing Survey we examine these issues. Over the 1983 to 2001 period, results indicate that gross of maintenance, housing depreciates at roughly 2.5 percent per year, while net of maintenance, housing depreciates at approximately 2 percent per year. Moreover, although the typical home appreciated at an annual real rate of roughly 0.75 percent, after allowing for depreciation and maintenance, the average homeowner experienced little capital gain."

4   Jacob Passy, "One big reason it's so hard for first-time buyers to find the right starter home," *MarketWatch,* (March 21, 2018), https://www.marketwatch.com/story/another-hurdle-for-first-time-home-buyers-there-are-barely-any-starter-homes-for-sale-2018-03-21.

5   Harding, Rosenthal, Sirmans, 197.

CHAPTER 4: CAN YOU HOLD ONTO YOUR RETIREMENT MONEY AND YOUR HOUSE?

1   "S&P/Case-Shiller U.S. National Home Price Index," *Economic Research, Federal Reserve Bank of St. Louis,* https://fred.stlouisfed.org/series/CSUSHPINSA.

2   "Understanding Deposit Insurance," *Federal Deposit Insurance Corporation,* https://www.fdic.gov/deposit/deposits/index.html. The Federal Deposit Insurance Corporation (FDIC) is an independent agency of the United States government that protects the funds depositors place in banks and savings associations. FDIC insurance is backed by the full faith and credit of the United States government. Since the FDIC was established in 1933, no depositor has lost a penny of FDIC-insured funds.

FDIC insurance covers all deposit accounts, including:

- Checking accounts
- Savings accounts
- Money market deposit accounts
- Certificates of deposit

FDIC insurance does not cover other financial products and services that banks may offer, such as stocks, bonds, mutual funds, life insurance policies, annuities or securities.

The standard insurance amount is $250,000 per depositor, per insured bank, for each account ownership category.

3   Denise Mazzucco, "Historical CD Interest Rates," *Bankrate* (April 19, 2016), https://www.bankrate.com/banking/cds/historical-cd-interest-rates-1984-2016/.

4   "CD Rates for July 2018," *Bankrate* (June 2, 2018), https://www.bankrate.com/cd.aspx. National rate for one-year certificate of deposit 2.3% as of June 24, 2018.

5   "Annuities," *Financial Industry Regulatory Authority,* http://www.finra.
     org/investors/annuities.

6   "How to plan for rising health care costs," *Fidelity Investments* (April 18,
     2018), https://www.fidelity.com/viewpoints/personal-finance/plan-for-
     rising-health-care-costs. Fidelity Benefits Consulting estimate 2018.

7   "Compare Long Term Care Costs Across the United States," *Genworth,*
     https://www.genworth.com/aging-and-you/finances/cost-of-care.html:
     Genworth Cost of Care Survey 2017.

8   "How Much Care Will You Need?" Administration on Aging, *U.S.
     Department of Health and Human Services,* https://longtermcare.acl.gov/
     the-basics/how-much-care-will-you-need.html.

9   "2018 Alzheimer's Disease Facts and Figures," *Alzheimer's Association,*
     https://www.alz.org/media/Documents/alzheimers-facts-and-figures-
     infographic.pdf.

10   Penelope S. Tzougros, *Long-term care insurance: How to make decisions that
     are right for you, 2 ed.* (Waltham, MA, Wealthy Choices®, 2016), 56-66.

11   Christopher Tarver Robertson, Richard Egelhof, and Michael Hoke, "Get
     Sick, Get Out: The Medical Causes for Home Mortgage Foreclosures," 18
     Health Matrix 65 (August 18, 2008), 66. http://media.cleveland.com/
     health_impact/other/medicaldebtandforeclosure.pdf.

12   Patrick Sisson, "How health care costs are linked to foreclosures," *Curbed,*
     (June 26, 2017), https://www.curbed.com/2017/6/26/15873206/
     bankruptcy-obamacare-medical-debt-foreclosures.

13   Penelope S. Tzougros, "Annuities- Retirement Guarantees, Promises or
     Traps," www.wealthychoices.com/blog

14   "Percent of Americans who own their home," *Statistic Brain Research
     Institute.* http://www.statisticbrain.com/percent-of-americans-who-own-
     their-home/.

15   "Snapshot of older consumers and mortgage debt," *Office for Older
     Americans, Consumer Financial Protection Bureau* (May 7, 2014), 8.

16   Kurt Fischer, "Seniors Have More Debt," *Money Counselor,* (March 18,
     2016), http://mymoneycounselor.com/seniors-have-more-debt.

17   Jennifer B. McKin, "Seniors face more foreclosures as reverse mortgages
     bite back," *The Eye,* (May 2, 2016), https://www.necir.org/2016/05/01/
     seniors-face-foreclosures-reverse-mortgages-bite-back/.

18   FICO scores may determine the interest rates you pay for car loans, credit

cards and other loans. It is useful to understand how they are calculated (https://www.credit.com). "What is a good credit score?" on https://www. myfico.com.

Chapter 5: Do You and Your House Pass the Test so that You Can Stay There?

1   Malka Young, LICSW, C-ASWCM leads the Healthy Aging programs offered by the Jewish Family Services of Metrowest in Massachusetts. A few of her areas of specialization are family caregiver coaching, living with chronic illness and family relationships and caring for aging parents (www. jfsmweldercare.org).

2   Claude McGavic was the Executive Director of the National Association of Home Inspectors in 2016. In August 2016, National Association of Home Inspectors ceased operations and many of its members joined the American Society of Home Inspectors (ASHI) (http://www.homeinspector.org/).

3   David Doerring, President of the National Association of Independent Fee Appraisers (NAIFA) term ending 6-30-18. The organization has transitioned to the American Society of Appraisers (ASA) with a new web address: http://www.appraisers.org/Disciplines/Real-Property.

4   John S. Marrazzo, SCGREA, IFAS, ASA, FRICS, IFA, MRICS, CTA, Past National President of the National Association of Independent Fee Appraisers (www.naifa.com.) His many designations relate to his appraising real property, teaching appraisal courses, consulting, and providing valuation services.

5   "Facts & Research," *American Automobile Association* (AAA), http:// seniordriving.aaa.com/resources-family-friends/conversations-about-driving/facts-research: "Specific physical, cognitive and visual abilities may decline with advancing age. However, there are large individual differences in the onset and degree of functional impairments, so **age alone is not sufficient information to judge driving ability**" [author's emphasis].

6   "Compare Long Term Care Costs Across the United States," *Genworth,* https://www.genworth.com/aging-and-you/finances/cost-of-care.html.

7   Suppose you bought your house for $50,000 and you sold it for $600,000—that difference (with certain adjustments) is taxed. You pay a capital gains tax. Suppose you die and the house is valued at $600,000— your heirs would not pay the tax on the gain. They receive the house at its value at the time of your death. That is a step up in basis. This is the

simplest description of these concepts. There is much more to know about capital gains tax and step up in basis.

CHAPTER 6: HEAR WHAT EVERYONE'S TALKING ABOUT: "DO I MOVE? OR DO I STAY?"

1   Kalliope Barlis, *Phobia Relief from Fear to Freedom,* (NY: Building Your Best, 2016). She is also the creator of Phobia Relief Day.

2   The Clare is a Continuing Care Retirement Community (CCRC) in Chicago, Illinois, offering residential units in independent, assisted, skilled care, or memory care.

CHAPTER 7: WHOSE MOVE IS IT ANYWAY?

1   Grace Lebow, Barbara Kane, and Irwin Lebow, *Coping With Your Difficult Older Parent: A Guide for Stressed out Children* (New York, Avon Books, 1999), 55.

2   Nina W. Brown, *Children of the Aging Self-Absorbed: A Guide to Coping with Difficult, Narcissistic Parents and Grandparents* (Oakland, CA, New Harbinger Publications, Inc., 2015), 6-7.

3   Carol-Ann Hamilton, *Coping with Un-Cope-Able Parents: Loving Action for Eldercare* (Bloomington, IN, Balboa Press, 2012), 105. Chapter 7.

CHAPTER 8: WHAT'S NEW IN HOUSING?

1   Elizabeth Cromley, "Apartments and Collective Life in Nineteenth-Century New York," *New Households, New Housing,* Karen A. Frank and Sherry Ahrentzen, Eds. (New York, Van Nostram, Reinhold, 1991), 41.

2   Ibid., 42.

3   Ibid., 43.

4   Ibid.

5   Laura L Carstensen, "A Hopeful Future," *Independent for Life: Home and Neighborhoods for an Aging America.* Eds. Henry Cisneros, Margaret Dyer-Chamberlain and Jane Hickie (Dallas, U. of Texas P, 2012), 21.

6   Ibid., 22.

7   Matthieu Lietaert, "The Growth of Cohousing in Europe," *Cohousing* (December 16, 2007), http://www.cohousing.org/node/1537.

8   Claire Thompson, "Cohousing: The Secret to sustainable urban living?" *Grist* (July 11, 2012), http://grist.org/cities/cohousing-the-secret-to-sustainable-urban-living.

9   Grace Kim, "How cohousing can make us happier (and live longer)," *Technology, Entertainment, Design* (TED), https://www.ted.com/talks/grace_kim_how_cohousing_can_make_us_happier_and_live_longer.

10 Amy Ellis Nutt, "Loneliness grows from individual ache to public health hazard," *Washington Post* (January 31, 2016), https://www.washingtonpost.com/national/health-science/loneliness-grows-from-individual-ache-to-public-health-hazard/2016/01/31/cf246c56-ba20-11e5-99f3-184bc379b12d_story.html.

11 Ibid.

12 Andy Dworkin, "Oregon among national leaders in number of assisted living facilities," *Oregon Live, The Oregonian,* https://www.oregonlive.com/news/index.ssf/2010/01/oregon_among_national_leaders.html.

CHAPTER 9: YOU MOVED WHERE? OFFBEAT AND IDIOSYNCRATIC HOUSING

1   "What is the Tiny House Movement?" *The Tiny Life,* https://thetinylife.com/what-is-the-tiny-house-movement.

2   Rene Rodriguez, "How small can you go?" https://www.miamiherald.com/news/business/real-estate-news/article208563364.html

3   Henry David Thoreau, "Where I lived," *Walden and Civil Disobedience* (New York: Penguin Group,1983), 135.

4   www.Couchsurfing.com; https://matadornetwork.com; www.globetreks.com; www.Seniorplanet.org.

5   Sarah Stevenson, "Is cruise ship retirement cheaper than assisted living?" *Senior Blog* (February 20, 2015), www.aplaceformom.com/blog/2013-2-2-cruise-ship-retirement-assisted-living.

CHAPTER 10: FROM "I'M NOT READY!" TO "IT'S TIME"

1   Sara Honn Quails, "What social relationships can do for health,"

Generations, *Journal of the American Society on Aging* (March 6, 2014), (www.asaging.org/blog/what-social-relationships-can-do-health).

2   Kathleen Mitchell, "Improve your mental sharpness. Bridge and other activities help to boost brainpower," *Northeast Ohio Parent* (December 22, 2016), 3. https://www.northeastohioparent.com/magazine/2016-editions/2016-february/improve-mental-sharpness-bridge-activities-help-boost-brainpower/.

3   Christopher Bergland, "Mental training boosts cognition and openness to experience," *Psychology Today* (January 12, 2014), 3, 5. https://psychologytoday.com/us/blog/the-athletes-way/201401/mental-training-boosts-cognition-and-openness-experience.

CHAPTER 11: WHAT TO DO WITH ALL THIS STUFF?

1   For help with the move, consider contacting National Association of Senior Move Managers (www.nasmm.org.) If you are moving into a senior community, ask who the staff recommends.

2   Consult your tax preparer and review IRS publication 523, which explains the capital gains tax that might apply when you sell your home. You may or may not be required to pay a capital gains tax. The price the buyer pays minus the price you paid when you bought your house is the gain. If you can substantiate what you paid for improvements, you can lessen the gap between your purchase price and the selling price, and therefore, potentially lower your capital gains tax. This is the simplest explanation. There is more to know.

CHAPTER 12: SUMMARY: YOUR HOME SWEET HOME DECISION GUIDE

1   "Compare Long Term Care Costs Across the United States," *Genworth*, https://www.genworth.com/aging-and-you/finances/cost-of-care.html: Genworth Cost of Care Survey 2017.

2   Oliver Wendell Holmes Sr. (1809-1894), born in Cambridge, Massachusetts, became a physician, professor, inventor, medical reformer and served as dean at Harvard Medical School. However, he was highly acclaimed in his day as a poet, humorist and novelist. One of his sons, Oliver Wendell Holmes Jr., is among the most well-known judges who has served on the United States Supreme Court.

Anthony M. Coniaris is a prolific Orthodox writer with over 78 books to his credit, President of Light and Life Publishing Company and a priest in the Greek Orthodox Church.

APPENDIX A MAINTENANCE LIST

1   John Riha, "How Much Value Does Regular Maintenance Add to Your Home?" *Houselogic* (March 9, 2010), https://www.houselogic.com/organize-maintain/home-maintenance-tips/value-home-maintenance.

APPENDIX D SAFETY CHECKLIST-
YOUR BODY AND YOUR HOUSE

1   Dorothy A. Drago, *Living Safely, Aging Well: A Guide to Preventing Injuries at Home* (Johns Hopkins, 2013).

INDEX

275

ACKNOWLEDGEMENTS

Ευχαριστώ

Debra Englander so thoroughly understands the process of writing that she stays out of the writer's way while both encouraging small ideas to develop and making precise edits that shape the book and take it to a higher level. It has been a privilege to have her editing and guidance for the second time. She and Martha Bullen moved the book from my computer to you with their expertise in marketing. Martha answered question after question even when she was on vacation. She explained the esoteric process of categories and how books get to their audience. Deb and Martha both know the world of publishing, but even more impressive is their wisdom, and kindness. Ευχαριστώ.

An enduring joy of this book for me is each of you who shared your stories about moving or staying or trying to decide what to do about the house. It was clear that you wanted your comments to help others and so you were honest, and willing to explain your deliberations even when they showed your mistakes. Each of you is very dear to me and I look forward to meeting with you again. However, I would not have met all of you without the chain of referrals started by Joy Silverstein, Eileen Schwartz, Gloria Bowman, Gayle Gordon, Kristen Viscum and many other friends.

Steve and Bill Harrison created Quantum Leap (QL) which is a cornucopia of benefits for speakers and writers. I learned so much from them and from the insights of their coaches and staff who each walked me thorough miles of this journey: Barb Early, Brian Edmonson, Tamra Richardt, Raia King, Geoffrey Berwind, Judy Cohen, Leeza Steindorf, Mary Giuseffi, Gail Synder, Dr. Rob Pennington, Rose George and Trish Troilo. Each deserves more specific thanks, but that will be at another time and place. QL is a community of writers and speakers who have become resources, friends and success stories to celebrate. Connie Merk, even while she was working on her own book with little time to spare, spent hours proofreading this book and offered significant improvements.

I thank you who read earlier versions of the manuscript, asked good questions, challenged some ideas, and supported the project: Dr. Susan Howards, Esq., Tricia Sinn, Frank Moffett, Judy Jose-Roddy, David Balekdjian, Heather Jarp, Carole Fawcett, and Leslie Bowden. Moving from the version that they read to the book you are holding was the creative work of Jerry and Michelle Dorris at Authorsupport.com.

I am grateful to each of you who found time in your busy schedules to read and review the book. You are helping the book makes its debut.

The greater thanks to the experts, the interviewees, and the many people who contributed to *Your Home Sweet Home* will come from you, the reader, if the book has served you well. We all hope that it does. Yasou.

Penelope Tzougros, PhD, ChFC, CLU

"The art of wealth begins by asking the right questions about your money and yourself. The better the questions, the better the answers, the better the results." The better you and I communicate about your values, worries, concerns, goals and timelines, the more suitable and individualized your financial plan will be. It will be flexible and make sense to you. You and I have the same goal of wanting you to have—on your terms—a creative, secure and satisfying retirement.

In 1986, after serving for thirteen years as a professor in New York and Boston, I joined Bay Financial Associates as a financial planner. Wanting to reach a national audience with my seminars, books, radio and television shows, I established Wealthy Choices® in 2000.

I specialize now on retirement income; how to turn whatever you have accumulated into income for life. Questions you generally need answers to are how to deal with Social Security, long-term care, your legacy, Medicare and the insurances related to Medicare, inflation and sufficient income and growth in your portfolio. A plan that addresses these issues in a helpful way can give you more confidence to face those hopefully happy and healthy retirement years.

Thank you for reading *Your Home Sweet Home*. For your sake, think through the issues and make the best decision for you. Don't wait until circumstances take away your choices, and make the decision for you. Decide, then go out and celebrate life.

Yasou!

Other books by the author:

Wealthy Choices: The Seven Competencies
of Financial Success (Wiley)

Long-term Care Insurance: How to Make Decisions That
Are Right for You. 2nd ed. (Wealthy Choices®)

Made in the USA
Middletown, DE
14 June 2021